Researching Conflict, Drama and Learning

John O'Toole · Dale Bagshaw ·
Bruce Burton · Anita Grünbaum ·
Margret Lepp · Morag Morrison ·
Janet Pillai

Researching Conflict, Drama and Learning

The International DRACON Project

Springer

John O'Toole
University of Melbourne
South Brisbane, VIC, Australia

Dale Bagshaw
University of South Australia
Adelaide, SA, Australia

Bruce Burton
Griffith University
Mt Gravatt, QLD, Australia

Anita Grünbaum
Västerbergs Folk High School
Sandviken, Sweden

Margret Lepp
University of Gothenburg
Gothenburg, Sweden

Morag Morrison
University of Cambridge
Cambridge, UK

Janet Pillai
Arts-ED
TTDI, Kuala Lumpur, Malaysia

ISBN 978-981-13-5915-6   ISBN 978-981-13-5916-3 (eBook)
https://doi.org/10.1007/978-981-13-5916-3

Library of Congress Control Number: 2018966120

© Springer Nature Singapore Pte Ltd. 2019
This work is subject to copyright. All rights are reserved by the Publisher, whether the whole or part of the material is concerned, specifically the rights of translation, reprinting, reuse of illustrations, recitation, broadcasting, reproduction on microfilms or in any other physical way, and transmission or information storage and retrieval, electronic adaptation, computer software, or by similar or dissimilar methodology now known or hereafter developed.
The use of general descriptive names, registered names, trademarks, service marks, etc. in this publication does not imply, even in the absence of a specific statement, that such names are exempt from the relevant protective laws and regulations and therefore free for general use.
The publisher, the authors and the editors are safe to assume that the advice and information in this book are believed to be true and accurate at the date of publication. Neither the publisher nor the authors or the editors give a warranty, express or implied, with respect to the material contained herein or for any errors or omissions that may have been made. The publisher remains neutral with regard to jurisdictional claims in published maps and institutional affiliations.

This Springer imprint is published by the registered company Springer Nature Singapore Pte Ltd.
The registered company address is: 152 Beach Road, #21-01/04 Gateway East, Singapore 189721, Singapore

This book is dedicated to:
The dozens of schools, hundreds of teachers, and especially the thousands of students who participated in DRACON, and informed, nourished and sustained all four national projects.

Foreword 1 (Conflict Mediation)

The core idea of *Researching Conflict, Drama and Learning: The International DRACON Project* is inspired. After reading it, you will wonder why we don't bring drama and conflict together more often. The authors explain how the fields of conflict studies and drama do actually overlap and share a lexicon: for example, words like *protagonist* and *antagonist*, used in conflict studies, are drawn from Greek drama. In practice, too, dramatic techniques like role-play are widely used not only to teach conflict transformation but also to examine students' grasp of processes like mediation. Reading this book, I was struck by the idea that techniques like role-play might be even more effectively used if those who teach and learn conflict transformation had more education in transformative drama.

The DRACON project explores the relationship between drama and conflict transformation in an impressively comprehensive way. The first part of the book lays down the conceptual foundations of the project. Theories of conflict transformation drawn from the academic field of conflict studies are explained, and then the theory and practice of transformative drama education is explicated. The secondpart of the book tells the stories of four action research teams, drawn from three different countries. A description of the local cultural and educational context provides a background for the reader: the school system, the student population, the researchers' expertise. Each chapter is then centred on reporting the action research: its aims, methods, the fieldwork and its analysis. Working in schools in very different cultural settings, each team developed its own program and teachers in particular will appreciate the variety of different creative processes used in the classrooms. Set across a time span of ten years, the research uses both quantitative and qualitative approaches, and results in findings which, taken together, make a substantial contribution to the teaching of drama and conflict transformation. The third part of the book reports on follow-up events that have occurred since the project officially finished, providing evidence of the capacity of DRACON to inspire and act as a catalyst across the globe. In terms of research, the book is very sound and thorough, demonstrating how different research techniques can be used to evaluate and refine courses in drama and conflict. The coverage of the issues and relevant theories and models is encyclopaedic.

The book raises a number of novel and interesting ideas. I will touch on several as examples to whet the readers' appetite. A person who is dogmatic and black and white in their thinking is not going to be a good candidate for mediation or similar conflict transformation processes. A key element of conflict transformation is the idea that conflict has a subjective dimension and the capacity to shift away from absolutes, to accept that different perspectives may be equally valid, and that events may look different if seen from a different angle is fundamental. This more fluid and flexible way of thinking is sometimes termed *dialectical* thinking. It is hard to think of a better way of extending a student's capacity to think dialectically than using dramatic techniques which, as the authors point out, literally play with roles to shift perspectives. In drama, the actor must be both close to a person, having empathy for the character being played, and distant, aware of how the performance comes across to an audience. Similarly, the mediator must tune in closely and listen empathically to one party, but also maintain distance, being aware of the needs and concerns of the other parties and the broader system in which the conflict is embedded. DRACON has opened a door to further research: looking at how drama can promote the kind of cognitive style and dialectical thinking that makes conflict transformation possible. Another point which interested me, and is neglected elsewhere in the academic literature, is the relationship between fact and fiction. Working directly with real conflicts may be too confronting and intrusive, especially when the teachers and researchers are adults and the participants are young people, so fiction, or somewhat fictionalised conflicts based on true stories, can be valuable material to work with. And young people's fiction, their popular culture, provides such a wealth of rich resources for understanding conflict. DRACON shows how drama brings conflict to life, and drama without conflict would have no life. So, whether you are a teacher, researcher, student or interested member of the public, please read on, learn and enjoy.

Brisbane, Australia

Hon. Prof. Diane Bretherton
School of Political Science and
International Studies
The University of Queensland

Foreword 2 (Drama Education)

Over recent months, I have been involved in the national monitoring of research outputs across New Zealand universities. It is an exacting role, requiring groups of academics to negotiate an overall score on an individual's research program over 6 years. As a committee, we often talk about the impact of research. Traditionally that has been measured by the quantum of references an article or chapter attracts, or about the esteem in which an individual is held. Increasingly, we are looking at new ways to understand how we might best understand the impact and relative quality of research.

Applying the kind of metrics that might be useful to understand the value of research, the question of the impact of the DRACON project might be best answered by thinking about the many thousands of people across the world who have benefited from their use of drama to better handle conflict. Students and teachers have come to find ways of naming and understanding the culturally conditioned nature of conflict, not just within their school settings but across their entire lives. That this has happened across the cultural diversity of Sweden, Malaysia and Australia speaks loudly of the care and thought in the initial design of the program and the flexible purposing across decades of implementation.

I was left wondering as I finished reading this book of the importance of serendipity in research—though it is not a metric we use to measure the quality of the research. By serendipity, I mean more than picking up on chance, but the ability to notice possibilities, to draw links across from happenchance and make something meaningful from the seemingly accidental. The spin-off tangential projects that DRACON generated might be its most consequential contribution. DRACON has spread to China strengthening NGO trainers, involves nursing training in Jordan, is working with African men in Adelaide to challenge cultural norms on domestic violence, and has trained senior management staff at Melbourne University. The wide range of tangential projects and the longevity of the overall project, adapting and changing as it meets new challenges, speaks of a team of researchers who understood the power of serendipity.

One of the impacts of this research is that we might better understand how open, dialogic international research projects, that allow freedom and autonomy for constituent parties, provide the opportunity for long-term relationships to deliver far more than original plans or visions.

I am often invited on to research teams that have clearly defined outcomes; it is one of the binds necessary for funding. My work and the work of the rest of the team are then constrained by the roles assigned at the beginning of the project, as we move onwards to the inevitable report that somehow justifies our work and our funding. What is strikingly different about the DRACON project is its open-endedness. In many ways, it has worked in the same way that a good process drama does. There was a hook, the pre-text that drew the ensemble together to work something out, but how that was done was determined in the making of the research rather than it being predetermined. The multiple and divergent outcomes suggest researchers who aren't just using arts-based processes but are working as artist/researchers. The artistry of this research is one of its strongest features. A willingness to be deeply curious, to engage in genuine collaboration, to be playful with ideas and take risks with new approaches, content to work with ambiguity marks researchers who act as artists.

Many years ago, John O'Toole and I sat with Dorothy Heathcote on a warm afternoon in Northampton. Dorothy knew John well, me not so well. She turned to me and asked, 'So, in New Zealand do children do things that matter, and in doing those things do they learn that they matter too?' I was silent for a long time. An easier question would have been about whether they did drama. The great gift of DRACON is that the children and teachers who were engaged in this project did work that truly matters in so many ways and that the whole project was motivated by a desire to let children know their lives matter. Perhaps Dorothy's questions might help other researchers frame their work so ethically.

This book is a record of an extraordinary project spanning continents and many years. It tells many variants of the story that there is much to be gained by having people engage in drama to handle conflict in their lives and much to be learned from research which artistically works on significant issues.

Auckland, New Zealand

Prof. Peter O'Connor
Faculty of Education and Social Work
The University of Auckland

Acknowledgements

DRACON Project Personnel

DRACON International

Mats Friberg (project leader 1994–2001); Horst Löfgren (project leader 2001–2005). The Swedish team has functioned as an informal editorial group with Löfgren and Birgitte Malm as managing editors.

DRACON Malaysia

Janet Pillai (leader, researcher); Latif Kamaluddin (researcher); Paul Jambunathan (quantitative researcher); Aida Redza (artist); Tan Sooi Beng (artist); Liew Kung Yu (artist); Leow Puay Tin (artist).

DRACON Sweden

Mats Friberg (teacher, researcher); Anita Grünbaum (teacher, researcher); Margret Lepp (teacher, researcher); Horst Löfgren (researcher, editor); Birgitte Malm (researcher, editor).

DRACON Adelaide

Dale Bagshaw (leader, researcher), Myk Mykyta (research associate); Rosemary Nursey-Bray (research associate); Ken Rigby (researcher).

DRACON Brisbane

Merrelyn Bates (mediation adviser); Bruce Burton (co-leader, researcher); Christine Hatton (teaching associate, Sydney); Morag Morrision (teaching and research associate, Brisbane); John O'Toole (co-leader, researcher); Maureen Owen (teaching associate, Brisbane); Anna Plunkett (teaching and research associate, Brisbane); Jane Sizer (administration and data analysis); Jean Will (administration and data analysis).

Thanks

The authors wish to acknowledge gratefully the support and assistance of the following organisations and people between 1994 and 2005:

- All the school and education system administrators, principals and policy officers in Australia, Malaysia and Sweden, who supported and sustained DRACON for over a decade.

DRACON Malaysia

- Universiti Sains Malaysia, Penang.

DRACON Sweden

- The Swedish Council of Scientific Research
- Malmö University
- University of Borås
- University of Gothenburg
- Västerbergs Folk High School.

DRACON Adelaide

- School of Psychology, Social Work and Social Policy, University of South Australia
- Centre for Peace, Conflict and Mediation, University of South Australia.

DRACON Brisbane

- Faculty of Education, Griffith University, Queensland
- Australian Research Council
- Multicultural Programs Unit, New South Wales Department of Education and Training; Hanya Stefaniuk, Shirley Coyle and Greg Maguire
- Education Queensland
- Costa Loucopoulos and Louise Gerondis.

Contents

Part I Background and Theory

1 Introduction 3
   The DRACON Story 3
      Background 4
      Sowing the DRACON Seeds—A Vision 4
      The DRACON Is Born 5
      The Shape of the DRACON 6
      Flight of the DRACON 9
   How to Read This Book 11
      Other DRACON Footprints 12
   References 12

2 Conflict Management, Resolution and Transformation 13
   Key Definitions 13
      Key Approaches to Conflict: A Historical Perspective 15
      The Components of Conflict 16
      Conflict-Handling Styles or Strategies 23
      The Conflict Process and Outcomes 25
   Conflict Interventions 27
      Direct and Indirect Conflict Interventions 27
      Third-Party Roles 28
      Transformation of Asymmetric Conflicts 29
      The Tasks of Conflict Interventions 32
   Approaches to Mediation 34
      A Problem-Solving Approach to Mediation 34
      Conditions for Effective Mediation 38
      Peer Mediation 39
      A Narrative Approach to Mediation 40
   References 41

3 Learning Through Drama ... 43
The History and Context in Schools ... 43
Learning, Social Control and Social Action ... 43
Modern Movements in Drama and Education ... 44
The Pedagogy of Drama ... 48
Drama and Transformation ... 48
Key Components of the Drama Process ... 49
Drama, Conflict and Pedagogy ... 58
Dracon's Central Drama Strategies ... 59
Process Drama ... 59
Theatre-in-Education ... 60
Forum Theatre ... 60
Enhanced Forum Theatre ... 61
Crossover in Movements ... 63
Conclusion ... 64
References ... 64

4 Bridging the Fields of Drama and Conflict Transformation ... 67
Connecting Drama with Conflict ... 67
Introduction ... 67
Drama and Conflict ... 67
Drama as a Holistic Model ... 68
A Conceptual Integration of the Fields ... 69
Towards an Integrated Model ... 75
Innovative Pedagogies ... 78
Transformative Learning ... 78
Transformative Mediation ... 80
Peer Teaching ... 81
Integration in the DRACON Project ... 84
References ... 85

Part II The Research Projects

5 Malaysia—Creative Arts in Conflict Exploration ... 89
Background ... 89
The Malaysian Cultural Context ... 89
The Education System in Malaysian Schools ... 91
Management of Conflict in Malaysian Schools ... 91
Educational Drama in Malaysia ... 92
Research Incorporating Conflict Handling and Processual Creative Arts ... 93
Aims and Rationale of the Research ... 94
Research Team and Participants ... 94
Research Design ... 94

	Research Cycle 1: Testing Potential	96
	Research Cycle 2: Testing Effectiveness	100
	Research Cycle 3: Enhancing Conflict Literacy	109
	Outcomes and Implications	113
	Cultural Implications	114
	Implications for the School Counselling System	115
	Conclusions	116
	References	122
6	**Sweden—Teenagers as Third-Party Mediators**	**123**
	Introduction	123
	Historical and Cultural Background	123
	The Swedish School System	125
	Drama and Conflict Handling in Swedish Schools	126
	Preliminary Student Survey	128
	Basic Strategies for Handling Conflicts	128
	Results—How Students Handle Conflicts	129
	Frequencies of Different Conflict-Handling Strategies	131
	Students' Basic Strategies for Handling Conflicts	133
	Developing a Classroom Program	134
	Third-Party and Mediator Roles	134
	Phase I: Six Classroom Studies	136
	Phase I Conclusions	140
	Phase II: Implementing the Program in Two Schools	142
	Overall Conclusions	148
	References	154
7	**South Australia—Adolescent Conflicts and Educational Drama**	**157**
	Secondary Schooling in Australia	157
	The Australian Cultural Context	157
	Schools and Drama in South Australia	158
	The South Australian Project	159
	Research Aims	159
	Adolescent Conflicts in Australian Schools	159
	What Adolescents Said About Conflict	160
	Stage 1: Focus Group Research	161
	Stage 2: The Survey Research	162
	Conclusions from the Focus Group and Survey Research	167
	The Classroom Study	168
	Research Methodology	168
	The Educational Drama Process	171
	Discussion	180

	Conclusions	181
	References	182
8	**Brisbane—Cooling Conflicts and Acting Against Bullying**	**183**
	The Background	183
	Genesis of the Project	184
	The Research	184
	Research Premises	184
	Research Aim and Questions	185
	Evolution of the Research	186
	Research Design and Methods	187
	The Action Research Cycles	188
	Selection of Schools, Teachers and Students	190
	The Pedagogy	191
	Teaching Conflict Literacy	191
	Acting Against Bullying	192
	Teaching Drama Techniques	193
	Peer Teaching	194
	Implementing the Programs	194
	Cycle 1, 1996 Queensland—An Urban Brisbane High School	195
	Cycle 2, 1997 Queensland—The Same Brisbane High School	195
	Cycle 3, 1998 Queensland—The Same Brisbane High School	197
	Cycle 4, 1999 New South Wales—A Rural High School and Feeder Primary Schools	198
	Cycle 5, 2000 NSW—4 Sydney High Schools and Feeder Primary Schools	200
	Cycle 6, 2001 NSW—8 Sydney and Regional High Schools and Feeder Schools	203
	Cycles 7–9 Queensland 2002–5—Twenty-Five Brisbane and Regional Queensland Schools	204
	Findings and Outcomes	206
	Outcomes from Cycles 7–9	206
	Conclusions and Projections	208
	Postscript	210
	References	215

Part III Past, Present and Future Impacts

9	**After DRACON: Persistence, Sequels and Echoes**	**219**
	Persistence: What Happened in the DRACON Schools?	220
	Sequels: The Continuing Impact	222
	Behaviour Change in Schools—DRACON: The Next Generation	222
	Training the Next Generation of DRACON Teachers	227
	Broader Educational Contexts	229

Adult Training and Professional Development	231
Building Individual and Community Resilience	235
Echoes: The Quest for Community and Cultural Change	238
The DRACON Quest Goes on	238
References	240
Appendix A	241
Appendix B	243
Index	247

About the Authors

John O'Toole was formerly Foundation Chair of Arts Education at the University of Melbourne, and previously Professor of Drama and Applied Theatre at Griffith University, Queensland. He has taught, lectured and researched drama and arts education for over forty years, with all ages and on all continents. He has written or co-written over 15 research and teaching textbooks, many of which are standard works, and three of which are published by Springer. In 2001, he was awarded the American Alliance for Theater and Education Lifetime Research Award, and in 2014 he was made a Member of the Order of Australia for his contribution to drama education.

Dale Bagshaw is now Adjunct Associate Professor, School of Psychology, Social Work and Social Policy, University of South Australia, and a mediation practitioner and trainer. From 1993 to 2009: Program Director for the Master/Graduate Diploma in Mediation and Conflict Resolution and Director of the *Centre for Peace, Conflict and Mediation* at UniSA, and from 2009 to 2016: Visiting Professor/Examiner with the Mediation and Conflict Intervention programs, National University of Ireland. She has received one international and two national awards for her services to the dispute resolution field. She co-edited the book: Bagshaw and Porter, *Mediation in the Asia-Pacific Region. Transforming Conflicts and Building Peace*, Routledge, 2009.

Bruce Burton is Professor Emeritus at Griffith University with an international reputation in the fields of drama education and applied theatre. He has been the recipient of six Australian Research Council Grants and is currently a lead researcher on a European Union Erasmus+ grant… He is the author of ten books, including two published by Springer in 2014 and 2015. He has received a national university teaching award in the Humanities and the Arts, and has been a Visiting Scholar at Cambridge University in the UK, and a Visiting Professor at the Sahlgrenska Institute at Gothenburg University in Sweden.

Anita Grünbaum was founder and Head of Education of Drama Pedagogues at Västerbergs Folkhögskola, Storvik, Sweden 1974–2002. She has had nearly 50 years' involvement in many aspects of drama development all over Sweden. Her research and book publications focus on drama among teenagers in school. She has been editor of the Swedish drama journal DramaForum 2004–2016 and author of hundreds of articles about drama in Sweden and abroad. Her main interests are process drama, drama for conflict handling, mediation and drama as a tool to learn about minorities. She is a trained psychodramatist.

Margret Lepp is Professor in Caring Science at the University of Gothenburg, Sweden and Adjunct Professor at Griffith University, Australia. She has published numerous original articles, books and chapters of books. She has used drama internationally as a teacher, researcher and consultant involving students, academics, patients, nurses and other health care professionals. She was a founder of the European Network Nursing Academies (ENNA) in 2007. She was the director of PhD students' affair in 2008–2010, and the Associate Editor of the *Scandinavian Journal of Caring Sciences* in 2008–2012. She is the project leader of a drama/theatre project in nursing education in Sweden and Australia.

Morag Morrison is Lecturer in Arts Education in the Faculty of Education, University of Cambridge, and Director of Studies for Education at St John's College, Cambridge. Morag was Course Manager for the M.Phil. Arts, Creativity and Education until 2018, and she has been involved in International Teacher and Professional Development projects in Kazakhstan and China. She has an Erasmus Teacher Exchange agreement with the Department of Caring Science at the University of Gothenburg, Sweden, and has received an award for her work in Nursing Education in Sweden. Morag continues to teach, research and publish in areas related to professional development and creative pedagogy through the arts.

Janet Pillai served as an Associate Professor at the Department of Performing Arts in University Sains Malaysia until 2013, and founded Arts-ED (2007), a non-profit organisation in Penang which provides arts and culture education for young people. Pillai specialises in arts education and creative pedagogies particularly for young people. She is currently an independent researcher and resource person who trains and programs community-engaged projects in partnership/consultation with community, local agencies, artists and professionals. Pillai has authored three books and numerous articles on arts and culture education and serves as expert resource person with UNESCO Bangkok and APCIEU Seoul.

Abbreviations

AAB	*Acting Against Bullying*
ACSS	Adolescent Conflict Style Scale
ARC	Australian Research Council
DASIE	Develop, Analyse, Support, Intervene, Evaluate model
DIAC	Drama in Acute Care
DIE	Drama-in-education
DRACON	DRAma and CONflict Resolution Project
EFT	Enhanced forum theatre
IDEA	International Drama/Theatre and Education Association
LISREL	Linear Structural Relations (analysis software)
MPU	Multicultural Programs Unit (NSW)
NGO	Non-government organisation
NSW	New South Wales
OECD	Organisation for Economic Cooperation and Development
Oxfam	Oxford Committee for Famine Relief
PhD	Doctor of Philosophy
PISA	Programme for International Student Assessment (tests)
RAD	Riksorganisationen Auktoriserade Dramapedagoger (Swedish Drama Teachers Organisation)
SIPRI	Stockholm International Peace Research Institute
TfD	Theatre for Development
TIE	Theatre-in-education
TO	Theatre of the Oppressed
UNESCO	United Nations Educational, Scientific and Cultural Organisation
UniSA	University of South Australia
WCC	Women's Centre for Change
WSARP	Whole-School Anti-Racism Program (NSW)

List of Figures

Fig. 2.1	Conflict triangle	18
Fig. 2.2	Styles of handling conflict	24
Fig. 2.3	Third-party roles	29
Fig. 2.4	Management approaches for asymmetric and symmetric conflicts	30
Fig. 4.1	Dynamics of the classic structure of Western drama	72
Fig. 5.1	Cultural values and attitudes in a Malaysian context	90
Fig. 5.2	Revealed and concealed in drama and conflict	115
Fig. 6.1	*Confronting* measurement model (Chi-square = 44; df = 32; $p < 0.08$; RMSEA = 0.030; GFI = 0.98)	130
Fig. 6.2	*Avoiding* measurement model (chi-square = 68; df = 40; RMSEA = 0.032; GFI = 0.98)	131
Fig. 6.3	**Fronting** measurement model (chi-square = 130; df = 78; RMSEA = 0.032; GFI = 0.97)	132
Fig. 7.1	Conflict resolution styles of Australian adolescents	166

List of Tables

Table 2.1	A contingency model of approaches to conflict intervention	33
Table 2.2	Phases of the problem-solving process	35
Table 4.1	Terms for components of conflict and drama	71
Table 4.2	Terms for the escalation of conflict and drama	71
Table 5.1	Shape and timescale of Malaysian DRACON project	95
Table 5.2	Changes in intensity of feeling across time	105
Table 6.1	Steps in developing and implementing the program	135
Table 6.2	Description of the program, sessions 1–12	142
Table 6.3	Participants involved in Phase II	143
Table 8.1	Brisbane project research questions	185
Table 8.2	Brisbane project action research cycles	189

List of Photographs

Malaysian Project

Malaysia 1:	Cycle 1: Students explore feelings through movement in school-related conflicts	117
Malaysia 2:	Cycle 1: Student-devised dance performance of school related conflict	117
Malaysia 3:	Cycle 2: Introduction to postcard theatre for exploring conflict situations	118
Malaysia 4:	Cycle 2: Using visual arts (comic drawing) to explore personal conflicts	119
Malaysia 5:	Cycle 2: Using visual arts (self-portrait) to explore individual conflicts	120
Malaysia 6:	Cycle 2: Participant explains her newspaper sculpture to her colleagues	121
Malaysia 7:	Cycle 3: Actors use a spin wheel of types of conflict in 'Stop! Look! Go!' TIE	121
Malaysia 8:	Cycle 3: An actor solicits opinions from students in 'Stop! Look! Go!' TIE	122

Swedish Project

Sweden 1:	Starting the Process—In a 'drama circle', the teacher introduces the procedures	150
Sweden 2:	Painting a conflict to share with the other students	150
Sweden 3:	'Third Party Sculptures'—protagonist and antagonist in action	151
Sweden 4:	'Third Party Sculptures'—two mediators in action with protagonist and antagonist	151
Sweden 5:	'Third Party Sculptures'—mediating is difficult!	152
Sweden 6:	'Third Party Sculptures'—The mediator practises on a teenage-mother conflict, with interested audience	152

Sweden 7: 'Third Party Sculptures'—the antagonists respond, with concentrated onlookers 153
Sweden 8: Peer teaching—A Year 8 student explains the ABC theory model to Year 7 peers 154

Brisbane Project
Brisbane 1: Acting Against Bullying... Will the bystanders intervene? 210
Brisbane 2: Acting Against Bullying... Enhanced forum theatre—emerging conflict. 211
Brisbane 3: Cooling Conflict... Manifest conflict—who can de-escalate it? 212
Brisbane 4: Cooling Conflict... Enhanced forum theatre—hot-seating a protagonist 212
Brisbane 5: Cooling Conflict... Spotting a latent conflict. 213
Brisbane 6: Cooling Conflict... Year 8 peer teachers demonstrate manifest conflict 213
Brisbane 7: Acting Against Bullying... The mediator investigates. 214
Brisbane 8: Acting Against Bullying... The mediator intervenes 214

Part I
Background and Theory

Chapter 1
Introduction

The DRACON Story

The real world of human conflict and the imaginary worlds of drama are closely tangled together in our thinking at every level—personal, communal and geopolitical. It clearly shows in our language—at least in English—and in our metaphors. Just think how often we hear and use clichés like 'What a tragic conflict…', 'This is a dramatic escalation…' and 'Let's not have a drama about this…'. They constantly colour our recounting of life's difficult moments, and think how many journalists would be bereft without these images!

Harnessing the power and familiarity of those dramatic ideas and images in order to help young people to address their real-life conflicts, albeit indirectly, has been the overarching purpose of DRACON, an international educational research project with a life and afterlife of over twenty years—and, as we shall demonstrate in the final chapter, it is still very much alive.

The DRAma and CONflict (DRACON) international project was an interdisciplinary and comparative action research project that commenced officially in 1996 and ended in 2005 with the publication of its 'final' report,[1] detailing a decade of mainly action research work conducted in four locations in three countries spanning the globe—Sweden, Malaysia and Australia. These countries were partly chosen because of important cultural differences and contrasts, and partly by happenstance—where those researchers with matching expertise and interests in the area happened to come across or already know each other.

---

[1] Löfgren and Malm (2007).

Background

Sweden is one of the earliest countries whose scholars and policy makers recognised the importance of peace and conflict studies. As early as 1964, the Swedish Prime Minister, Tage Erlander, puts forward the idea of establishing a peace research institute. In 1996, the Stockholm International Peace Research Institute (SIPRI) was founded to commemorate Sweden's 150 years of unbroken peace. The Department of Peace and Development Research at the University of Gothenburg was a leading centre of interdisciplinary and action-oriented enquiry.

Peace and conflict studies can be classified as a pedagogical activity (dealing with the teaching of conflict literacy) as well as a research activity (aiming to create new knowledge about conflict and conflict handling). By the 1970s, the field had become well established as research within the social sciences in universities in many countries, including Sweden, Malaysia and Australia. However, the pedagogical aspect of teaching conflict literacy was not as far advanced as the theoretical research development. One contributing factor is likely to be that higher education has been resistant to changing the relationship between theory and practice, and university thinking is itself still largely characterised by a traditional pedagogy based on lectures, tutorials and end-of-course tests (Christie & de Graaff, 2017). Research shows that a major problem with 'traditional' pedagogy at the tertiary level is that it encourages students to take a surface rather than a deep approach to their learning (Marton, Hounsell, & Entwistle, 1984).

Sowing the DRACON Seeds—A Vision

Interestingly, the beginnings of the DRACON project can be attributed to a Swedish industrial consultant and engineer, Jöns Andersson, who worked for a time in Southeast Asia. Andersson retired from engineering but retained his contacts with Southeast Asia. In the 1990s, he became acquainted through Swedish researchers Mats Friberg and Jens Allwood with a cross-cultural peace research project involving Malaysia and Sweden. The project was part of a larger project entitled 'Culturally conditioned models of conflict resolution in Sweden and Malaysia' organised by the Department of East and South-East Asian Research Studies, University of Gothenburg (1988–1994). Andersson came to understand from Friberg that the teaching of peace studies faced a challenge in that while peace research had great conflict theories to work with, it lacked an animated language and pedagogy that could teach conflict literacy.

Andersson had been interested in amateur theatre in Gothenburg from the 1970s and had been further inspired by Inger Johnsson, a pioneer in the development of the Education of Drama Pedagogues in Sweden. In the early 1990s, Andersson was introduced to Malaysian theatre practitioner Krishen Jit and they talked about the possible use of theatre, and specifically educational drama, as a teaching and learning tool. After observing a creative arts program with young people, organised by the company *Five Arts Centre*, Andersson was highly inspired by what he saw as a potential link between the academic and practical fields of drama and conflict resolution. He proceeded to organise contacts between Swedish conflict researcher Friberg and Janet Pillai, the educational drama programmer at the Five Arts Centre, and a lecturer at the local University of Sains Malaysia, Penang, Malaysia.

In July 1992, Andersson attended the first International Congress of Drama/Theatre and Education (IDEA '92) in Oporto, Portugal. Andersson was highly inspired by what he saw as a potential link between the academic and practical fields of drama and conflict resolution. Here, he connected with Margret Lepp from Malmö University, Sweden, then a PhD student in pedagogy with a focus on applied drama in nursing education. They decided to meet again in Sweden to further discuss possible plans for a drama and conflict management project. A meeting was set up with Friberg, who later became the first project leader of DRACON International from 1994 to 2001.

Andersson's vision and determination to link the two disciplines of conflict resolution and drama and bring experts together cannot be understated. Sadly, he had no further influence on the development of the project because of his death in 1995. Christie and de Graaff (2017) state that while both educationalists and engineers seek to understand phenomena and solve problems connected with them, educational researchers focus on phenomena and problems that involve people, whereas engineers tend to focus on material objects and effects. It can be surmised that as an engineer, Andersson may have professionally perceived the potential of drama and observed the effects of active learning while observing the Malaysian drama program with children.

The DRACON Is Born

In spite of Andersson's demise, the seed for a fascinating interdisciplinary venture had been planted. Starting at the drama end, in 1994 Malaysian drama educator Pillai reached out to invite Latif Kamaluddin, a conflict management specialist from the University of Sains, to become part of the Malaysian DRACON team, along with four artists: a dramatist, a visual artist, a dancer and a musician.

Coming the other way, the Swedish team of conflict specialists felt it was necessary to have experts in drama and pedagogy. In 1995, Anita Grünbaum, who was a drama education specialist and Head of drama teacher education at Storvik College, was invited to join the team, as was another expert in pedagogy, Horst Löfgren, Professor of Education at Malmö University.

At an international meeting in Aldinga, South Australia, in 1996, it was decided to extend the Swedish-Malaysian research cooperation, with two Australian teams joining the project, one in Adelaide, South Australia, and the second in Brisbane, Queensland. Like the original projects, the Australian teams were drawn from opposite starting strengths and expertise, with conflict management leading in Adelaide and drama in Brisbane. The core South Australian DRACON team consisted of Dale Bagshaw, a conflict resolution specialist from the University of South Australia in Adelaide, and Ken Rigby, an expert on bullying in schools, also from the University of South Australia, with Rosemary Nursey-Bray and Myk Mykyta, drama consultants and teachers, providing the drama input. The Queensland team initially comprised John O'Toole and Bruce Burton, both drama specialists from Griffith University in Brisbane, with advice from conflict management specialist Merrelyn Bates from the Griffith Justice Administration team. As this program grew to become the largest, longest-lasting and most widespread of the DRACON research projects, three more researchers were incorporated: Morag Morrison, then a local Brisbane teacher; Anna Plunkett, a PhD student; and as the program spread interstate to New South Wales, research associate Christine Hatton from Sydney. These three were all specialists in drama education.

Essentially, all four DRACON teams were responsible for financing their own research throughout. From 2001 to 2005, Löfgren assumed leadership of the DRACON International project and the Swedish team was given a grant from The Swedish Council of Scientific Research for three years' research to complete the Swedish studies and to draw the country findings together. Lofgren invited a PhD student, Birgitte Malm from Malmö University, to join the Swedish team, who together with Löfgren co-edited the final report.

From these beginnings, all the authors of this book were directly and intensely involved in the DRACON project, through to its formal completion in 2005, and some of us have continued, indirectly or sporadically, right through to the time of writing, as will be detailed in Chap. 9.

The Shape of the DRACON

As previously mentioned, DRACON International was formally established in 1996 by this core group of researchers from two disciplines, three countries and four teams, with the formal brief:

DRACON is an interdisciplinary and comparative action research project aimed at improving conflict handling among adolescent school children by using the medium of educational drama.[2]

The essential hypothesis underlying this project is that drama can be an effective way to learn about conflict handling or management—more commonly labelled at the time of writing this book as conflict transformation—not conflict resolution. These decisions will be explained in the next three chapters, because early in the project there was some discussion about drama's capacity for actual conflict resolution, meaning solving participants' real everyday life conflicts. This concept was rejected at the outset by some of the Australian drama specialists who were only willing to join

---

[2]Löfgren and Malm ibid, p. 13.

the project on the condition that direct management and resolution of conflicts in real life were excluded. The Malaysian project did try dealing partially with student's real conflicts using a multi-arts approach, but found it problematic. The reasons for these difficulties and the Australian refusals are addressed in detail in Chap. 4, Bridging Conflict and Drama. For the rest of the project, the consensus was that we would use drama indirectly, as a strategy for helping students to understand the nature of conflict, and perhaps give them some useful tools to later understand, manage or transform their own conflicts.

In the early years of peace and conflict studies, the idea of joining the fields of conflict transformation and drama, either in theory or practice, was almost unheard of. The cautious tendency to keep the two fields separate now seems strange given that drama and conflict are two words that have always had a lot in common that is recognised in common parlance—as we have mentioned, and as will be examined in detail in Chap. 4.

From the outset, cultural and intercultural contexts and factors of conflict were a major priority of DRACON International; this is hardly surprising, given the cultural diversity of the teams, but it also flowed on naturally from its earlier forebears. As we have mentioned, a group of Swedish and Malaysian researchers had cooperated for some years on a comparative study of how conflicts are handled in different social and cultural contexts in Sweden and in Malaysia. The project *Culturally conditioned models of conflict resolution in Sweden and Malaysia* lasted from 1988 to 1994 (Allwood & Friberg, 1994). DRACON carried over an important idea from this earlier study: that culture matters in conflict transformation. Therefore, the DRACON project adopted a comparative and cross-cultural approach and inherited the idea of international research cooperation organised on a symmetrical basis between independent national teams. In an early meeting, the team members discussed the opportunities afforded for useful three-way comparisons and contrasts between the ways in which these three nations with quite disparate social and cultural histories were coming to terms with their ongoing challenges of multiculturalism and changing population profiles. Conflict is an inevitable component of intercultural and cross-cultural encounters, and there were opportunities to compare how conflict has been managed traditionally and contemporarily in the schools in those societies.

The DRACON research focused on adolescents in the context of school. It is well understood that young adolescents in transition from childhood to adult life often experience tensions and difficulties in handling conflicts. DRACON team members, who were predominantly educators, strongly believed it would be appropriate to introduce the concept of conflict literacy to young adolescents and that the school was the most strategic arena for learning, practising and spreading conflict competence. The DRACON research teams focused on a sample of school-going adolescents aged 13–15 years to increase their conflict handling skills and knowledge using educational drama methods.

The whole of the DRACON research was based on five basic hypotheses:

- It is possible to improve conflict literacy and conflict handling through drama.
- The school is a strategic arena for learning conflict handling and literacy skills.

- Early adolescence is a critical period for learning conflict resolution strategies, as there is a high frequency of conflicts.
- Ways of viewing and handling conflicts are culturally conditioned.
- Empowerment of students is needed in order to build up self-help as well as intervention capacities.

The main aim of DRACON has been:

to develop an integrated program using conflict handling as the theory and practice, and drama as the pedagogy, in order to empower students through an integrated, school-based program to manage their own conflict experiences in all aspects of their lives.[3]

We developed these aims into the following eight general research questions as a guide for all four DRACON teams:

- What are the most common types of conflicts among adolescents? How do they perceive their conflicts and how do they behave in typical conflict situations?
- How can adolescents explore their own conflicts through the medium of drama?
- Can the development of relevant drama methods and programs in schools improve adolescents' capacities for handling conflicts?
- How resilient are these drama methods and programs? Will they function under troublesome conditions, such as in 'problem' classes and in ethnically divided schools?
- Can the same or similar drama programs be used for school teachers and counsellors to stimulate their participation as facilitators in the drama programs?
- Under what conditions and to what effect can the drama programs be implemented in a whole school? Can they be taken over and run by the school itself, and under what conditions?
- What kind of observations/measurements can be developed for studying the long- and short-term effects of drama programs?
- What are the effects of different background or contextual factors (national and ethnic cultures, school systems etc.) on the design and outcomes of the field studies?[4]

These questions were in general adhered to throughout, although each team pursued their investigation in distinct and individual ways, and tweaked the questions—and re-calibrated their order of priority—as necessary to fit the team's own cultural, research and school contexts. This was inevitable, as action research was the chosen central research method, and a characteristic of action research is that it provides its own momentum and changes of direction.

---

[3]Löfgren and Malm ibid, p. 422.
[4]Löfgren and Malm ibid, p. 29.

Flight of the DRACON

As a first task, each of the four country teams developed its own action research cycles relevant to its schools and adolescent situations. These included developing research methods that could map students' conflicts, and the strategies used by students for handling their own conflicts.

The second task was to study the effects of various educational drama exercises for the purpose of conflict exploration or intervention at individual, class and whole-school levels.

The third task was to develop and test integrated drama programs, giving adolescents in the three different countries the opportunity to handle conflicts in a more constructive way or simply to develop conflict literacy.

Throughout the research process, a fourth major task conducted at inter-country level was to examine and compare conflict handling processes in different cultures and examine which educational drama methods worked best or were most culturally appropriate.

The action research base and commonly agreed research questions allowed the whole project to grow and develop organically, which entailed variations. The contextual differences, the different balances of expertise in the four teams and those accidents of happenstance led to divergences that were useful to the organic growth of the project as a whole, and meant that the comparative elements of the research could only be informal, each team illuminating the other's research. The common research questions and philosophy kept a level of unity among this variegation, and contingencies sometimes worked towards commonality.

- The distinctive primary strategy used in Malaysia, namely professional theatre-in-education with writers and teams working with schoolchildren in a broad arts-based program of school visits, was not able to be replicated in any of the other projects. However, the insights gained, particularly into the cultural components of conflict, and adolescent responses to the arts, formed touchstones for all the other projects, and provided a valuable model for the Brisbane team when it ventured briefly into the field of theatre-in-education.
- Initially, the Swedish and Queensland teams found themselves independently experimenting with the same improvised drama strategies of forum theatre and process drama, and they came up with fieldwork programs very similar in structure to each other. After the formal conclusion of DRACON, these have fused into a now quite widely used new genre of class-based drama, christened within the project as 'enhanced forum theatre (EFT)' (see Chaps. 3 and 8).
- The intensive preliminary survey work on conflict mapping and bullying in schools carried out early by the Adelaide team flowed directly into the later excursion into drama and bullying that was entered into by the Brisbane team and significantly informed all the projects in the area of bullying—a frequent cause of conflict in all cultural contexts.

The whole DRACON project was in fact characterised by considerable diversity of approach, scale and longevity, partly due to the different cultural backgrounds, interests and expertise of the various team members, but partly also to the contingencies affecting all the teams at different times, relating to funding, sponsorships and all the usual uncontrollable variables of large and international qualitative research. Different levels of funding and availability of school and university systemic support created different scales of action research fieldwork; different strengths of expertise led to disparate proportions of the project researchers' time and energy spent on developing the theory and the practice in each location.

However, throughout the project in general there was an effective and sufficient network of communication that kept the national projects working in synchronicity and accord. There were two major components to this network, one formal and one informal. To further the aims and operation of DRACON, international meetings including all four teams, each lasting several days, were held annually throughout the project. There were eight in all, in all three countries (Australia, Malaysia and Sweden), but mainly in Penang, Malaysia, as the approximate geographical mid-point. Intellectually and organisationally, these meetings were crucial for many reasons: to ensure that philosophically the projects were aligned; to develop together our conceptual and theoretical understandings that underpinned our practice; to exchange information and findings, and advise each other about the ongoing structures and activities of the individual projects, and to share successful strategies and techniques; and as much as anything to cement and maintain the personal relationships and sustain commitment to the overall vision. These informal relationships were the other major component that glued the project together—as the members grew to know and trust one another, and understand each other's way of working, we established connections both inside and beyond DRACON. This was particularly true of the drama specialists, all of whom have since worked with each other independently in other related and unrelated contexts. The project was not all plain sailing, of course, with so many individual perspectives, cultures and histories coming together on such a complex project for so long. However, only once during the formal DRACON decade was there a major clash of personality or philosophy, leading to a breakdown of communication and the unfortunate withdrawal of one key original member of the project. This single instance did not otherwise affect the outcomes of the project or the network of relationships.

We have learned much from our individual and combined experiences about the essential characteristics of international research collaboration and the strategies that make it work. These characteristics were succinctly summed up in an earlier article resulting from the research[5]:

- valuing diversity and developing cooperative goals
- engaging in self-reflection and reflexivity
- practising collaborative dialogue
- taking time and building trust.

---

[5]Bagshaw, Lepp and Zorn (2007), p. 333.

How to Read This Book

One of the defining features of DRACON was its open and dialogical nature. The insights and discoveries made by the four teams were not locked into formal comparisons, but informed each other in a ten-year ongoing conversation among all the participants—the teachers, schools, educational and conflict transformation theorists and above all the students. As participant members of all four teams, the authors have tried to capture something of the dialogue of learning, the development of new theory and practice, and something of the stories. We hope we are presenting a coherent picture of DRACON as a unified whole, so the book has a clear shape, divided into three parts. However, we have not tried to meld the writers' contributions into a uniform style, hoping to preserve something of the conversation and each project's idiosyncrasies.

Along with this introductory history, Part 1 comprises three chapters. Chapter 2, with its natural home in the previously mentioned academic field of 'conflict studies', explicates the theories of conflict with which we worked, and the theoretical developments generated in the project. Chapter 3 explains the relevant theory and practice of the growing field of drama education—and again, the major developments made within the DRACON project. Chapter 4 offers a theoretical bridge between the two fields—the bridge that we spent our whole time spanning in our practice. The word 'transformation' is a current keyword, both in conflict studies and educational pedagogy, and we will show how it provided a central conceptual link for us.

Part 2 is comprised of four 'country' chapters, telling the story of each of the four projects: Malaysia, Sweden, South Australia and Queensland. Each contains a brief preliminary description of the local cultural and educational background for the reader at least to grasp the basics of that particular context: the school system, the student population, the researchers' expertise and what they brought to the project. Each chapter is then centred on reporting the action research: its aims, methods, the fieldwork and its analysis. The chapter then concludes with the immediate findings and outcomes of the project. This structure has been used as a general guide, but the balance is different in each chapter. Malaysia completed three cycles that also included other art forms besides drama. Brisbane completed nine cycles, in three waves. South Australia completed one cycle of action research fieldwork, and its major contribution was its theoretical survey research. Sweden provided a more even balance of theoretical development and fieldwork than any of the other projects. These four chapters do not present every detail of the original DRACON International research. We have selected those aspects we believe will be useful and interesting to academics and practitioners in the relevant fields of drama and conflict transformation, and to the general reader.

Part 3, comprising just one chapter, looks beyond the end of DRACON to what has happened since 2005: to the many follow-ups, spin-offs, tangential programs and related projects that have occurred, and are still occurring, right across the globe, in countries far removed from the three original nations. These are explored in terms not of their direct relation to whichever country project spawned or inspired them, but to the main themes that have emerged and that we ourselves have derived from the project.

Other DRACON Footprints

This book is attempting to tell the general and interested reader for the first time the whole story of DRACON, as seen through the eyes of the majority of its participant researchers and practitioners, and told by them. There are other previous publications that deal with particular aspects of the project, or some of the emerging themes. These are mainly for specialist audiences, and full details can be found in Appendix A. The Swedish and the Queensland projects each produced a textbook for teachers based on their work. Others of the authors, as well as other scholars and practitioners, have written about the follow-up and spin-off projects that are described in Chap. 9. Details of all these can be found in Appendix B. For dedicated social science researchers, the complete details of all the theoretical and practical research, and all the findings and statistics of all four projects, can be found in the already cited Final Project Report.

What follows here is the book of the DRACON.

References

Allwood, J., & Friberg, M. (1994). *Culturally conditioned models of conflict resolution: A comparative analysis of Malaysia and Sweden.* Göteborg: Padrigu.
Bagshaw, D., Lepp, M., & Zorn, C. R. (2007). International collaboration: Building teams and managing conflicts. *Conflict Resolution Quarterly, 24*(4), 433–446.
Christie, M., & de Graaff, E. (2017). The philosophical and peadgogical underpinning of active learning in engineering education. *European Journal of Engineering Education, 42.*
Löfgren, H., & Malm, B. (Eds.) (2007). *DRACON INTERNATIONAL: BRIDGING THE FIELDS OF DRAMA AND CONFLICT MANAGEMENT. Empowering students to handle conflicts through school–based programmes.* Malmö: University of Malmö. http://dspace.mah.se/bitstream/2043/5975/1/drac06nov.pdf
Marton, F., Hounsell, D., & Entwistle, N. J. (1984). *The experience of learning.* Edinburgh: Scottish Academic Press.

Chapter 2
Conflict Management, Resolution and Transformation

Key Definitions

Approaches to handling conflict have been labelled in many ways, including conflict management, conflict resolution and conflict transformation, and this specialist field of scholarship and practice has developed since World War II. The field then expanded after a slow beginning in the 1950s and 1960s. Different social sciences converged in the analysis of conflicts as well as in the quest for improved ways of handling or approaching conflicts. Practitioners in many applied fields, such as family mediation, labour management relations and international diplomacy, learned from each other's theories and processes. Increasingly, 'conflict' is understood as a generic term that applies to social clashes on many levels, from the interpersonal to the international. A basic idea is that all conflicts are similar enough in their structure and dynamics to make it possible to develop general concepts and theories of conflict as well as generic procedures for handling conflict.

There are many different definitions of conflict, suggesting that conflict can be *constructive* or *destructive* and involve *action* or *no action*. Deutsch, a leading theorist, stated that 'a conflict exists whenever incompatible activities occur … An action that is incompatible with another action … in some way makes the latter less likely or less effective' (Deutsch, 1973: 10). Others suggest that a conflict can arise when two or more people or groups perceive their needs, interests, views, values or goals as being different or incompatible, whether or not they propose to take action. Conflict can also arise when there are 'scarcities of certain resources such as power, influence, money, time, space, popularity, position and rivalry' (Johnson & Johnson, 1991: 303). On a more positive note, conflict can be seen as creating an opportunity for intimacy, change, growth and learning.

Christopher Moore highlights that conflicts are based upon a number of factors. *Value-based* conflicts can be caused by different criteria or priorities for evaluating ideas or behaviour, different goals and different ways of life, ideology or religion. *Structural* conflicts are caused by negative patterns of behaviour or interaction; unequal control, ownership or distribution of resources; unequal power and authority;

geographical, physical and environmental factors and time constraints. *Relationship* conflicts can be caused by poor or miscommunication, stereotyping, strong emotions or repetitive negative behaviour. *Data-based* conflicts are caused by lack of information and misinformation, different views on what is relevant, different interpretations of data and different ways of assessing or processing data. *Interest-based* conflicts can be caused by different procedural interests, psychological interests and substantive interests that form the substance of a dispute (Moore, 2003).

Postmodernist, narrative theorists offer a different perspective on conflict. They view conflict as an inevitable by-product of diversity and the operation of power, contests over whose meanings or stories are privileged, rather than the result of the expression of personal needs and interests:

> … conflict is likely because people do not have direct access to the truth or the facts about any situation. Rather they view things from a cultural position … they develop a story about what has happened and continue to act into a social situation out of the story they have created. (Winslade & Monk, 2000: 41)

From this perspective, dominant discourses in the *social, economic, cultural* and *political context* influence the way that a conflict is perceived, defined, handled and processed.

The literature often distinguishes between realistic or necessary conflict and unrealistic or unnecessary conflict. In *necessary conflict,* there are substantive differences expressed as opposed needs, goals, means, values, rights or interests. These substantive aspects may be dealt with in negotiation or mediation, although where there are value conflicts the most that can often be achieved is for people to agree to disagree. *Unnecessary conflict*, however, stems from ignorance, error, historical tradition and prejudice, dysfunctional organisational or group structures, competitive attitudes and behaviours, hostility, or the need for tension release—factors which to a significant degree can be prevented and controlled. These aspects of conflict do not form the substance of a conflict, but get in the way of effective conflict management. They need to be dealt with before effective negotiation can occur on the substantive issues. Sometimes counselling or time is needed before mediation can begin, or counselling can occur alongside mediation in order to assist one or both parties to handle the emotional aspects of their dispute.

The language we use when we describe our conflict handling interventions is important. John Paul Lederach points out that popular conceptions of the term 'conflict resolution' promote the idea that conflict may be undesirable and should be stopped at the expense of justice, whereas in ongoing relationships, conflict remains. The term 'conflict management' is too 'narrow' and 'technical', suggesting that we can control conflict (Lederach, 1995: 16). 'Conflict transformation', however, is more closely linked to peace-making than conflict 'resolution' or 'management'. The term 'transformation' addresses the ongoing, longer-term conflicts and the potential need for structural changes.

Conflict transformation best describes the approach we took in the DRACON project. It may be defined as any method, process or procedure which is intended to transform a conflict into a less costly form of interaction between the conflicting parties—for example, the transformation of a painful and unproductive quarrel between two people into a creative dialogue. In this chapter, we will study conflict handling in general, independent of whether or not it is intended to lead to conflict resolution, conflict management or conflict transformation.

Key Approaches to Conflict: A Historical Perspective

Conflict is a natural and inevitable part of all human relationships and therefore certain approaches to conflict have been present from the very beginning of human existence.

Collaborative, non-coercive approaches to conflict were born as an academic field of study and research in the 1950s in the West, starting in the USA. The interdisciplinary field of peace and conflict research pioneered new studies of international conflicts but was slow to move into practical applications because of the complex nature of international conflicts. However, the whole field of conflict resolution gained a new momentum in the 1970s because many people started to apply non-coercive and participatory methods of intervention to intra-national conflicts such as family quarrels, industrial disputes, conflict in the workplace, neighbourhood conflicts and so forth.

In general terms, the trend has gradually moved away from expensive, time-consuming, public, adversarial legal procedures such as formal arbitration and adjudication. In the latter processes, the conflict is settled by coercive means without giving serious consideration to the causes of the conflict or the needs and interests of the people involved. Increasingly, approaches to conflict now emphasise cooperation rather than competition. Collaborative and consensual outcomes are reached through 'problem-solving', 'controlled communication', 'workshops', 'family or group conferencing', 'facilitation', 'conciliation', 'mediation' and so forth. Specialist centres for conflicts and disputes have been set up across the Western world and increasingly people are choosing to get help from mediators and others with a different type of competence—people with special education and training from diverse backgrounds such as law, psychology, social work, counselling, human services, organisational studies and the social sciences.

Traditional Western approaches to dispute resolution tend to be individualistic, confrontational and retributive, based on an adversarial culture of law. Central to this culture is the concept of universal legal rights. On the other hand, alternative approaches are inspired by a more communitarian culture, which emphasises the long-term interests and relationships of people embedded in a community. This leads to restorative justice models of dispute resolution in which incompatibilities are shared in a constructive environment in order to increase understanding and improve the communication and/or the relationships between the parties. It's important to emphasise that in Asian and other communitarian cultures, views and approaches to conflict and its resolution are underpinned by collectivist, cultural and religious principles (Bagshaw and Porter, 2009).

Alternative dispute resolution processes, such as mediation, privilege the concept of voluntary 'win–win' solutions to conflicts—a pragmatic concept going beyond the value-laden ideas of 'right or wrong' or 'good and bad' that often lead to win–lose outcomes. In mediation, it is assumed that under certain conditions mutually satisfying processes and outcomes to conflicts can be found when parties voluntarily come together to identify disputed issues, explore their mutual interests and develop new creative options and new ways of relating to each other. They themselves carry the main responsibility for the management of their conflict. This approach is favoured where people want to be in control of their own decisions and where the preservation of an ongoing relationship is needed, as adversarial processes tend to irrevocably damage relationships.

The conventional approach to conflicts used in most schools can be compared to legal methods of conflict management. The disciplinary code of the school often corresponds to the law. Disciplinary school codes may prohibit behaviours such as bullying, vandalism, name-calling and teasing. Teachers can be viewed as being like 'police' and 'judges' in the system. The school Principal represents a higher authority to whom the most serious cases are referred. However, as schools have experienced more and more problems with student conflicts and violence this hierarchical disciplinary system has proved to be inadequate. Since the 1980s, alternative approaches to conflict management have slowly penetrated into the educational systems of many Western countries.

Some schools have built comprehensive conflict management systems. First of all, they have tried to create a supportive school climate conducive to conflict prevention. Secondly, they have introduced conflict-handling skills to the students and staff. Thirdly, they have introduced collaborative procedures for solving conflicts, such as *peer mediation*, in which some students are selected and trained to mediate conflicts between their peers. However, in most cases the new methods have been seen as complementing the disciplinary system. The DRACON project grew out of these developments. We were searching for new and creative ways to empower adolescent school children to manage their own conflicts.

The Components of Conflict

Before presenting the basic concepts underpinning approaches to conflict, we have to understand what conflict is. Conflict can be positive and is necessary for good decisions and for growth, change, learning and intimacy to occur. However, the term 'conflict' has many negative connotations, such as dispute, argument, debate, disagreement, contradiction, crisis, incompatibility, clash, struggle, fight, violence, tension, hostility, dissonance, war and so forth. These terms all cover some aspects of conflict but not the whole. Disagreement for instance is not necessarily conflict as people can agree to disagree. Hostility and tension are not conflict if they can stay on the level of feelings and emotions without developing into destructive action. Incompatible goals are not conflict if the parties refrain from pursuing their goals. In these cases, we may talk about *latent conflict* in the sense that the situation has the potential to develop into *emerging, manifest* or *real conflict.*

Latent conflicts are characterised by underlying tensions that have not fully developed and have not escalated into a highly polarised conflict. Often, one or more parties may not even be aware of the conflict. Here approaches such as giving information, education or counselling tend to be most appropriate, with an emphasis on prevention and early intervention. Mediators, for example, can help people identify the nature of the conflict, who is involved or affected, the needs, issues and interests involved and possible procedures for resolution, management or transformation.

Emerging conflicts are conflicts where the parties are identifiable, they acknowledge that there is a problem and most issues are clear, but no workable negotiation or problem-solving process has developed. Parties tend to adopt a particular strategy or style for handling the conflict at this stage and again may be assisted by timely access to information, education, counselling and/or mediation or conciliation which assists them to manage their relationship and to process or transform their conflict in a constructive manner.

Manifest conflicts are those in which the parties who are actively engaged in an ongoing dispute may have adopted strategies or styles and started to negotiate and may have reached an impasse or stalemate. Manifest conflict has been defined as 'a social situation involving perceived incompatibilities in goals or values between two or more parties, attempts by the parties to control each other, and antagonistic feelings by the parties towards each other' (Fisher, 1990: 6). The word 'perceive' is very important in this definition as a particular person or party might decide to interpret the other person's actions as not really aimed at him or her, not really negative or not of importance anyhow. Such a conflict situation can be characterised as *unilateral* conflict. The subjective character of this situation indicates that a conflict is a social construction. Conflicts do not 'just happen' to people. They are constructed by the participants in interaction in a particular cultural context and are influenced by their definitions and perceptions of the situation.

Conventional wisdom says that it takes only one person to make a conflict but two to solve it. However, from a constructivist perspective one would argue the opposite, that it takes two to make a real conflict and only one to solve it.

The definition of manifest conflict presented above indicates that conflict in the generic sense involves at least four components:

- parties or actors to the conflict
- attitudes towards each other and the relationship
- behaviour towards each other
- contradiction or the substantive content of the conflict.

If we take for granted the first component—the parties—we arrive at the following formula: *Manifest Conflict = Attitudes + Behaviour + Contradiction* or in short: *Conflict = A + B + C*. In this formula, A stands for negative attitudes, B for destructive behaviour and C for contradiction. Manifest conflict can be seen as a triadic construct. Of the three, the behavioural component is the only clearly visible or manifest aspect of the conflict. Attitudes and incompatibilities, on the other hand, are more or less

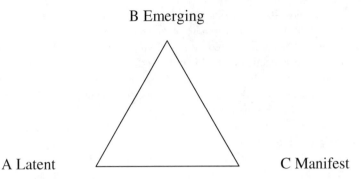

Fig. 2.1 Conflict triangle

hidden, sometimes even to the parties themselves, e.g. as unconscious hostility to the other person. The three components together form the *conflict triangle*.

A latent conflict is said to exist if there is no conflict behaviour, but there are contradictions and/or hostile attitudes. A conflict is usually latent before it becomes manifest and there is always a possibility that a latent conflict is transformed into a manifest one. A manifest conflict can also have latent aspects, for example, when the parties hide their true attitudes towards each other (Fig. 2.1).

This is the beginning of the so-called ABC theory of conflict, originally proposed by Galtung (1996). The simple ABC formula is worth remembering as it highlights the significant features of the definition of conflict given above.

There is no generally accepted theory of conflict, only a vast number of different approaches and a few efforts at synthesis. Each approach provides a different lens through which to view conflict and suggests a particular approach to its resolution, management or transformation. The authors of this book favour an eclectic approach, believing that all theories have something valuable to contribute to our understanding of conflict as a multidimensional phenomenon.

Parties to the Conflict

In every manifest conflict, there are people involved who we call 'parties', commonly pitted against each other. Depending on the number of independent actors, a distinction can be made between *bipolar, triangular and multi-polar* or *multi-party* conflicts.

The parties can include a variety of people, individuals or groups, factions within the groups, allies, spectators, perpetrators and victims, mediators, authorities, advocates, family members, separating couples. If the main parties are individuals, we talk about *interpersonal conflicts*; if they are collectives, we are dealing with *intergroup conflicts* such as tribal fights, fights between families, industrial disputes or international wars. There are also *intra-personal conflicts*, that is to say two subpersonalities of the same tormented person are fighting for supremacy within one psyche. When a person is helping another person with an intra-personal conflict, it is not called 'conflict resolution' but 'therapy'.

Conflicts at school that concerned us in the DRACON project tended to be interpersonal or inter-group conflicts, but there may have been an intra-personal dimension to these conflicts as well. It is not always easy to separate intra-personal, interpersonal and the inter-group conflicts.

Some well-known theories explain conflicts as originating from the nature of the parties, such as realist theory and transpersonal theory. *Realist theory* says that conflict is caused by the antisocial nature of humans, our aggressiveness and hunger for power. The legal system (adjudication) is an offshoot of realist thinking to which has been added the idea of universal rules (law) applying to everyone (equality in court). These rules are enforced by the state, which is assumed to have a monopoly on the legitimate use of violence within its territory.

The *transpersonal theory of conflict* suggests that people are driven by egoistic desires generated by an individuated sense of self. According to transpersonal theory, there is a possibility of ultimately transcending power struggles by a process of spiritual development. When we drop our sense of an individuated self and surrender to the greater whole, we are in tune with the Dao (the Way) as the Chinese say.

According to *socialisation theory*, people's behaviour in conflicts depends on how they have been socialised. Harsh socialisation, such as physical violence and emotional deprivation, can produce aggressive adults who are prone to create conflicts around them. Some people are assumed to have 'wounds' from childhood. Conflict resolution processes that treat the root causes rather than the symptoms attempt to heal the psychic wounds of participants through some sort of individual or group therapy. According to this view, interpersonal conflicts are closely related to intra-personal conflicts. Every theory about the nature and causes of conflict holds a key to the way the conflict is perceived and handled.

Contradiction or Content of the Conflict (the C-Component of Conflict)

The content of the conflict can be referred to as 'bones of contention', incompatible goals and values, contradictory interests, disagreement on substance, specific grievances, substantive issues and so forth. If there are many substantive issues, the conflict is termed *diffuse*, whereas a conflict with only one issue is called *specific*. What appears at first sight to be a conflict between two parties over one issue is often a complex conflict between many parties over a variety of issues. A divorce, for instance, may include not only husband and wife but also lovers and children, relatives and friends, and the disputed issues not only involve decisions about income and habitation but also questions about their future relationships, how to share responsibility for children, division of property and so forth.

Interest-based theories argue that conflicts arise because people pursue incompatible interests or values. *Interests* are concrete and divisible, and therefore, conflicts of interests can often be solved through a *compromise*, sometimes called 'splitting the difference'. *Values* are abstract and indivisible and difficult to trade through a bargaining process, e.g. one party wants a socialist order and the other a liberal one. Value stands against value and the winner takes all. In both cases, we are dealing with *zero-sum* or *distributive* conflicts—what one party wins the other loses. However, most real-life situations involve *mixed motive conflicts*. Workers and employers have a common interest in the profitability of the firm and at the same time opposing interests in the splitting of the profit. In such systems of 'antagonistic cooperation', for example in a school class, there is always some space for negotiations.

Problem-solving is an approach to conflict that focuses on dissolving the contradictions of the conflicts. It has become one of the major approaches to conflict within the alternative dispute resolution field. It offers a fairly linear and rational approach to resolution if the parties agree to see the conflict as their shared problem. The basic technique consists of focusing on the needs, interests and goals of the parties that underlie their positions, then generating a variety of creative options and designing outcomes that meet the needs of all concerned, commonly known as a *'win–win'* solution. For example, if both parties want to have the one orange available it can look like a zero-sum game. However, if through discussion they reach an understanding of *why* each party wants the orange (the needs), it may turn out that what one person really wants is the juice from the pulp and what the other needs is the peel to produce marmalade or to decorate icing on a cake—the situation can then become a *positive-sum* (or 'win–win') *outcome*.

Conflict Attitudes (The A-Component of Conflict)

The attitudes that the conflicting parties have towards each other and to themselves have at least two components—*cognitive* (assumptions about and images of the enemy and of the self), and *emotive* (positive or negative feelings). Other words for the A-component are hostility, tension, dissonance and so forth. The typical pattern of attitudes in conflicts is that we perceive ourselves as intrinsically right and/or good and the other party as wrong and/or evil. The other is blamed, criticised, judged and/or labelled. This fundamental asymmetry of the 'self-other' images can be explained by *depth-psychological theories*, at least partly, as resulting from repression and projection. Each person excludes from her consciousness the unwanted aspects of herself (the *shadow*) and automatically attributes them to the other party. This mechanism of *projection* can also be called scapegoating. Often the negative attitudes are not even directed towards the original source of the frustration; for example, a man scolded by his boss at his job takes it out on his wife when he comes home. Such conflicts are called *unrealistic, projected or displaced*.

The image of oneself is as important as the image of the other. For a group conflict to emerge, each party has to develop a sense of shared identity. Often the shared identity within each group is taken for granted by the participants as well as the analysts. However, *constructivism* claims that the identity of a party or the nature of the issue is a social construction that evolves with the conflict itself. In some group conflicts, especially ethnic conflicts, people have socially constructed a history and a common ancestry and created myths about differences that were not really there from the start. The 'self-other' separation is often reinforced through a process of *social polarisation*, in which people on both sides of the conflict cut all links with people on the other side. The boundaries between the groups are strengthened through discourses of inclusion and exclusion and the construction of images of the other as 'the enemy'. Solidarity within the groups is emphasised. Persons who socialise with the 'enemy' are regarded as traitors.

Applied to the personal level, *social constructivism* leads to the idea that the self is not an inner essence, but a multiple set of identities constructed in large measure by people's group affiliations and cultural backgrounds. According to constructivism almost everything in a conflict situation is socially constructed—the identities, the interests and values of the parties as well as the events, facts and realities of the conflict. In this view, people are storytelling creatures—they not only tell stories, they live them too. The stories that guide people's lives are constructed from the discourses available in the culture. From a *narrative view*, conflict arises between people when they construct incompatible stories, stories that lead to diametrically opposed readings of the events in the conflict. The facts of the situation are not so important, because people don't have direct access to the objective 'truth' of any situation. Conflict can also arise when some voices are marginalised and others are privileged, in particular, where there are gender, class, race or ethnic differences.

From the point of view of subjectivist theories, the approach to conflict focuses on changing subjective perceptions and constructions rather than objective interests. If we accept the Buddhist view that conflict is in the hearts and minds of people, then it is in the hearts and minds that resolution comes about.

Conflict Behaviour (The B-Component of Conflict)

In manifest conflicts, the parties try to control each other through different types of behaviour, both verbal and non-verbal. An important threshold has been reached when physical violence becomes a part of the picture. Sometimes words like action-reaction, attack–defend, struggle, clash and fight are used to describe this component.

While psychological theories tend to focus on the cognitive and emotional processes and perceptions that influence conflict behaviour, *interactionist theory* focuses on the behaviour itself. According to behavioural theories, the behavioural component (verbal and physical) should have a favoured status in conflict theory, as all conflicts are constituted and sustained by the behaviours of the parties involved. It is important to notice that conflict behaviour cannot be understood by studying the individual behaviours of the parties in isolation. A significant feature of conflict behaviour is that it develops in cycles of actions and reactions.

Conflict involves communication, both verbal and non-verbal. *Communication theories* focus on the use of language, gestures, symbols and structures of discourse, how people argue, take turns in producing messages, etc. It is a commonplace observation that each individual always brings unique experiences and meanings to any conversation. How then is it possible to reach agreement on the meanings of the messages in situations coloured by fear and mistrust? How do the parties convey meaning and coordinate the management of meaning? Interpretations of a message in a conflict will be shaped by the context, the nature of the relationship as well as the self-concept and culture of each individual. Misunderstandings are inevitable in conflict situations.

Theories of communication have identified a number of barriers to communication or *communication killers* that tend to provoke the other into defensive responses or aggression—such as using threats, orders, criticism, name-calling, demanding, blaming, judging, patronising, diagnosing motives, interrogating and persuading with logic. Marshall Rosenberg (1999) called the language we normally use in conflicts *wolf language*. He invented an alternative language called *giraffe language* with a potential to transform conflicts into peaceful dialogues. Giraffe language is a language for compassionate communication where you can speak your mind without creating hostility. The two primary skills needed when speaking this language are *appropriate assertiveness* (clearly expressing to the other 'I'-messages) and *compassionate listening* (empathically receiving 'you'-messages from the other).

When adversaries engage in contentious behaviour, they may eventually use physical violence against each other. This is usually preceded by a number of serious verbal threats. When physical violence erupts, a new dynamic is generated. The logic of war takes over. Now the parties treat each other as 'inanimate objects' and construct 'the other' as the enemy. The fight itself has a brutalising effect on the parties and their relationship, often bringing out the worst qualities in each. At this level, the conflict feeds itself in a vicious circle of violence, resistance and revenge that it is very difficult to break out of.

Feminist theories in the modernist genre view gender-based conflicts as a consequence of patriarchy and challenge men to address their violent behaviour. Postmodernist feminist theories also focus on the importance of language and power in the construction of gendered identities and the place of conflict therein. Feminists are concerned with gendered nature of abuses of power within relationships, such as is evident in domestic violence and much of the violence, sexual harassment and bullying in schools. Dominant constructions of masculinity in schools, for example, are often associated with the ability to provoke and win fights, misogyny, and with abusive behaviours towards girls and towards boys who display feminine qualities or behaviour; this has been demonstrated by a large research project carried out by the author in South Australia (Bagshaw, 2004).

In violent conflicts, interventions require first of all a *security approach*. Before choosing an appropriate intervention, screening for violence and imbalances and abuses of power should occur. This is necessary to keep the antagonists safe and to prevent one person from dominating, controlling or harming the other. Conflict interventions on lower levels of intensity include introducing rules for behaviour.

Sociocultural Context of Conflicts

The sociocultural context of conflicts includes a number of components of the conflict situation, such as the power and resources of the parties, the presence of allies, mediators, bystanders and authorities, the institutions for dealing with conflict available in the culture, the social structure, the organisational and cultural conditions, etc. Almost all conflicts have *structural* elements. They have to be understood not only from a micro-perspective but also from a macro-perspective. Therefore, the DRACON approach to student conflicts has not treated interpersonal conflicts in isolation from the rest of society. Cultural dimensions such as age, gender, sexuality, social class, ethnicity, ability and race have been considered when relevant, along with organisational and institutional factors, such as teacher authority, student rights, the structure of the school class, the whole-school atmosphere, school policies and so forth.

The DRACON team also paid a lot of attention to the *cultural* understanding of conflicts. Our reasoning is simply that conflict is a form of social action and social action carries meaning. Thus, conflicts are always located within a system of meaning or a cultural context. When a culture legitimates violence through discourses of inclusion and exclusion based on myths, or a particular worldview, approaches to conflict require cultural understanding more than anything else. The existence of cultural differences between groups can be a challenge. The value systems of the groups may clash but even more important are the communication barriers that follow from different understandings and systems of meaning. As we have pointed out, mutual understanding is rare in many conflicts and training in cross-cultural communication can be a decisive factor when intervening in conflict between different cultural groups.

Conflict-Handling Styles or Strategies

Conflict-handling styles refer to the strategies the parties use to deal with the other party. Do they try to dominate the other party, avoid the conflict, give into the other or try to find a compromise? Do the parties aim for a mutually satisfying solution? *Styles* are the particular orientations used by individuals or groups, which guide the specific moves or countermoves (*tactics*) used to enact the strategy.

There are several conceptualisations of conflict styles. The simplest model is the *FFF model—fight, flight and freeze* (Cornelius & Faire, 1989). The fight and the flight modes are the most common reactions. They occur frequently in human conflicts even if there is no physical threat. A fourth option is to *flow*. We need to take a more creative attitude to the conflict if we assume that all people involved in a conflict situation have an equal right to exist and therefore a right to their own viewpoints. The cardinal rules of 'flowing' in conflict situations are:

- Do not coerce the other. When attacked, do not attack back.

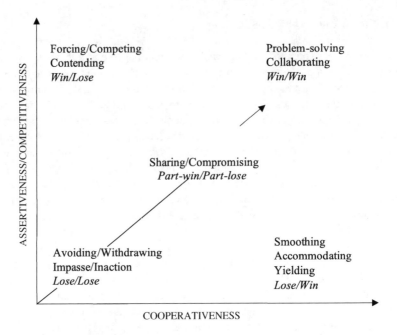

Fig. 2.2 Styles of handling conflict

- Do not walk away. Be 100 per cent present in a conflict situation.
- Talk it out. Be attentive and assertive at the same time.
- Make a deal that satisfies both parties (a win–win solution).
- If you can't make it on your own, turn to an impartial third party.

Thomas and Kilmann (1974) constructed a different but related conceptualisation of conflict styles. When we are in a conflict situation we are concerned about two dimensions:

- the intention to satisfy our own needs (assertive) and
- the intention to satisfy the needs of the other (cooperative).

By combining these two independent dimensions, we arrive at five conflict styles as ideal types (see Fig. 2.2):

- Competing (lion): high in assertiveness and low in cooperativeness.
- Accommodating (camel): low in assertiveness and high in cooperativeness.
- Avoiding (turtle): low in both assertiveness and cooperativeness.
- Compromising (fox): intermediate on both dimensions.
- Collaborating (owl): high in both dimensions.

There is no assumption that collaboration is the 'best way' of handling conflicts under all conditions. Collaboration seems to be the most effective style when the parties are dependent on future cooperation, the time pressure is not too high, they trust each other and resolving the issue is important to both of them.

Thomas and Kilmann suggest that there is a positive but not very strong relationship between personality type and conflict style. Each person uses more than one style, depending on the situation they are in, but we usually have one style we use most, particularly in a crisis or an argument with people we are close to. In an earlier project, we have shown that the different styles are differentially used in different cultures. Malaysians tend to favour avoiding and accommodating styles. Swedes also avoid and accommodate, but less so than the Malaysians; they are relatively more into competition and collaboration (Friberg, 1996).

We developed an instrument (based on Johnson, 1997) to measure adolescent styles in the South Australian DRACON project and found differences between the styles used by males and females (See Chapter 8). Johnson had developed a typology of styles, which is closely related to Thomas and Kilmann's, but the two underlying dimensions are different. Johnson (1997) assumes that we are concerned about two things in a conflict with others:

- getting what we need or want, and/or
- the relationship with the other person.

This typology leads also to five basic conflict styles. He calls them forcing (shark), smoothing (teddy bear), withdrawing (turtle), compromising (fox) and problem-solving (owl) when mentioned in the same order as above.

We used the three conceptualisations of styles in the DRACON project, and therefore, all of them have been included here.

The Conflict Process and Outcomes

Resolved or not, the conflict leads to an outcome such as withdrawal, impasse, stalemate, agreement, physical damage or an improved relationship. Conflict is a transformer, a process that leads to changes on many levels. For instance, the use of a particular style of conflict handling has some predictable effects on the outcome of the conflict with respect to both the relationship and the contradiction. The withdrawing and forcing styles of conflict handling are not concerned with enhancing the relationship, or the needs or interests of the 'other', and can therefore be seen as self-serving and competitive, usually leading to 'lose–lose' or 'win–lose' outcomes and to a deteriorating relationship. Smoothing, compromising and problem-solving styles, on the other hand, all involve taking the needs and interests of the 'other' into account, to varying degrees, and can therefore be described as co-operative. Smoothing and compromising, however, involve giving up some or all of your own interests and needs in order to preserve the relationship with the 'other'.

Compromise, in particular, is often understood to be an ideal form of conflict management. However, it always leaves the parties somewhat frustrated, as they have to give up something. The problem-solving style strives for a 'win–win' outcome that takes into account the needs and interests of all parties to the conflict, at the same time preserving or enhancing the relationship between them. This outcome can be beneficial but it is not always easy to achieve. It takes more time and requires a willingness to listen in order to understand the other parties' needs, interests, fears and concerns.

The Conflict Process

How does conflict change and develop over time? What are the incidents or critical events that help *escalate* (intensify) and *de-escalate* the conflict process? The focus here is on the interaction between the parties over time. Normally, we can distinguish between three phases of the conflict: the origin, the escalation and the resolution, de-escalation or transformation phases, although these are not always linear.

The most recent advances in theories of conflict have focused on the subjective side of conflict. Conflict resolution theories, social–psychological theories and communication theories have been integrated within a general theory of *escalation* (Glasl, 1982, 1999; Jordan, 1997). This theory explains the general dynamics of conflicts over time and is also very useful in finding ways of preventing or resolving conflicts. It is specifically applicable to interpersonal conflicts, but recently a number of higher-level variables have been added to the theory at inter-group and international levels. Efforts have also been made to integrate projection theory, personality theory and transpersonal theory into the framework.

Using the concepts of ABC theory, we can describe the basic process of the conflict escalation theory as running through three major stages:

1. Phase of discussion. The attention of the parties is on C rather than A and B.
2. Phase of polarisation. A dominates over B and C.
3. Phase of destruction. B dominates over A and C.

In the initial *discussion phase* the emphasis is on the contradiction (C). The parties have differing conceptions of the issues at stake, and each tries to persuade the opposing party to change their views and perceptions. They may continue to have respect for each other, although the means used for persuasion become increasingly 'hard' in nature. The idea is to find a solution together with the opposing party.

At a certain stage in the conflict process, the parties begin to feel that it is useless to try to discuss things with the other. This is the beginning of the *polarisation phase*. Now the opposing party has become the major problem (A), and the original issues (C) fall into the background and lose their saliency. The relationship and communication between the parties become poisoned by negative feelings, attitudes and malicious images of the other. Trust declines rapidly between the parties. If the conflict moves even further, it eventually reaches the third phase, the *destruction phase*. In this phase, one or both of the parties turn to verbal or physical violence (B) and attempts to annihilate the other, or at least cut down the size of the opponent by violent means.

The theory of escalation is of relevance to conflict handling, as the discussion, polarisation and destruction phases require different approaches and methods.

Conflict Interventions

The terms 'conflict resolution', 'conflict management' and 'conflict transformation' have a lot of relatives such as agreement, settlement, modus vivendi, ceasefire, conflict termination, reconciliation, conflict handling, problem-solving, de-escalation, cooling, exploration, treatment, outcome, solution, peace-making, peace-building, peace-keeping and so forth.

By *conflict interventions,* we mean all methods that can erase, reduce or transform the conflict into a less costly form of interaction, less costly in terms of the ongoing relationship, feelings, health, safety, time, money and resources in general. Conflict intervention can be about de-escalation of conflicts. It is about limiting destructive behaviour (B), decreasing emotional tensions (A) and transcending contradictions (C)—in short, *cooling* the conflict. This does not mean that it is always easy to find a smooth path from a high-intensity conflict situation to a calm one. Usually, there are many 'ups and downs' on the road to harmony.

Sometimes a conflict can be so *frozen,* with all tensions kept under the surface, that it is impossible to work on the conflict directly. In this case, conflict interveners need to heat it up before real work can start. This can occur if the parties are encouraged to express their subjective positions and feelings for each other assertively, not submissively or aggressively. The conflict has to be made manifest or brought out into the open before resolution work can begin. This principle of intensification of conflict before resolution is also familiar to drama workers as will be seen later in this chapter.

It is seldom the case that a conflict is completely resolved in the sense that all latent aspects of the conflict are eliminated. It is more often the case that the conflict is transformed, controlled or managed or that people agree to disagree. The original conflict can be *transformed* into a new type of conflict, sometimes called a *meta-conflict,* which takes a less destructive form. For example, a physical fight between mafia gangs is converted into a juridical struggle in court. In order to emphasise this, we prefer the term 'conflict transformation' to 'conflict resolution' or 'conflict management'.

Direct and Indirect Conflict Interventions

An important distinction can be made between *direct* and *indirect* conflict interventions. If direct, the conflict is a recognised and intended focus of a procedure and, if indirect, an unrecognised or unintended consequence of other activities. A thousand small frustrations and unresolved conflicts in everyday life contribute to the building of diffuse tensions. Every culture has accepted methods of releasing or displacing tensions. The phenomenon of *running amok* is an example from Malaysia. Malay culture in general emphasises self-control and constant restraint but provides people with an accepted way of 'breaking loose and going mad', which is interpreted as 'spirit possession' (Karim, 1990).

In the dominant cultural traditions of Sweden and Australia drinking with friends, engaging in sport or sexual activity can operate as outlets for tensions, particularly for men. Physical activity can release energies that otherwise could have been fuel for conflicts. However, displays of masculinity among groups of men, including in sports' teams, have been linked to sexual violence towards women, as in the cases of sexual harassment, domestic violence and gang rape, brought to public attention in Australia and the UK.

The distinction between direct and indirect approaches to conflict is very important when analysing the role of educational drama in conflict resolution. As will be elaborated in this book, we think drama has most relevance as an indirect approach to conflict management. The direct procedures are basically negotiation procedures. *Negotiation* can be defined as a verbal interaction in which two or more parties seek to reach an agreement on a contentious issue.

Third-Party Roles

The process or procedure used to intervene in a conflict situation can be defined as a culturally available system of norms or institutions that, if introduced into the conflict at a particular moment, transform it into a new conflict or a situation that is less damaging than the original conflict. The basic distinction is between *self-help procedures*, namely procedures that can be used directly by the involved parties, and *third-party intervention procedures* that are dependent on intervention by an outsider. If the parties cannot solve the conflict by direct negotiations, one or more impartial third parties can be called in, such as a counsellor, facilitator, negotiator, conciliator, mediator, arbitrator or judge. Other parties may also be involved in a bipartisan way, such as supporters, bystanders or advocates. It is worth noticing that the term 'third party' is a misnomer as the original conflict can be between more than two direct parties. On the other hand, the phrase recognises that an additional actor(s), even if impartial, is always a party with its own interests in the conflict.

Any third-party role can be described by two major dimensions—partiality and power—as is shown in Fig. 2.3.

Our empirical data show that when people in general, and school children in particular, intervene in conflicts they often take the roles of ally, supporter or advisor, which are partial third-party roles. These roles are usually motivated by power and loyalty considerations. Each party to the original conflict builds up a coalition of supporters and allies against the other party—especially when the conflict has reached the polarisation phase. The result is often further intensification and escalation of the conflict.

Conflict resolution in *symmetric conflicts*, where there is a roughly equal balance of power, requires the intervention of third parties who take an impartial stance. Mediation, for instance, is built on the idea that the conflicting parties voluntarily

Conflict Interventions

	Impartial	Partial
With coercive power	Administrator Arbitrator Adjudicator or Judge	Ally or partisan
Without coercive power	Facilitator Conciliator Mediator	Supporter Advisor Advocate

Fig. 2.3 Third-party roles

accept the service of a mutually acceptable, impartial third party. The mediator controls the process and the way that the parties communicate, and does not give advice, but the parties control the content (what is discussed) and the outcomes. Mediation will not work if mediators have a conflict of interest, or are perceived as favouring one of the parties, or as having a vested interest in one party, the issues in dispute or the outcome.

Transformation of Asymmetric Conflicts

Power is always a major consideration when intervening in conflicts. The greatest challenges occur when intervening in *asymmetric conflicts*, that is conflicts where there are significant differences of power which are not amenable to mediator intervention.

Power is rarely static and can shift during the mediation process, depending on what is under discussion. There are many different bases of power, including the power to reward or coerce, charismatic or referent power, informational and expert power. The power of language or discourse is also important to consider—people can be marginalised by dominant discourses, which ignore or discount their cultural values and ways of viewing the world.

If one party persists in dominating, abusing or exploiting the other it is inappropriate to choose or to proceed with mediation, as the process relies on each party's competence to negotiate a fair outcome for themselves. A judge, on the other hand, has the power to make and enforce decisions. In most cases, the formal adjudicative legal process can assist in the management of conflict where there are large differences in power, in particular where the laws are progressive, the judges are enlightened and parties have equal access to legal assistance. However, this is not always the case.

A number of renowned thinkers and practitioners in the fields of conflict studies and dispute resolution agree that where there are major imbalances of power, conflict interveners should support the weaker party—but only as long as that party remains

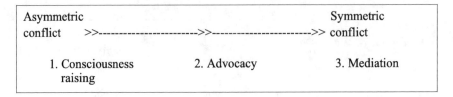

Fig. 2.4 Management approaches for asymmetric and symmetric conflicts

weak. The challenge is to find non-violent roles that are effective in bringing about genuine peace. The educator and the advocate are two relevant third-party roles for asymmetric conflicts. When it comes to self-help, in such conflicts the whole repertoire of *non-violent action* developed by Mahatma Gandhi and others is relevant.

When conflict is latent and people are unaware of power imbalances and injustices, consciousness-raising is a necessary condition. The task of the educator is to overcome ignorance and raise awareness of the nature of the conflict as a first step in the process of restoring equity. Conscious awareness leads to demands for change, and the next task becomes advocacy—giving voice to the less powerful. If successful, consciousness-raising and advocacy will lead to a change in the balance of power. The weaker party will be empowered to speak in a context that encourages the stronger party to listen. In this way, an asymmetric conflict can be transformed into a symmetric one. For example, mediators can provide access to information and links to counsellors, support persons or advocates for a weaker party where there are imbalances of power (see Fig. 2.4).

Where imbalances of power are gender-based, such as where there is sexual harassment, bullying and/or domestic or family violence, feminists urge that the processes chosen be subject to public scrutiny and/or that, where private processes such as mediation are chosen, special procedures be put in place to support the weaker party and to ensure safety. This would include measures such as using two specially trained and gender-aware co-mediators; ensuring safety before, during and after the mediation; applying strict rules for behaviour in the sessions; using 'shuttle' mediation or separate sessions; linking the weaker party to advocates and support persons; making sure that parties have equal access to information and expert advice before making a decision and so forth.

Whether a conflict should be regarded as asymmetric or symmetric is often a knotty question. The power imbalance may be subtle, hidden, fluid and/or difficult to define. From a constructivist perspective power is not a completely objective property that can be attributed to a relationship independently of how the actors define the situation and how it is defined in a particular culture. The Western culture of egalitarian individualism colours how the concept of power is used by Westerners. In the East, collectivism and vertical relations are often seen as natural and some people have an emotional need to be protected by father figures. For them, power imbalance is not a problem in itself, only the abuse of power.

There is often a grey zone in which it is unclear if the third party should act as a partial advocate or an impartial mediator—it is impossible to be both. The challenge is to empower the 'oppressed' person to speak his/her truth and at the same time to empower the 'oppressor' and listen to his/her truth. A certain form of impartiality—respecting both parties as human beings—is necessary in order to get the 'oppressor' involved in the conflict intervention process; however, the parties have to be approached in an asymmetric way. Family mediators in the Western world have struggled with this issue in divorce mediations where there are often gender-based imbalances of power, in particular where there is ongoing domestic violence.

The theory of asymmetric conflicts is of relevance to the handling of student conflicts in schools. International research has shown that bullying in schools is quite widespread. *Bullying* has been defined in many ways. Rigby has based his definition of bullying on a variety of published views of what bullying is:

> Bullying involves a desire to hurt + hurtful action + power imbalance + an unjust use of power + evident enjoyment by the aggressor and generally a sense of being oppressed on the part of the victim. (Rigby, 2002: 51)

Thus, bullying by definition involves an asymmetric balance of power. If the students are more or less equal in power we do not call it bullying but a conflict, quarrel or fight. According to the PISA report, every sixth student in Sweden is exposed to bullying a couple of times every month. The situation is similar in other OECD countries. The frequency of bullying in compulsory schools has increased (OECD-PISA, 2015). When we were implementing the DRACON project in South Australia, approximately 50% of schoolchildren reported that they had been bullied at least once during a year, with one child in six reporting being bullied on a weekly basis (Rigby, 2002).

Bullying has been treated in a number of very different ways. These have been summarised by Rigby (2002). Generally, responsibility for bullying has been attributed to the 'bully' or 'bullies'. Efforts have been made to change their behaviour, either by imposing sanctions or by counselling methods or by both. Efforts have also been directed towards changing the behaviour of victims, for example by helping them to act more assertively or to refrain from acting provocatively. Other approaches have focused upon the influence of peers and friendship groups and have made use of problem-solving techniques. Pikas's (2010) *Method of Shared Concern*, for example, proposes the use of interviews with individual members of a bullying group in which the interviewer shares his or her concern for the victim. This procedure, he has found, can help towards the resolution of bully/victim problems in secondary schools, especially if further meetings involving all the participants are convened and mediation techniques employed.

Such problem-solving methods contain elements that are consistent with the approach taken by DRACON; however, DRACON was not originally focused on bullying. It was our ambition to develop drama-based intervention programs which had the potential to reduce the frequency of bullying as well as other unwanted conflicts at schoolQuery. The Brisbane subproject has focused specifically on bullying since 2002.

The Tasks of Conflict Interventions

We now turn to symmetric conflicts. The bulk of the conflict intervention literature is targeted at these types of conflicts and impartial third-party roles. As we have seen, there are many such roles, including counsellor, negotiator, facilitator, conciliator, mediator, arbitrator and judge. What determines whether a particular role is effective in solving a symmetric conflict? The answer in part has to do with the nature of the conflict and its level of escalation. Let us first investigate what the third party can do in order to transform the conflict. According to the ABC model, conflict intervention implies three main tasks:

- *Conflict termination* (focus on the B-component): putting an end to destructive behaviour, such as through an agreement on ceasefire or ground rules for respectful behaviour. This task implies a security approach oriented towards the control of violence and the creation of a safe space where the parties can feel physically and emotionally secure.
- *Reconciliation or conflict transformation* (focus on the A-component): dispersion of negative feelings and images of each other. This task calls for a 'process' approach in the sense that the negative feelings and stories have to be processed until the emotional and/or communicative bond between the parties is transformed or healed.
- *Conflict settlement or resolution* (focus on the C-component): reaching an agreement on the substantive issues at stake in the conflict. This third task requires an issue-oriented approach. This involves identification of the mutual issues in dispute, analysis of the underlying perceptions, meanings, interests, needs or fears, the creative generation of a range of new options and negotiation of a mutually satisfying outcome.

These three tasks are quite different and require specific methods and skills. Here it is very important to make distinctions between the *phases* of a conflict, because each method of conflict intervention must always be chosen, or adapted to the stage of escalation.

Any conflict intervention process may be described as a conflict escalation process 'run backwards'. The first task is to stop any violence. Security takes priority. It is very difficult to try to change the negative attitudes that the parties have towards each other if fighting still continues. The second task is to achieve a measure of reconciliation or mutual understanding between the parties. The 'self-other' polarity must be overcome before the underlying contradictions can be handled in a reasonable way. At the polarisation stage, people have often 'dug into their trenches', with strongly held positions (or solutions) that are fixed or entrenched, and with no understanding of the perceptions, meanings, interests or needs underlying their own position and that of the other. They attack each other, rather than the problem, and it becomes impossible to carry out a rational dialogue about the substance of the dispute. This is the reason why the *security approach* should be followed by a *process approach,* which, in turn, can successively be transferred into a negotiation process, preferably between the parties themselves.

Conflict Interventions

Table 2.1 A contingency model of approaches to conflict intervention

Phase of conflict	I. Discussion phase (C)	II. Polarization phase (A)	III. Destruction phase (B)
Approach to management	Issue-oriented approach (settlement)	Process-oriented approach (reconciliation)	Security-oriented approach (termination)
Method of management	Self-help Collegial help Mediation (of issues)	Socio-therapeutic consultation, Mediation (of relationship)	Coercive intervention, Adjudication, Arbitration
	F-a-c-i-l-i-W-o-r-k-	-t-a-t-i-o-n -s-h-o-p-s	

These theoretical considerations can be summarised in a so-called *contingency model of approaches to conflict intervention*. Table 2.1 shows how the effective uses of a number of conflict resolution methods are contingent on the level of escalation of the conflict (Table 2.1).

The contingency model indicates that there are serious limitations to self-help as a method of conflict resolution. The participants have a chance to solve the problems themselves without external help if the conflict is still in the discussion phase (C). When the conflict has escalated into the polarisation phase, self-help becomes very difficult because the participants see the 'other' as the major problem and have adopted fixed positions on the issues. 'Self' and 'other' are treated in an asymmetric way; therefore, solutions suggested by the other are automatically rejected as being partial. An impartial third party has an essential role to play on this level.

When it comes to the nature of the conflict itself, mediation is needed mostly in the earlier phases of the escalation of a conflict or dispute—in the *phase of polarisation* and in the *phase of discussion*. The *phase of destruction* lies beyond the range of mediation and the issue of violence itself should never be mediated. In the polarisation phase, subjective factors such as cognitive rigidity, stereotyping, hostile emotions and dysfunctional communication play a greater role than the content of the conflict. In the discussion phase, when the content is still in focus, the most difficult contested issues to reconcile are issues involving basic needs, values, identities and worldviews. Some value-based issues can only be resolved by agreeing to disagree.

We have seen that if the parties cannot solve the conflict by direct negotiations, an impartial *third party* can be engaged, such as a facilitator, conciliator, mediator, arbitrator or judge. When compared to arbitration and litigation, mediation is a relatively voluntary, informal, private and collaborative approach to resolving or transforming conflict, with the third party (mediator) in charge of the *process* (how the conflict is resolved) and the disputants in charge of the *content* (what is discussed) and *outcomes* (what is agreed to). While mediation is a voluntary, facilitative process, both arbitration and adjudication are *determinative* processes and for that reason are of less interest to the DRACON project. In determinative processes, the parties leave it to the third party to find a fair solution to the conflict on the merits of the opposing positions, and the third party imposes a solution. In adjudication, the third party also enforces the decision.

According to Rosenberg's (1999) model of *non-violent communication,* reconciliation is about the establishment of a heart-to-heart connection through the use of appropriate language. The mediator in this case works as a 'translator'—translating the 'wolf language' of the parties into 'giraffe language'.

Similar processes are used in an approach called *transformative mediation* in which the focus of the mediator is on the opportunities for personal growth that unfold at every moment of the mediation (Bush & Folger, 1994; Folger & Bush, 2001). The guiding words for this process are 'empowerment' of the parties and their 'recognition' of each other. Postmodernist theories also underpin an approach to mediation, called *narrative mediation*, in which the focus is on deconstruction and reconstruction of the socially constructed, 'problem-saturated stories' that parties bring to the mediator (Winslade & Monk, 2000, 2008). The transformative and narrative models of mediation have some features in common with educational drama, especially the focus on the process itself, not the outcome.

Approaches to Mediation

A Problem-Solving Approach to Mediation

Mediation is an approach to conflict that has some features in common with facilitation in educational drama. As we have pointed out, there are many models of mediation. Here we will describe a basic problem-solving, interest-based approach, which is outlined by many authors (Gilman, 2017; McCorkle & Reese, 2005; Moore, 2003). The problem-solving process is easy to follow, commonly used and is sometimes incorporated into other approaches, and so for this reason, we have taught it to our DRACON students. We also refer in this section to a transformative approach and make special reference in the final section to a narrative approach to mediation, as we believe they are most closely aligned to educational drama.

From a problem-solving and interest-based perspective, the term mediation is commonly defined as a process by which the parties, together with the assistance of an acceptable, impartial person or persons, voluntarily and systematically isolate issues in need of mutual consideration, develop a range of options, consider alternatives and reach a consensual settlement that will take into account the interests and needs of all concerned. Mediation is a process that emphasises the parties' responsibility for making decisions that affect their lives. The mediator manages the process but does not get involved in or influence the decisions.

The problem-solving process can be divided into three main phases—preparation, intervention and consolidation—and then further subdivided into twelve stages as shown in Table 2.2. It must be stressed that the process is more circular in its application than this linear presentation shows. The mediator may need to return to

Approaches to Mediation

Table 2.2 Phases of the problem-solving process

I. Preparation phase
- Inviting the third party
- Conflict assessment
- Agreement on the ground rules and procedures
- Creating a safe space

II. Intervention phase
- Exploring the presenting problems or issues
- Identifying mutual issues to be addressed
- Inventing and designing options
- Developing principles for deciding
- Assisting negotiation
- Developing a preliminary or trial agreement or negotiating text

III. Consolidation phase
- Reality testing
- Implementation, review and revision

and renegotiate or consolidate earlier stages from time to time as the process unfolds and as each issue is dealt with. In what follows we will give a short description of each phase of the problem-solving process and where possible indicate how the transformative and narrative processes are different.

Preparation Phase

Invitation to the Third Party

The initiative for starting the mediation process lies with the parties themselves. This requires conflicting parties to jointly acknowledge that they cannot solve the conflict themselves and that they want to be helped by a mutually acceptable, impartial and skilled third party. Access to the conflict can be a major issue for the third party, as he/she has no power to pull the parties to the negotiation table. Parties may be mandated to attend an information session but cannot be mandated to participate or settle, as it is a voluntary process.

Conflict Assessment

The third party makes a preliminary investigation of the conflict to find out if the parties are voluntary, the power imbalances are amenable to third-party intervention and the conflict is ripe and to determine which types of intervention processes are appropriate. This is often done separately by interviewing relevant parties to the conflict, in particular where there is the potential for imbalances or abuses of power.

Agreement on the Ground Rules and Procedures

If the initial assessment indicates that mediation is appropriate, the mediator tries to create a commitment to the mediation process and ensures the appropriate selection of a mutually acceptable third party or parties. The mediator must be given the power to control and manage the process and establishes agreed-upon ground rules with the parties, which can include 'listen when the other is speaking and do not interrupt', 'speak for yourself not the other person', 'share all relevant information' and 'treat each other with respect'.

Creation of a Safe Space

The mediator preamble and 'ground rules' lay the foundation for the mediation process. The parties must trust the mediator and believe that they have a *safe space* in which they can explore the conflict on a new level. The problem-solving process is feasible only if the parties are voluntary, and there are no serious disturbances in the communication process, the balance of power and the emotional climate. When safety is in question, the mediator may use 'shuttle' mediation, where the parties are in separate rooms, if necessary at separate times, and the mediator takes messages between them.

Intervention Phase

The intervention phase begins when all parties for the first time are brought to a common session with the mediator in order to do the agreed work on the conflict itself, unless separate sessions or 'shuttle' mediation have been chosen as the preferred options. The parties are empowered by the mediator to identify and consider the interests, needs and fears underlying their positions and their goals, resources and decision-making processes, independently of any potential outcomes of the mediation. The intervention phase can be divided into five subphases.

Exploring the presenting problems or issues

Exploration usually starts with *storytelling*. Each participant gives his or her version or perspective of the conflict, identifies what is negotiable and non-negotiable and outlines what they want to achieve in the mediation. In this early stage, the mediator builds trust in the process by actively and equally listening to each of the participants' views, by discouraging interruptions and negative comments and by using strategies such as empathic responding, summarising, reflective questioning and reframing in order to develop mutual understanding of why the other person has taken a particular position on the issue or issues to be addressed.

Identifying mutual issues to be addressed

If the participants stick to and defend their original positions, movement is impossible. The facilitator therefore assists the parties to move from the positions taken at the beginning by encouraging them to focus on the needs, fears, interests, wants and concerns underlying their position. When positions are translated into interests or needs, through techniques such as reflective questioning, reframing, needs analysis or conflict mapping, the parties are more able to release their defensive stances and develop empathy. The redefined problems or issues take the form of how to best satisfy the mutually defined interests and needs of the parties—their interests are no longer defined as exclusive of the other.

Inventing and Designing Options

This can be the most creative stage of the problem-solving process. The parties are encouraged to generate as many proposals or options for consideration as possible before choosing between them. This can be done through the technique of *brainstorming*, where every idea is listed without ownership, discussion or evaluation, even if an idea seems to be absurd. Criticism, discussion and ownership of an idea are forbidden at this stage of the process.

There are many other techniques the mediator can also use to generate options, including asking each of the participants reflective questions such as 'What are you prepared to do differently to assist the others to agree to what you want?' and 'What would you like the other persons to do differently to assist you to agree to what they want?' Another technique is to ask each person to come up with a 'yes-able proposition'—that is, a proposal the others are likely to agree to.

Assisted Negotiation

If misunderstandings, misperceptions, miscommunication, differing values, resentments and rigid positions have been discussed, clarified, deconstructed or dealt with, the participants know and understand each other's interests and needs, and there is a whole set of new creative options to choose between, the parties are ready for fruitful negotiations aimed at reaching an agreement. It is unethical at any stage for the mediator to give the parties advice as this is *their* agreement, but the mediator can act as 'the devil's advocate' at this stage.

Preliminary Agreement

By this stage of the process, the parties are usually able to reach a provisional, preliminary or trial agreement on options to address the major issues of the conflict. It is desirable for agreements to be recorded to avoid future misinterpretations or misunderstandings. Writing agreements is the responsibility of the mediator, whose task is to ensure that agreements are couched in clear, accurate, positive, mutual and specific terms, where possible using the language of the parties.

Consolidation Phase

Reality Testing

Often time is needed for testing the agreement and making necessary adjustments after a trial period. 'Sleeping on the decision' before signing the final agreement is good advice. The parties may also wish to consult with significant others.

Implementation, Review and Revision

There are sometimes unforeseen factors and new developments or changes that might jeopardise an agreement. The parties can fall back into old patterns of behaviour over time or new factors or situations may emerge, making it necessary to amend agreements. The best agreements provide for flexibility, as situations rarely stay the same. Consolidation means planning recurrent reviews of the agreement, setting up ongoing support systems, renewing consultations and so forth.

Conditions for Effective Mediation

There are necessary conditions for reaching an agreement through informal processes such as mediation. Here we will explore some of the prerequisites with regard to the parties and their relationships, the nature of the conflict, the mediator and the context. As to the parties, a basic condition is their capacity to act in their own legitimate self-interest. The purpose is to enable the participants to engage in a constructive dialogue concerning the substantive, psychological or procedural issues they bring to the mediator and ultimately to reach agreements and/or continue to handle their disputes without assistance. This requires a willingness to negotiate, some minimal skills in communication on the part of the participants and a roughly equal balance of power. Mental illness and/or drug or alcohol addictions can jeopardise the success of the process. In these cases, the mediator may refer the client(s) to therapy or medical treatment.

Mediation works best when the parties have an ongoing relationship with each other. If there is no need to co-operate in the future, or there is a perception that nothing is to be gained from a negotiation, the incentive to engage in the process decreases considerably. In ongoing relationships, power should not be severely unbalanced. To a certain extent, power shifts according to what is under discussion and a mediator can sometimes balance power by using shuttle mediation and/or ensuring that people have equal time, equal access to information, abide by ground rules, have access to an advocate or support person and so forth. However, a mediator cannot jeopardise his or her impartiality by becoming an advocate for one party.

Most importantly, for mediation to work, the parties must be voluntary and have a common wish to reach an agreement or some sort of mutual understanding. This cannot be taken for granted even if the parties turn up at the negotiation table. Traditional religious attitudes or rigid beliefs can also make it difficult, if not impossible for people to move from their position on some issues. A willingness to see the other person's point of view, even if eventually to agree to disagree, is essential.

The mediator must be acceptable to both parties and have the necessary education, training, skills, values, cultural background and personality for the process to work. It is too easy to aggravate the conflict by making a few simple mistakes or by appearing to be biased.

The first essential condition for the mediator is an impartial attitude and behaviour, both perceived and actual. The second condition may be the attitude of empowering the participants to make their own decisions. The third is to be a patient, effective listener and communicator. For this to happen, the mediator must be comfortable in the presence of conflict. Fourthly, a mediator should convey an attitude of acceptance of all the participants and accommodate and respect sociocultural differences. Finally, the facilitator needs to have a positive attitude to conflict, a sense of humour and an ability to think laterally and creatively.

Peer Mediation

Peer mediation as a particular application of mediation was of special relevance to the DRACON project. Peer mediation has become widespread in recent years, particularly in primary schools in Western countries such as Australia and the USA. This social innovation was being introduced in some Swedish schools during the DRACON project, but was almost non-existent in Malaysia. The dominant models used for peer mediation have been the problem-solving approach and the narrative approach. The pioneers of peer mediation have claimed outstanding benefits from implementing programs in schools for many types of student-to-student conflicts.

Up to the mid-90s, only a few research studies had been conducted on the effects of peer mediation programs in schools—some had presented positive results, others more negative ones. The South Australian DRACON research team received negative reports about peer mediation in focus groups from many Year 9 students from a wide range of schools. The students had appreciated peer mediation in their primary schooling, but did not find it useful for their age group (13-15 years) in secondary school. There were many reasons provided, including that their conflicts were too serious, that boys found it 'sissy' and preferred to solve their own disputes, that they did not trust their peers as mediators and that their peer groups were more important. They preferred older students and teachers to mediate their disputes. In seven secondary schools, there was no evidence that peer mediation worked and in some instances it appeared to have made conflicts worse.

Well-known authorities on conflict resolution in schools in the USA and Australia, however, have since found a significantly lower incidence of conflicts in some secondary schools that had a peer mediation program compared to schools that lacked such programs. It is necessary to keep up-to-date with the latest research. It is important to point out that the necessary conditions for successful implementation of peer mediation programs are not always in place in schools. One of the most important conditions is that there is an adult program coordinator based in the school and trained in mediation. This person oversees all aspects of the program's operation, selects the peer mediators, functions as their mentor and decides whether a particular conflict should be a case for the disciplinary system or for peer mediation. As has been explained, not all conflicts can be mediated, in particular where the parties are involuntary or there is a severe imbalance of power, a history or threat of violence or abuse, addiction to drugs or mental illness. Mediation in such cases can lead to failure as parties are required to be competent to negotiate fair outcomes for themselves unless a support person or advocate comes with them..

A central weakness of some *peer* mediation projects is that they select and train just a few older students as mediators. While peer mediators develop a valuable understanding of conflict management themselves, there is little evidence that the rest of the students in the school are similarly empowered, especially in secondary schools. Research has demonstrated that when all the students in a school are taught peer mediation and conflict-handling skills, the program can have a preventive effect, even on destructive conflicts such as fights and bullying at the school. It has been argued that a peer mediation program should also include a serious effort to change the experiences of young people at home and in the community as well as at school, which would involve training *all* students to be part of any program, with community involvement as an essential element. In part, the DRACON approach was based on these insights. We argue that a 'whole-school' approach is desirable, involving all students, teachers and if possible the parents and broader community.

A Narrative Approach to Mediation

We end this chapter with special reference to narrative mediation, which we consider to be the most relevant approach to conflict transformation for the DRACON project. Research evidence suggests that young people in Western secondary schools are heavily influenced by the dominant discourses of their peers, for example in the social construction and performances of their masculinities and femininities. Research has demonstrated that dominant discourses on 'macho' forms of masculinity, in particular, contribute to destructive conflicts and violence in schools (Bagshaw, 2004). Therefore, the narrative approach to mediation was relevant to use in our programs.

As previously explained, narrative mediation is based on postmodernist, social constructivist thinking, which challenges the view that an individual has an essential essence or identity, instead arguing that we have multiple identities, which are fluid and 'mapped onto us by the social and cultural world around us' (Winslow & Monk, 2000: 37). The narrative approach to conflict acknowledges that discourses, stories or 'truths' are constructed from a particular social and cultural view of reality, in a particular historical time and place. A leading narrative therapy theorist, Michael White, stated that: 'We enter into stories, we are entered into stories by others and we live our lives through stories' (White, 1989: 6). From a narrative perspective, language (as discourse) is viewed as a precondition of thought and gives meaning to our everyday interactions. When they talk, people are constructing their world. In this sense, language is performative.

The word 'narrative' refers to a mode of thinking as described by Jerome Bruner:

> … people construct their intentions and enact their 'performances of meaning' with the characteristics of a well-formed story rather than with facts, realities, or cause-and-effect logic (Winslade & Monk, 2000: 52).

From the narrative perspective, there is no universal truth—there are many 'truths'. Socially constructed stories serve to mediate, shape and create our truths or realities. People make meaning in story form and in any conflict one would expect different narratives to describe the same situations or events in the conflict. All parties to a conflict, and others, will have their own stories or versions of the 'truth'. The mediator works with the parties to create an alternative but plausible story in a way that makes sense to the participants. No one story is true but out of the complexity of stories can emerge a range of possible future stories.

Power is viewed differently from a narrative perspective and is closely aligned with discourse. Not all stories or voices are equal—some are privileged and others are discounted or marginalised. Conflict is seen to be an inevitable product of the operation of power in the modern world, closely related to knowledge and whose meaning gets to be privileged. Dominant discourses in a culture specify what is 'normal' and what can be talked about, in what way, by whom and in what contexts. The voices of disempowered people or minority groups tend to be subjugated or silenced by the voices of people in power. Conflict will develop when power and privilege are threatened or resisted.

In mediation, as in drama, cultural stories are being produced and reproduced, performed and re-enacted and these stories can be unpacked and reshaped to create a different world or view of self and/or reality. The narrative mediator's task is to assist people in conflict to deconstruct their various perspectives of a conflict and to expose the multiple truths or realities. Deconstruction involves 'unpacking' taken-for-granted assumptions and unquestioned 'truths' or inevitable realities that are reflected in the stories people bring to mediation. In assisting the parties to view things from a new and different perspective, 'the familiar is rendered strange, the gaps or inconsistencies in a story are highlighted, and opportunities to resist an unquestioned truth are made clear'. The mediator emphasises 'curious exploration rather than simple acceptance', helping to create new meanings to events and rendering background assumptions visible and open to revision (Winslade & Monk, 2000: 43).

The DRACON project rests upon the belief that, using a narrative approach, educational drama can provide the opportunity and context for young people to deconstruct and reconstruct their histories, identities, stories and meanings in relation to their conflict.

References

Bagshaw, D. (2004). *Verbal abuse and adolescent identities. Marking the boundaries of gender* (Doctor of Philosophy Research Thesis), University of Melbourne, Melbourne.

Bagshaw, D., & Porter, E. (Eds.). (2009). *Mediation in the Asia-Pacific Region. Transforming conflicts and building peace*. New York: Routledge.

Bush, R., & Folger, J. (1994). *The promise of mediation: Responding to conflict through empowerment and recognition*. San Francisco: Jossey-Bass.

Cornelius, H., & Faire, S. (1989). *Everyone can win. How to resolve conflict*. East Roseville: Simon & Schuster.

Deutsch, M. (1973). *The resolution of conflict: Constructive and destructive processes.* New Haven and London: Yale University Press.
Fisher, L. (1990). *"Training Issues" in Centre for Conflict Resolution seminar papers. Mediation: Current controversies and future directions.* Victoria: Maquarie University.
Folger, J. P., & Bush, R. A. B. (Eds.). (2001). *Designing mediation approaches to training and practice within a transformative framework.* New York: The Institute for the Study of Conflict Transformation.
Friberg, M. (1996). *Conflict resolution in Sweden and Malaysia—A survey of cultural conditioning.* Paper presented at the Second International Mediation Conference: Mediation and Cultural Diversity, Adelaide.
Galtung, J. (1996). *Peace by peaceful means. Peace and conflict, development and civilization.* London: Sage Publications.
Gilman, J. E. (2017). *How to resolve conflict. A practical mediation manual.* Lanham, Maryland: Rowman & Littlefield.
Glasl, F. (1982). The process of conflict escalation and roles of third parties. In G. B. J. Bomer & R. B. Peterson (Eds.), *Conflict management and industrial relations* (pp. 119–149). The Hague: Kluwer Nijhoff Publishing.
Glasl, F. (1999). *Confronting conflict.* Bristol: Hawthorn Press.
Johnson, D. W. (1997). *Reaching out. Interpersonal effectiveness and self-actualisation* (6th ed.). Boston: Allyn and Bacon.
Johnson, D. W., & Johnson, F. P. (1991). *Joining together. Group theory and group skills.* Englewood Cliffs, NJ: Prentice-Hall International Inc.
Jordan, T. (1997). Review of F. Glasl, Konfliktmanagement. Ein Handbuch für Führungskräfte, Beraterinnen und Berater. *International Journal of Conflict Management, 8*(2), 170–174.
Karim, W. J. (1990). *Emotions of culture: A Malay perspective.* New York: Oxford University Press.
Lederach, J. P. (1995). *Preparing for peace. Conflict transformation across cultures.* New York: Syracuse University Press.
McCorkle, S., & Reese, M. J. (2005). *Mediation theory and practice.* Boston, New York & San Francisco: Pearson.
Moore, C. (2003). *The mediation process. Practical strategies for resolving conflict* (3rd ed.). Jossey-Bass: San Francisco.
OECD-PISA. (2015). *Knowledge and skills for life: Results from PISA 2000*, Paris.
Pikas, A. (2010). New developments of the shared concern method. *School Psychology International, 23*(3).
Rigby, K. (2002). *New perspectives on bullying.* London: Jessica Kingsley.
Rosenberg, M. B. (1999). *Nonviolent communication. A language of compassion.* Encinitas: PuddleDancer Press.
Thomas, K. W., & Kilmann, R. H. (1974). *Thomas-Kilmann conflict MODE instrument.* Tuxedo, NY: Xicom.
White, M. (1989). *The externalising of the problem and the re-authoring of lives and relationships.* Summer: Dulwich Centre Newsletter.
Winslade, J., & Monk, G. (2000). *Narrative mediation. A new approach to conflict resolution.* San Francisco: Jossey-Bass.
Winslade, J., & Monk, G. (2008). *Practicing narrative mediation. Loosening the grip of conflict.* San Francisco: Jossey-Bass.

Chapter 3
Learning Through Drama

The History and Context in Schools

Drama is the art form that most explicitly mirrors and explicates human conflict. Conflict is part of the basic business of drama, which exists to depict and explore human relationships. Keywords and concepts are shared between drama and conflict resolution, and the very words *protagonist* and *antagonist* that are used to label the main parties in a conflict derived from Greek drama. A central element of all drama is *tension*, and dramatic action consists of *dialogue, opposition, negotiation and argumentation*, all of which are employed in the drive towards resolving the tension. The classic structure of the majority of traditional Western drama, known by scholars as the 'dramatic curve', usually describes the escalation and de-escalation of conflicts, and the end of the curve is dubbed the resolution. In educational drama as in real-life conflict-handling situations, how tension is managed and resolved offers insights for learning and change.

Learning, Social Control and Social Action

Historically, drama has a long and equivocal relationship with education, and almost as long—and equivocal—an association with conflict management, social control… and also social activism. The traditional Indian drama handbook Natya Shastra is explicit: 'Drama originated because of the conflicts that arose in society when the world declined from the Golden Age of harmony, and therefore a drama always represents a conflict and its resolution'. (New World Encyclopaedia—see also Chap. 4).

Drama and theatre have always been used by rulers to assist in generating and maintaining a stable and harmonious congruence of thought and social purpose. This has been true of governments from ancient Rome—'Bread and Circuses', as the poet Juvenal (Satire 10, line 81) pungently put it—to modern Singapore—'The Theatre that Governs' as theatre director Kuo Pao Kun (1996) equally succinctly labelled this useful quality. In 330 BC, Aristotle observed and attempted to define the stabilising effect of drama on an audience, explaining it in terms of catharsis, purging socially dangerous excesses of pity and fear.

By contrast, Plato (c. 360 BC) a generation earlier warned of the potentially disruptive effects of drama. Official ambivalence to theatre is always present. Governments and non-governmental agencies welcome the power of theatre to speak to the community and influence its attitudes to health and to the environment, but they look nervously on its potential to stir those communities into unrest (Kuo Pao Kun spent time in gaol for his social activist views). It is part of the two-headed nature of drama and theatre not just to reflect and celebrate society, but to interrogate it—to ask awkward questions as well as providing happy endings.

Not only that, but it must be noted that drama may also be traduced into assisting the escalation and maintenance of conflict itself: practising for war is in no small measure carried out through dramatic simulations and enactments.

Modern Movements in Drama and Education

The Twentieth Century

Throughout the twentieth Century and into the twenty-first, interest in the educational and social effects and possibilities of drama has been growing. From the 1920s in Vienna to the 1960s in the USA, Jacob Moreno and his associates developed the psychodrama (Moreno, 1946) and sociodrama (ibid. 1960) movements. Both were predicated on the assumption that drama may be used to assist in the restoration of personal, psychological and social stability. Both movements used forms of role-play: psychodrama to stabilise and normalise disturbed individuals, and sociodrama to assist groups, and both movements are still active and influential. Psychodrama is widely used in mental health settings, and sociodrama developed into the massive adult role-play training movement still popular in commercial and managerial settings.

The rise of progressive education throughout the twentieth century led to the growth of educational uses of drama in schools. From the turn of the twentieth century, educators in many countries started to find in drama a pedagogy to accomplish the liberal progressive education whose proponents were attempting to centre the curriculum on the personal and social development of the child. In England a radical school principal, Harriet Finlay Johnson, wrote *The Dramatic Method of Teaching* (1907), based on her work with village elementary schoolchildren that included both role-play and Shakespeare. In the USA, Winifred Ward developed the hugely influential Creative Dramatics (1930)—a movement that is still popular in the USA—with the aims of providing a controlled emotional outlet, an avenue of self-expression, encouragement of the creative imagination, growth in social understanding and cooperation and giving students experience in thinking on their feet and expressing themselves fearlessly. In Sweden Esther Boman, the principal of a progressive girls' school, used drama to 'focus on aspects of the curriculum and on personal problems in the girls' own lives' (1932—see Hagglund, 1999).

All of these movements were based on the active learning power of *doing* drama, and all of them espoused improvisational methods to permit children to become active participants, not just audiences—albeit with a range of forms of participation, and for different purposes.

Child Drama and Developmental Drama

In the 1950s, the charismatic teacher Peter Slade set up a centre in Birmingham, UK to focus attention on the significance and natural structures of children's own dramatic play, allowing those to create the conditions for classroom learning. This he described in his internationally influential book *Child Drama* (1954). He also founded the still-active Dramatherapy movement, a more group-centred variant of psychodrama.

In the 1960s, Slade's equally influential associate Brian Way (1967) extended this idea into harnessing the dramatic instinct in a more organised way, through structured theatrical exercises, to provide a developmental progress for the individual child. The philosophical drive came largely from Rousseau through Dewey and the progressive education movement—crystallised in Richard Courtney's *Play, Drama and Thought* (1968). Theatre itself was downplayed in favour of children exploring drama for themselves in the private context of the classroom itself, with no external audience.

Drama-in-Education

These ideas became the springboard for the even more influential ***drama-in-education*** movement, again initially centred in the UK. The pioneers of this movement, Dorothy Heathcote and Gavin Bolton followed Slade's lead by starting their drama work on the basis of extending children's natural dramatic play into improvised drama, but to some extent they were reacting against both Slade and Way. Slade's declared reliance on letting the children freely lead the dramatic play sometimes led, in the classrooms of his less charismatic followers, to chaos, puzzled children and little in the way of learning. Heathcote had little patience with all of this. Like Brian Way, Heathcote and Bolton believed in structure, but not in Way's rather mechanistic patterns of dramatic exercises. They set out to build the children's ideas into intellectually and emotionally strong dramatic experiences; Heathcote's phrase 'building belief' is now part of the drama teacher's lexicon, and she happily agreed with libertarian critics that she used 'manipulation'. This drama had a strong social and group orientation.

In all drama-in-education, participants are collaborative learners engaged in learning by shifting role perspectives in a fictional or fictionalised context. Heathcote's most distinctive pedagogical innovation was the 'mantle of the expert', where to achieve the goals of the drama, the participants as characters in role had to learn to carry out tasks and make decisions demanding real expertise. This shifted the balance of power and responsibility in the classroom on to the students. Drama was there to create genuine dialogue and social learning: understanding of the world and each other.

For a long time, the dominant mode of drama-in-education was group 'living-through' role-play, with no concept of an external audience. In this kind of role-play, the participants become entirely absorbed in the dramatic context as characters, empathising with the situation and their role, making it up as they go along, in concert with the other characters—the members of the class or subgroup. More recent drama educators have woven into this group-based empathic role-play a broader range of theatrical techniques, exercises and conventions, not least to provide the participants with the opportunity of exploring the context with a measure of emotional distance.

Both pioneers were themselves masterly, though very contrasting, teachers whose fame quickly spread. Heathcote's dazzling and revolutionary practice was seen in numerous films (e.g. 1971) and attracted teachers and drama workers to her side from all round the globe, who spread the word. With Bolton's meticulous theorising of the practice in *Towards a Theory of Drama Education* and later writings (1979, 1984; Heathcote & Bolton, 1995) they quickly created a worldwide movement. Many of their early followers and successors refined the practice and the theory, creating manageable classroom learning strategies that are still current, pre-eminently the composite drama form that is nowadays more commonly known as **process drama**. This is still widely used, mainly in educational settings.

Emanating from the UK, DIE became most strongly established in Anglophone and English-friendly education systems, such as those in Scandinavia and former UK colonies like Australia. Not surprisingly the Brisbane, Adelaide and Swedish DRACON projects were all based on DIE philosophy and made use of some of its forms.

The early DIE pioneers were also influential in a complementary and contemporaneous movement in the field of young people's theatre known as **theatre-in-education** (TIE), which like DIE spread internationally. TIE commonly refers to a participatory form of theatre for young people provided to school students by external companies and groups. It started in regional theatres in the UK and was closely allied to the DIE pioneers and their aims; TIE's early practitioners similarly set out to visit schools in order to utilise the power of drama—through theatre—to open up, explore and influence learning, providing 'a dynamic means of gaining new understanding' (Bolton, 1979, p. 112).

Contemporary TIE is now a widely used extension of schooling worldwide across all age levels and many subject areas. It can also involve groups of students attending a performance at a specific site. Some education systems have established sites such as farms, environmental centres and historic villages which combine theatre performance with hands-on experience. Theatre in museums has become a major form of theatre-in-education in a number of countries in Europe, North America and Asia, where students travel to museums to see performances and take part in intensive role-play days, with activities such as costumed improvisations of an historical event and battle re-enactments.

TIE was the form used by the Malaysian DRACON project and is described in more detail below.

Theatre of the Oppressed

Developed contemporaneously with DIE but on the other side of the world, and also now a worldwide movement, was ***Theatre of the Oppressed*** (TO). TO was founded by the Brazilian theatre director Augusto Boal. Directly inspired by Paolo Freire's *Pedagogy of the Oppressed* (1970), Boal set out to develop a community theatre practice that has become, in effect, a pedagogy. TO's original aim was to help the poor and disenfranchised to liberate themselves by revealing through theatre the nature and conquerability of the things that oppressed them. One of Boal's most celebrated techniques was *forum theatre* described in more detail below.

Boal subsequently acknowledged the problems for a visiting theatre company playing to localised audiences; these included the possible irresponsibility of a fly-in, fly-out experience leading to uncontrolled responses, and the limitation of only being able to work at the communal level. His later theory and practice included alternative forms which concentrated more on the individual, such as 'image theatre' and what he termed 'Rainbow of Desire' (1995). This involves a group with their leader engaging in workshop drama exercises, whose purpose is to assist individuals to deal with their own 'cops in the head' that provide much of what oppresses them. This method of theatre and therapy is now widely used within economically developing world contexts where it is seen to have the therapeutic potential of using theatre to transform life.

Boal's work was focused on adults and liberatory rather than educational. His workshop exercises were based on acting techniques rather than play forms familiar to children. However, his work is increasingly finding application in schools. Both the Brisbane and Swedish DRACON projects made use of forum theatre, with modifications.

Theatre for Development and Applied Theatre

Other significant influences on the DRACON project were approaches drawn from ***Theatre for Development*** (TfD). TfD refers to a process of creative problem-solving and community empowerment using theatre. Communities, usually with the assistance of professional theatre makers, draw on standard theatrical forms as well as their own specific cultural traditions, to address issues of concern in their own communities. Interchangeable terms have historically included Theatre for Social Change, Theatre of Liberation, Cultural Action Theatre, Protest Theatre and Popular Theatre. Most of these draw inspiration from Latin American liberation theology and the work of Paulo Freire and Augusto Boal, and some also from DIE and TIE. Now these forms are most commonly aggregated under the umbrella term *applied theatre*, a phrase coined and defined in the 1990s to encompass all these forms of drama based in communities of all sorts that have the aim of effecting some kind of social change.

Most applied theatre targets issues within the fields of health, environment, education and politics. It locates the creative process within specific social, cultural and political contexts; it uses familiar cultural forms and processes as a participatory medium, to raise collective consciousness and promote self-determination and change.

The Pedagogy of Drama

Drama and Transformation

The continuing action research of the DRACON project, since its inception and beyond, has confirmed the power of drama as a learning medium. Drama pedagogy has been utilised to stimulate insight and understanding first in all four DRACON settings, and then in spin-off projects in areas as diverse as professional learning in health care and working on resilience with the survivors of natural disasters (see Chap. 9). As Brown et al. put it, 'participatory drama opens spaces to explore lived experience, imaginations, emotions and possible solutions' (2017, p. 8).

At the time when the DRACON project was conceived, the power of drama as a powerful pedagogy was increasingly being recognised and acknowledged. Alongside the expansion of drama as a school subject in some education systems like the UK, Australia, Canada and the Scandinavian countries, there was an increasing global awareness among school policy leaders that as well as enhancing learning, drama had the power to generate profound aesthetic experience that could transform students as individuals. Beyond schools too, this same realisation was leading to the complementary worldwide applied theatre movement.

Understanding how drama generates engagement is central to understanding its transformative potential. Michael Fleming argues:

> In successful drama the ... process of bringing about explicit awareness and making discriminations which are fundamental to human concerns is happening far more intensely because the art form serves to select, focus and heighten the feeling context. (2005, p. 38)

Fellow UK drama educator Jonothan Neelands identifies how dramatic transformation functions to stimulate learning:

> Theatre can offer young people a mirror of who we are and who we are becoming. Theatre can be a dynamo for social change by providing the space to imagine ourselves and how we can live differently. Theatre can be a lens through which young people can discover the embodied relevance of the real in their curriculum. (In O'Connor, 2010, p. 155)

Furthermore, the aesthetic nature of both classroom drama and theatre performance is notably a result of transformative processes—processes underpinned by concepts such as empathy, imagination and creativity. Understanding how drama operates in relation to these concepts provides the clues to its power as a transformative medium.

Key Components of the Drama Process

Improvisation and Games

Those twentieth and twenty-first century educational movements referred to above have all been based on the concept of participant learning and children creating their own drama, so they have mostly abandoned what Aristotle would have recognised as the educational function of drama (namely the performing and viewing of a script) for the diverse forms of dramatic improvisation. There have been three major and connected sources of inspiration.

One of these has been the use of acting exercises, many of which are improvisatory, even when rehearsing a set script. Indeed, from the middle of the twentieth century, adult theatre itself started rediscovering the potential of improvisation not only in rehearsal, but also in performance. In the USA Viola Spolin (1963) and then her son Paul Sills used improvised acting exercises and games as the basis of the popular Chicago performance genre known as 'long-form improv'. UK theatre director Johnstone (1979) added the spirit of competition to the same exercises to create the even more successful genre of Theatresports. All forms of dramatic improvisation demand careful and continuous focus on the subject of the drama, the creative use of imagination, and immediate and sensitive reading of the group process—teamwork with the other participants. All participants have to be equally engaged and to have accepted the 'agreement to pretend', the contract inherent in together entering a fictional situation.

Games are the second of these drivers of improvised drama in school classrooms. Spolin saw the educational potential in theatre games and published a version of her handbook for schools (1986). Dramatic or quasi-dramatic games are already in the DNA of children, with their close connection to the dramatic play of early childhood. Though—like play—games are not traditionally encouraged in classrooms, they have the advantage for teachers of immediately engaging children's attention, and also being structured, with recognisable rules.

Games have been immensely popular in drama classrooms, in all the movements referred to above, from Finlay-Johnson's Dramatic Method to Boal's Theatre of the Oppressed. Games have a number of purposes in drama and were extensively used in all the DRACON projects:

- They create a sense of the group, with defined rules for all, and defined goals for the activity;
- That in turn leads to group trust, a vital prerequisite for that agreement to pretend;
- The result is uncertain, so they contain dramatic tension;

- They can change the energy level of a group—liven up a lethargic class or calm a frenetic one;
- They can interestingly introduce a theme that may be explored dramatically.

Role and Role-Play

The third and as far as DRACON is concerned the most significant wellspring of improvised drama is role-play (a feature of improvisation and many games, in any case). In many ways the 'grown-up' manifestation of children's play, role-play is so much a part of the basic dramatic urge, and so crucial to the learning in DRACON that its psychological and sociological roots need to be explored.

The psychological act of identification is crucial to human learning and development. Identification involves conscious and unconscious changes of behaviour through the deliberate adoption of other people's behaviour, ideas and feelings as one's own (Coleman, 2015). Identification allows us to both think and feel as another person, to experience a range of cognitive and affective states not directly accessible to us. In drama, this enhancement of experience and sense of self occurs through role, the fundamental act which is at the heart of drama, where participants take on the behaviour, perform the actions and speak the words of other characters in fictional or fictionalised situations. We *play with* these roles, as we *play* them *out*, so we accurately call this ***role-play***.

The power of identification to generate deep learning through the act of taking role is not restricted to the field of drama. For decades, academics, educators and trainers from many disciplines have identified the importance of role in personal development and learning. We know that the knowledge and techniques of creating a role can enhance the presentation of self in everyday life, through what sixty years ago Goffman (1956; Raffel, 2013) called impression management. In the field of psychotherapy, 'an individual's identity is seen as constructed through the roles they perform in various contexts' (Newman, 2017, p. 3). Education theorist Bruner (2005) believed that we achieve real insight through taking on and expressing roles that provide us with passionate experience. Finally, having the opportunity to construct and explore a range of effective personal roles in a rehearsal for life can be profoundly influential in developing a sense of identity and self-confidence (Erikson, 1965).

For the process of drama to operate, participants must first imagine or accept a fictitious role, and then behave as if this fiction were a reality. The experience generated by this taking on of role is, in one sense, authentic first-hand experience, because the actor is directly and actively involved in both becoming and doing, creating a level of commitment to the reality of the experience. However, the participant is also consciously involved in pretence, using identification and the substitution of action for reality. The participants are acting the role, but also perceiving their actions, consciously observing and controlling their involvement in the drama. As education theorist Lev Vygotsky famously described young children acting in role: 'the child weeps in play as a patient, but revels as a player'. (1933/1974, p. 548) He termed this phenomenon *dual affect*. That concept is now embedded in the theory and practice of educational drama, and acknowledged as crucial in theatre theory, too.

This two-way process of relatedness is also key to the participant/percipient interaction described by Augusto Boal as 'metaxis' (1979). Metaxis is a framed activity in the sociological sense, separated from the more usual world of everyday interactions. Carroll (1988, p. 13) defines it as '...a mental attitude, a way of holding two worlds in mind, the role and the dramatic fiction, simultaneously in the drama frame.' The coming together and the resulting emotional frisson between these two worlds gives drama of this kind much of its tension and its learning potential.

The experience of identification through role in drama can provide the form of learning that Erikson (1975, p. 173) describes as insight: 'the act of seeing into a situation and into myself at the same time.' Antonin Artaud, one of the major adult theatre innovators of the twentieth century, described the experience of identification that occurred while in role as a form of enhanced awareness:

> While I live, I cannot feel myself living, but when I am acting, then I feel I am existing ... theatre is like heightened waking, where I guide fate. (1993, p. 101)

Empathy and Distance

Drama fundamentally depends on a particular form of identification that is equally central to conflict resolution: **empathy** (the ability to identify not only cognitively but also affectively with others), to 'step into others' shoes' to some degree, and temporarily see the world from an alien viewpoint. Drama actually works through the simultaneous operation of both empathy and distance. As many writers on drama have pointed out, Vygotsky's 'dual affect'—better known in theatre studies and psychodramatic theory as 'aesthetic doubling' (e.g. Courtney, 1968, p. 192)—permits both emotional identification and closeness to the conflict, and at the same time dispassionate awareness of the elements of that conflict.

To permit the 'contract' referred to above, an emotional 'safe space' has to be created. In all the various forms of role-play that we used in DRACON (process drama, participatory TIE and EFT—see below) the participants need focusing, and sometimes warming-up into an appropriate mood and physical readiness where they are able to embody their roles with ease, and unconsciously step into and out of those empathic shoes, as called for by the dramatic context or the drama teacher.

As soon as the participants are asked to take a role, even if this is just a generalised shift of viewpoint ('Imagine this has happened to you—how do you react?') it is crucial that they are enabled to focus intellectually and emotionally, so that they can operate and respond with empathy, and simultaneously with distance. Particularly if they are asked to adopt a realistic, personalised or complex role where they will be expected to empathise and respond as a specific character who is perhaps very alien to their own disposition, it is crucial that appropriate preparation activity time and space be allowed for this process, known as 'enrolment'.

There is also a compelling contemporary case for the significance of empathy in transformative learning and the particular potency of dramatic transformation. Recent research provides insights into the fundamentally empathic, cooperative nature of human beings:

> Discoveries in evolutionary biology, neurocognitive science, and child development... reveal that people are biologically predisposed to be empathic—that our core nature is not rational, detached, acquisitive, aggressive, and narcissistic, but affectionate, highly social, cooperative, and interdependent. The realization that we are an empathic species, that empathy has evolved over history, and that we are as interconnected in the biosphere as we are in the blogosphere, has profound implications for rethinking the mission of education. (Rifkin, 2013, p. 2)

It is both the nature and the function of drama to encourage participants to seek affective experiences and feel empathy, to make vivid use of their imaginations and to be intuitive. Furthermore, creative engagement in drama may involve a genuine divergence of intense feeling and thought expressed through the drama process; it can equally allow the empathic and creative affirmation of the common beliefs of a group involved in the process.

Reflection

When stepping out of the kind of realistic dramatic role that may be involved in exploring conflict, if it has been strongly empathic the participants may also need a little time and even a structured 'derolment', to process the emotional content. The emotions kindled in a drama are quite real, though invested in a fictionalised dramatic context and should not carry over into the real-life context, other than as what is primarily cognitive reflection. Reflection has been described as the ability to examine one's own actions, thoughts and feelings (Newell, 1992), and thinking purposefully to gain new insights, ideas and understanding. In drama-in-education, the key to learning is not only the experience itself but also the reflection related to that experience.

Drama generates its own meanings, which cannot easily be reduced to simplistic resolutions and assumptions nor written down as discursive text. However, it is possible, and in some cases necessary, to reflect upon the meanings, those personal to each participant and those shared by the group. In the case of inexperienced participants, particularly in role-play exercises, this reflective process may need to be carefully structured and even to begin within the dramatic fiction itself. Whether there is a teaching, counselling or clinical purpose, this is crucial to make explicit the nature of the experience just shared, and what useful knowledge may be derived from it.

In genres of role-play, reflection may follow the drama (known as *reflection-on-action*) or be interwoven with the drama itself (known as *reflection-in-action*). Reflection-on-action usually takes the form of discussion about the experience the students have just had. It can, however, involve turning the original 'lived-through' drama into a performance for an audience, or even transforming the experience or the feelings it evoked into other art forms, such as into drawing or dance. Reflection-in-action can begin within the drama itself and may itself include re-enactment, theatrical conventions or performance. A commonly used reflection-in-role strategy is to ask the participants to create original writing in the roles of the characters, such as personal diary entries or letters to an editor. However it is managed, reflection is invariably a distinct and necessary phase of processing the drama to make it into usable knowledge. For the three predominant genres of drama pedagogy used in DRACON (*process drama, theatre-in-education (TIE)* and *enhanced forum theatre (EFT)*, a reflective phase was built-in. The reflective phase is always important in process drama, and often in TIE, where the audience is invited to engage with the participants, either in role, or in discussion following the performance. In EFT, the form we specifically devised and refined for the Brisbane and Swedish projects, it turned out to be even more integral and consequential than we had imagined. In several ways, reflection-in-action was built into the structure of the drama, and as well as this, reflection-on-action, in the form of discussion, frequently supplanted and replaced the drama itself, crystallising the explicit cognitive and social learning for the students.

Cooperation and Trust

Drama of all kinds is a group activity, dependent on organised teamwork, and generally non-competitive—apart from occasional oddities such as Theatresports and ancient Greek Drama Festivals (and some school drama festivals). The teamwork must extend to all the participants and that includes the theatre audience. Obviously the playwright, actors, director and designer and theatre team must all be working on the same project in synchrony, and the audience needs to 'tune in' to the play. There is, however, a deeper bond between all of them—the bond of accepting a shared fiction, without which the play cannot happen at all. This goes right back to children's social play, the 'agreement to pretend' that has to happen if the players are to step into those others' shoes and create a shared dramatic situation and context. This is sometimes known as 'the dramatic contract' or in schools 'permission to play'. For adults, though it is rarely made explicit this contract is clear: the creative team affirm it when they agree to join the production and the audience sign up for it when they buy their tickets. In dramatic genres where there is no external audience, the drama must still start with the agreement to pretend.

Based on Bakhtin's theory about dialogism Eva Hallgren uses the concept of *postupak* to explain the central acting behaviour in role-taking within an improvisational frame. She describes postupak as 'a goal-oriented action that contains open, not completely defined offers' (2018, p. 256), directed towards another person and waiting for an answer in role. It is a complicated creative process, serious and at the same time playful, involving teacher and children in role making offers to and answering each other.

This can be trickier in schools and classrooms, particularly with classes unused to social learning or socially dysfunctional. The 'safe space' may be much harder to create, as some of the DRACON class teachers and facilitators discovered. Where there is little cohesion or group learning experience, shedding one's real-life role protections and trusting other people to respond in the same way leaves one vulnerable. Safer to keep up one's guard and offer nothing—especially as there may be real conflicts within the class, or with the teacher—and anyway, isn't school about real life, not pretending? As students move into adolescence this protective need grows stronger, and if they are not already used to drama it may be hard to get them to drop their guard.

Generating trust is the most basic prerequisite of all for drama, and sometimes it has to be taught. Teachers may have to use serious group social engineering tactics (usually in the form of games and group exercises) before anyone is ready to sign the contract. Drama's most basic requirement is just an 'empty space', as Peter Brook (1968) reminds us, which must then be turned by that dramatic contract into a place made special to allow the participants to make the agreement to pretend. So, as we have seen, the special place must also be a 'safe space' where the students are trusting enough to sign the contract and invest their emotions in empathy. The simplest and most common manifestation of this special space is in the drama classroom. At the beginning of a lesson and during class discussion and planning, the students, whatever their age, are normally grouped in a circle, including the teacher, usually seated at the same level, rather than the conventional classroom formation of the students, all sitting, facing the teacher, who is often standing or on a raised level. This in itself signals a democratic power shift and an invitation to take an equal part in discussion and decision-making, as well as permitting all participants eye contact with each other. The importance of this safe space in the DRACON classroom explorations of conflict we will discuss in the next chapter.

Narrative and Tension

Of all the basic elements of drama, *narrative* and *dramatic tension* are the two which come together most naturally and integrally in exploring and depicting conflict, its causes and effects. As we have already analysed in Chap. 2, contemporary social constructivist philosophy acknowledges and conceptualises humans as 'storytelling creatures… that not only tell stories, they live them too' (Section "Conflict Attitudes (The A-Component of Conflict)"). We construct our very reality and sense of meaning in the form of narrative. Drama is just a way of making and depicting plausible narratives for us to observe our behaviour and explore cause and effect: why we behave as we do, and what this does to the personal, social and physical worlds we inhabit. This narratising gives shape to the welter of our lived experience—making it into a comprehensible story by finding a beginning, selecting a simplified train of events or significant ideas to follow and looking for a meaningful conclusion to the story.

The dramatic fictions of drama-in-education are not 'just made-up' stories, but narratives that must be in some way authentic—not 'real' but realistic. The situation, characters and dramatic action are always one degree removed from reality—as a representation of that reality, not the real thing—or else it is not drama. This is a particularly important distinction to make in a context like DRACON, where students who like all of us experience unpleasant real-life conflict are being asked to step into the shoes of people in conflict. Our DRACON conflict narratives were of three kinds. Some of the stories were in fact taken from the participants' own reports of their real conflicts, but only of those beyond the DRACON classroom; they were then fictionalised in ways described elsewhere in the book to make them safely 'second-hand'. Some were third-hand, developed from stories collected by the participants through questionnaires, interviews with other students, even the media, etc. Those that were entirely 'made-up' had to pass stringent tests of their authenticity, through the students' own and shared ability to believe in them according to their own experiences.

Tension drives the narrative; it is the element that prevents the story reaching its conclusion until something significant emotionally or intellectually has emerged. Tension keeps the participants or audience interested, slows down the action and makes the story worth the telling. From the point of view of the dramatist, in simple terms tension is the force or forces that prevent the characters in the story reaching their goals without some form of change or development in themselves or in the dramatic context, or both.

For the dramatist, conflict of one sort or another is among the most productive forms of tension (making it hard for the characters to realise their goals, and therefore productive of development or change). That's why it is also among the most time-honoured across cultures. The Natya Shastra's claim about conflict as the mainspring of all drama may not be quite true—as there are other forms of dramatic tension, such as dilemma, ritual, suspense, discovery, secrecy and mystery (Haseman et al. 2017)—but some of these, such as dilemma, are frequently bound up in conflict too. That is why the factual realm of conflict and the fictional world of drama share the word for their ideal conclusion: 'resolution'. This will be discussed in more detail in the next chapter.

Language and Dialogue

Dialogue is of course a word almost synonymous with drama. Language is one of the twin basic instruments of dramatic expression (the body being the other), and dialogue is what makes language dramatic. We expect any drama we watch or take part in to be to a large extent comprised of dialogue, usually spoken but sometimes implied (as in a monodrama or a soliloquy). Sadly, it has traditionally been less essential to formal education. Throughout the history of schooling worldwide, the emphasis, sometimes the sole emphasis has usually been on the one-way transmission of knowledge, skills and morals from those who know to those who don't. This has on the whole been compounded by the invention of printed books, which are monologic, and the computer screen, only slightly less so. Add to that the advantages of one-way communication for controlling students' thoughts and behaviour, and the economic advantage that more one-way traffic demands fewer teachers and less time. This is a cruel simplification that nonetheless has some truth—just thinks of a conventional secondary school classroom or university lecture hall in any era, even today.

Contemporary teachers, education theorists and even education systems are trying to find ways to restore dialogue; they are driven by the recognition that learning is not a commodity to be handed on, but an ongoing, dynamic, social and dialogical construction of knowledge and understanding. Drama is one of those possible ways. All the historical and current movements of drama education mentioned above have been at times welcomed, at times feared, just because they are dialogic. Restoring dialogue is also of the essence in handling and resolving conflict, so education and conflict transformation go hand in hand in making dialogue central to their goals.

Movement, Gesture and Embodiment

The body, its senses, feelings and movement form the other twin instrument of dramatic expression. Unfortunately, in traditional schooling systems, the transmission of knowledge has been seen as a purely cognitive absorption activity. It can thus best be achieved with everybody sitting down and facing the same direction, where the distractions of movement, of social interaction and of emotional response can be minimised. Again, just think of a conventional secondary classroom almost anywhere. But contemporary educators and some education systems know that learning is not like that; they are backed up by current discoveries in neurology, which show that the brain, senses and emotions are inseparable in learning and in cognition itself (e.g. Damasio, 2018). So of course those educators are looking desperately for embodied education practices. Again, drama provides a complete and holistic solution.

Imagination

> The imagination is, indeed, increasingly recognized as one of the great workhorses of learning, and its development is seen frequently as one of the proper constituents of any adequate educational program. (Judson & Egan, 2012, p. 38)

A number of key elements that constitute the operation of the imagination are inherent in the drama process:

- Imagination is a form of consciousness where individuals conceive of an object and then perceive it as an abstract representation to generate meaning
- Imagining is a complex synthesis of subject and object, created by the individual out of a range of different experiences to enrich understanding
- Imagination involves intuitive and affective dimensions to provide meaning that transcends cognitive understanding.

It is essentially the use of the imagination applied through the creative lens of aesthetic engagement that allows participants in drama to experience intense awareness, heighten our perceptions and discover embodied relevance. Through the use of the dramatic imagination, participants are able to conceive of and experience not only a range of roles beyond our immediate experience but also a range of situations, contexts and issues we have not yet encountered. Through this we extend our own understanding of human behaviour and the world we live in. Using our imagination in this way, we can actually create our own versions of the world. By animating these, our understanding of the nature of being human is enlarged and we are made aware that the lives and experiences of others carry meaning for our own.

By drawing on our own experiences and by using our imaginations, participants in drama can also recreate situations and environments that are part of our history, and our relationships with other people. Alternatively, drama allows us to imagine completely fictitious experiences, people and environments. Using the drama process to act in an imagined environment or situation, we extend and transform our original experiences through thinking, feeling and behaving as if the imagined experiences were real, while being fully aware that we are constructing and reconstructing a fiction. This is the process of metaxis in operation. Drama education pioneer Richard Courtney argues that it is crucial to real learning: 'Nothing has reality to the human being unless he realises it completely—lives it in the imagination—acts it.' (1968, p. 273)

Creativity

Creativity is a crucial element in the functioning of drama, and in the process of drama. Drama communicates aesthetically and cognitively—its conception and reception rely on key human characteristics and drives. While we might recognise creativity in a work of art, and therefore consider its maker creative, creativity is not a unique gift or innate in a select few. Recent research suggests that we are all creative to some extent and that creativity is a fundamental human ability:

> The capacity to be creative, to produce new concepts, ideas, inventions, objects or art, is perhaps the most important attribute of the human brain. (Andreasen, 2011, p. 1)

The creative process in action consists of being inventive, having the ability to problem-solve, problematise, think and reflect laterally and respond in ways which provide fresh insights and lead to original outcomes. Working through drama stimulates the same cognitive and affective dimensions that work in the production of a creative response. It is both the nature and the function of educational drama, comprising as it does group-based activities where there is no clear distinction between players and audience, to encourage participants to seek affective experiences and feel empathy, to make vivid use of our imaginations and to be intuitive. Furthermore, creative engagement in drama may involve a genuine divergence of intense feeling and thought expressed through the drama process, and it can equally allow the empathic and creative affirmation of common beliefs by the group involved in the process. There is also a selective element in the drama process where only those things of significance to the participants are chosen for representation. In this way convergent thought can be as valuable as divergent thought in the process of creativity.

The interactive nature of educational drama is also conducive to creativity, involving shared commitment to the improvisation or representation of the perceptions and intentions of the whole group. This form of cooperative, aesthetic activity stimulates the ability to intuit feelings and thoughts that occur in the minds of others, which is apparent in the high-level creativity revealed in neurological research. Bernie Neville explains that in the holistic endeavour that characterises the drama process:

> Conscious and unconscious processes are integrated and what we do together intuitively is far more appropriate and creative than what was produced by our usual modes of thought. (1989, p. 12)

In essence, the deep aesthetic learning generated by engagement in the arts involves an act of the imagination, both cognitive and affective, and an intense engagement in a creative process. This combination results in the creative construction and reconstruction of perceptions of the world, both physical and human. In drama, deep learning occurs through the imaginative and creative process of assuming roles and creating transformations that generate the experience of metaxis, the balance between the fictitious roles and contexts in the drama and the real perceptions and understanding of the participants.

Drama, Conflict and Pedagogy

The fundamental nature of how drama operates, and the processes underpinning its power as a learning medium, share much with those of conflict management. Mediators identify three classic phases of conflict: 'latent', 'emerging' and 'manifest'. They construe the phases and factors involved in escalation, and work towards de-escalation and resolution. Furthermore, all the areas of situation and relationship that are explored by dramatic action are central to real-life understanding and stable relationships. Drama is about the clashes and conflicts of personality, of values, of attitudes, of emotions, of interests both internal and environmental, of status and power, of philosophy and ideology, of ethics and morals.

Drama offers living, breathing models to define and diagnose the nature of conflict, as well as to present the circumstances that motivate adversaries to take particular action. In retelling/re-enacting, the participants expose their needs and clarify their motivations for certain actions they have taken. The pedagogical intention in using dramatic models of conflict is to deconstruct the simplistic classifications and assumptions that dominate perception and perspective-taking. Drama provides the participants with three distinct perspectival experiences: first, the opportunity to explore the viewpoint and attitude of the protagonists; second, to deconstruct the enemy image by playing the antagonists; and third, to view the conflict situation more objectively by playing the third parties, such as bystanders and other stakeholders in the conflict.

These central connections between drama and conflict mediation will be addressed in more detail in the next chapter.

Dracon's Central Drama Strategies

Process Drama

The Brisbane, Swedish and Adelaide DRACON projects made considerable use of the DIE approach now most commonly referred to as ***process drama***. In process drama participants are collaborative learners, engaged in learning by shifting role perspectives. The work is unscripted and open-ended, based on forms of improvised role-play. In this way drama is used as a learning medium first and foremost, and its ultimate dramatic form is less important. The usual distinctions one would expect to find in a dramatic production give way to a more egalitarian group of collaborators. The participants are all engaged together in role as characters in the dramatic context not performers for an external audience, so they are simultaneously actors, playwrights, directors and audience. Their engagement is in the service of self-reflection, collaborative meaning-making and problem solving. Process drama is a distinctive dramatic form or genre insofar as it is exploratory and investigative, and its shape evolves and unfolds as each stage builds upon the last. It is always to some extent open-ended in nature, allowing room for multiple participant perspectives to play out. Participants take on roles relevant to the topic or theme being investigated and explored.

Despite its improvisational nature, process drama does have a focus—it is shaped by the teacher who identifies a learning area or theme and selects a sequence of drama strategies to support the investigation. The teacher often takes part, in a convention known as 'Teacher-in-role', a technique mainly developed by Dorothy Heathcote, guiding the dramatic action from within the drama. In the case of the DRACON project, the learning area was 'Conflict', and more specifically fictional or fictionalised conflict that directly related to the experiences of participants. Roles and relationships within the drama were based on real experiences. Having the opportunity to explore alternative perspectives on an event through role-play provided a springboard for learning, and the teacher's role was critical to 'find ways in which to connect pupils to content and enable them to develop responses to it through active engagement and reflection' (Bowell & Heap, 2001, p. 7).

While teachers have a central role in shaping the participants' engagement in process drama, it can be argued that problems or issues that have personal meaning naturally incite interest and stimulate a drive to explore them. Student engagement underpins experiential learning, and since one of the core characteristics of process drama is collaboration and role taking, the form lends itself to a pedagogy which seeks to develop an experiential approach to understanding alternative perspectives. That understanding is fostered through empathy, and the insights that the students gain through this dramatic form of experiential learning can be deep and meaningful.

> In successful drama the ... process of bringing about explicit awareness and making discriminations which are fundamental to human concerns is happening far more intensely because the art form serves to select, focus and heighten the feeling context. (Fleming, 2005, p. 38)

Process drama in schools has been used in cross-curricular learning and has also proved a powerful approach to explore and deepen students' understanding of text of all kinds. In the context of DRACON, it was used as a medium for personal and social learning.

Theatre-in-Education

Theatre-in-education (TIE) was the form that the Malaysian DRACON team adopted, as there was no tradition of DIE or familiarity with it in their schools, and no drama teachers.

> Internationally, TIE is now characterised by its diversity of practice, and also by the shared aim of educating young people in ways that transcend the straight performance of a play and actively engage them in their own learning. (Vine & Jackson, 2013)

TIE's mission in its early days was defined, in the subtitle of the first book on the subject, as providing 'new objectives for theatre—new techniques in education' (O'Toole, 1977). TIE characteristically involves a group of actors who may also be teachers (some of the performers describe themselves as 'actor-teachers') visiting a school and working with groups of students, rather than just performing to them. This can involve both scripted and improvised performance, where the students are often engaged as characters in the drama. They share process drama strategies like Teacher-in-role; their participatory programs, usually in the students' classrooms, often involve the students integrally in the dramatic action as characters, making decisions and even deciding on the ending of the play. The actor/teachers also conduct discussions and workshops with the students to introduce or reinforce the knowledge and understanding generated by the performance work.

Both DIE and TIE have been from their inception characterised by a focus on sceptical and social activist interrogation of the society and its mores, usually with the leader's or teacher's underlying intention of contributing towards changing those mores. Issue-based classroom drama and theatre for many years became the norm, strongly influenced by the theatrical and educational ideas of revolutionary playwright Bertold Brecht, and of social learning theorist Lev Vygotsky. Particularly in secondary schools, TIE has traditionally focused on social and political subjects, investigating issues such as injustice.

Forum Theatre

Boal's most celebrated technique, *forum theatre*, is now widely used throughout the field of applied theatre in economically developing world, health and educational contexts. In a forum theatre performance, a company of actors rehearse and re-enact on stage a story of oppression provided by the audience. They then invite the audience as 'spect-actors' to intervene directly in the scene as characters—thus disrupting the 'set' playtext—and offer the oppressed protagonist alternative behaviours or courses of action, in order to find the most effective method of dealing with the oppression. Since the oppressors cannot be expected voluntarily to change their behaviour, a key constraint is that the spect-actors can only intervene as the protagonist. This usually leads to extended discussion, and according to the aims of Boal, encourages the audience to take liberatory action in real life to overcome the oppression.

This classic 'Boalian' forum theatre was used by the Swedish and Brisbane DRACON projects early on, but both discovered the same limitations of the form when applying it to conflict handling. This led to the evolution of the most prominent and sophisticated drama strategy used in the project, that has also turned out to have considerable longevity (see Chap. 9), so it is worth describing in a little detail.

Enhanced Forum Theatre

This form of participatory theatre was based on Boal's forum theatre, modified in two key ways, and augmented by some elements of process drama. **Enhanced forum theatre** (EFT) was developed during the Brisbane DRACON project, where forum theatre and process drama were both being used as alternative strategies. The research team, seeking to compare the advantages and disadvantages of each, were observing some limitations in each form that appeared to be complementary—and the same problems were noted by the Swedish team.

- Participants were reporting that they found forum theatre was easy to master, to implement in class and to peer teach. However, it frequently led to superficial exploration of conflict. Originally designed by Boal to address oppression rather than conflict, the classic forum theatre structure invites direct audience intervention in the conflict without close investigation of its context or causes, and also demands that the protagonist alone is responsible to take action. We found that this led to simplistic resolution of the conflicts. Worse, it could encourage entirely inappropriate conflict handling practices. In real life, conflicts are often better de-escalated and settled away from the battleground and the heat of the strife, and with the agency of third parties.
- In contrast, the participants and their teachers were finding the form of process drama much more difficult even to understand, let alone to structure, lead and control. It was particularly challenging for students tasked with the design of new dramas in their peer teaching contexts. However, those participants, both teachers and students, also affirmed that process drama engendered much deeper engagement with the conflict situation, and more thoughtful and reflective student discussion.

The Brisbane research team put the two forms together, and created a hybrid ('enhanced') form that was easy for both teachers and students to manage, to create workable conflict-based dramas for exploration. It also allowed for much deeper and more sustained examination and discussion of the conflict situations. The Swedish team adopted many aspects of EFT in their project, with variations to suit their own context.

Using Boal's basic forum theatre structure, EFT diverged from his model in a number of key ways. Each play was structured in three scenes not one, depicting the three stages (latent, emerging and manifest) of a particular conflict. Those stories were sometimes generated from students' own stories using drama activities, and sometimes by prior discussion or student surveys. They were always fictionalised and thus distanced from direct experience, with a prescribed time gap between scenes, to ensure that the conflicts being explored were substantial and complex, instead of the evanescent or flashpoint conflicts often impulsively chosen by younger students.

Members of the audience were invited to intervene in the role of any character, not just the protagonist. In everyday conflicts, very often the protagonist has less power or will to de-escalate a conflict than others not so directly involved.

The enactments were controlled by a 'Host' (Boal used the term 'Joker'), and performed two or three times, to incorporate the following key process drama techniques that provided more contextual background and so deepened the response and discussion.

- *Hot Seating*. Any character from the play could be put in the 'hot-seat' and questioned by the audience to explore their background and motivations.
- *Thought Tracking*. A scene would be frozen for the Host or audience member to ask characters what was in their mind at that moment.
- *Role Circle*. The Host or the audience could ask questions relating to the conflict to all the characters in turn, as well as characters important to the conflict but not previously seen—also played by the actors.
- *Scene 4*. This further step was perhaps the most important extension of the forum, since conflicts can seldom be solved neatly or easily by a single intervention, and to imply this—as classic forum theatre does—teaches poor conflict handling. Usually, real-life mediation involves working with the antagonists and others outside the scene of the conflict, to identify with them what can be traded to de-escalate it. Once a piece of EFT had been worked through a number of interventions without full resolution (as was usually the case), the Host divided the audience into subgroups to identify another point in time, perhaps with characters mentioned but not present in the scenes shown, when the conflict might be better mediated or resolved. That scene was then acted out either by the actors or occasionally the audience group themselves—or just discussed.

One of Boal's techniques remained central: the control mechanism that he labelled 'magic'. If the dramatic action or interventions became improbable or any of the interventions out-of-character (such as the antagonists being reconciled through a million-dollar lottery win), any participant—audience, actors or Host—could freeze the action with the call 'Magic!'. The audience and actors would then discuss the scene's credibility, and if necessary take a vote before the action could proceed. This led to many richly pedagogical, student-led discussions.

As may be seen, EFT incorporated considerable reflection, both in-action and on-action. The hot-seating, the audience interventions and resulting discussions about appropriateness and magic were rich examples of reflection-in-action. The Scene 4 strategy started off the same way, but we found that frequently the discussion spontaneously took over and the drama itself just disappeared in even richer reflection-on-action.

EFT proved highly amenable to effective peer teaching. The older ('Key') class used the technique themselves to learn about conflict, and then they identified conflicts likely to be of concern to their younger peers. Using this as a basis the Key Class devised one or more pieces of EFT, with which they then initiated the peer teaching, reinforcing their own understanding of conflict as they did so. They followed that by helping the younger ('Focus') Class to construct their own EFT for enactment, so that the younger students were simultaneously clarifying their understanding of the conflict concepts and practising the techniques. These students in their turn, with their teacher, prepared EFT performances for their target peer group. The EFT was slightly simplified as the process descended through the primary school.

Crossover in Movements

Overall, the movement towards drama as a learning method has consolidated its pedagogy and diversified its practice since 1996, when DRACON began, establishing a strong foothold in the schools, especially in English-speaking countries and some European ones. In some developing countries, particularly in Africa, the movement has had a major influence on the equally fast-developing field of applied theatre. At the time of DRACON, drama and theatre workers were extending the pedagogy into social therapy in some war-torn countries, such as Northern Ireland, Israel and the Balkans—with promising but equivocal results (e.g. Fyfe, 1996; Schonmann, 1996; Knezevic, 1995). In DRACON, drama was explicitly not used as a direct medium for conflict handling or transformation, as it had been in all of the above contexts of national conflict. All the DRACON projects used drama as a method to provide school students with a basic cognitive understanding of conflict, and some tools that they might use to transform future conflicts.

There is now extensive crossover in these movements, particularly in the incorporation of TO techniques like forum and image theatre into the broader movement of DIE. In the use of structural and organisational strategies to build engagement and shape participant experience, there are links to the role of the teacher in process drama. This is the case in both Sweden and Australia, for example, where educational drama has been for a long time established in schools and tertiary education. In Malaysia, there is as yet virtually no drama in schools within the curriculum; however, both these approaches are understood and practised where possible, in special projects, and within the small tertiary drama sector.

Conclusion

As the DRACON project evolved in slightly different dramatic forms in the different countries involved, it became apparent that drama was an extraordinarily powerful tool to generate engagement in learning about conflict and to enable participants to develop competence in managing conflict in their own lives. Furthermore, drama provided an effective range of strategies and approaches for exploring and understanding conflict that could be adapted and applied in a range of contexts. Improvisation, the creation of a range of genres of role-play, process drama, and forum theatre were some of the key drama approaches we adopted that proved most effective in enabling young people to investigate and manage conflict. One of the major outcomes of the DRACON project was to identify those forms of drama best fitted for exploring and learning about conflict transformation, and then to modify them into new drama forms, such as EFT, to generate consistently effective knowledge and skills of conflict handling and transformation in the participant students.

References

Andreasen, N. (2011). *A journey into chaos: Creativity and the unconscious*. Mens Sana Monographs (pp. 42–53). Medknow Publications.
Aristotle. (c.330BC). *The art of poetry. Sections 6–11, 13*. Variously published.
Artaud, Antonin. (1993). *The theatre and its double*. Montreuil: Calder.
Boal, A. (1979). *Theatre of the oppressed*. London: Pluto.
Boal, A. (1995). *The rainbow of desire*. London: Routledge.
Bolton, G. (1984). *Drama as education*. London: Longmans.
Bolton, G. (1979). *Towards a theory of drama in education*. London: Longman.
Bowell, P., & Heap, B. (2001). *Planning process drama*. London: David Fulton.
Brook, P. (1968). *The empty space*. London: McGibbon & Kee.
Brown, K., Eernstman, N., Huke, A. R., & Reding, N. (2017). The drama of resilience: Learning, doing, and sharing for sustainability. *Ecology and Society, 22*(2), 8. https://doi.org/10.5751/ES-09145-220208. Accessed June 2, 2018.
Bruner, J. (2005). *In search of pedagogy: The selected works of Jerome Bruner 1957–1978*. London: Routledge.
Carroll, J. (1988). Terra incognita: Mapping drama talk. *NADIE Journal, 12*(2), 13–21.
Coleman, A. M. (2015). *A dictionary of psychology* (4th ed.). Oxford: Oxford University Press.
Courtney, R. (1968). *Play, drama and thought*. London: Cassell.
Damasio, A. (2018). *The strange order of things: Life, feeling, and the making of cultures*. New York: Pantheon.
Erikson, E. (1965). *Childhood and society*. Harmondsworth: Penguin.
Erikson, E. (1975). *Life, history and the historical moment*. New York: Norton.
Finlay Johnson, H. (1907). *The dramatic method of teaching*. London: Nisbet.
Fleming, M. (2005). *Starting drama teaching*. London: David Fulton.
Freire, P. (1970). *Pedagogy of the oppressed*. New York: Seabury.
Fyfe, H. (1996). Drama in the context of a divided society. In J. O'Toole & K. Donelan (Eds.), *Drama, culture and empowerment* (pp. 61–69). Brisbane: IDEA Publications.
Goffman, E. (1956). *The presentation of self in everyday life*. New York: Random House.

References

Hagglund, K. (1999). A glimpse into the early days of drama education in Sweden: The work of Ester Boman. *Research in Drama Education, 4*(1), 85–100.

Hallgren, E. (2018). *Clues to aesthetic engagement in process drama—Joint action in a fictive activity* (Dissertation). Stockholm University.

Haseman, B., & O'Toole, J. (2017). *Dramawise reimagined.* Sydney: Currency Press.

Heathcote, D. (1971). *Three looms waiting.* (Film). Director Richard Eyre. London: BBC Films.

Heathcote, D., & Bolton, G. (1995). *Drama for learning: Dorothy Heathcote's mantle of the expert approach to education.* Portsmouth, NH: Heinemann.

Johnston, K. (1979). *Impro: Improvisation and the theatre.* London: Routledge.

Judson, G., & Egan, K. (2012). Elliot Eisner's imagination and learning. *Journal of Curriculum and Pedagogy, 9*(1), 38–41.

Juvenal (c.130). *Satires.* Variously translated and published.

Knezevic, D. (1995). The healing power of theatre. In P. Taylor & C. Hoepper (Eds.), *Selected readings in drama and theatre education* (pp. 6–13). Brisbane: NADIE Publications.

Kuo, P. K. (1996). Uprooted and searching. In J. O'Toole & K. Donelan (Eds.), *Drama culture and empowerment* (pp. 167–174). Brisbane: IDEA Publications.

Moreno, J. (1960). *The sociometry reader.* New York: Beacon House.

Moreno, J. (1946). *Psychodrama* (Vol. 1). New York: Beacon House.

Neville, B. (1989). *Educating psyche: Emotion, imagination and the unconscious in learning.* Melbourne: Collins Dove.

Newell, R. (1992). Anxiety, accuracy and reflection: The limits of professional development. *Journal of Advanced Nursing, 17*, 1326–1333.

Newman, T. (2017). Creating the role: How dramatherapy can assist in re/creating an identity with recovering addicts. *Dramatherapy, 2*(3), 106–123.

New World Encyclopaedia. (2018). *Natya Shastra.* http://www.newworldencyclopedia.org/entry/Natya_Shastra. Accessed May 9, 2018.

O'Connor, P. (Ed.). (2010). *Creating democratic citizenship through drama education: The writings of Jonothan Neelands.* Stoke on Trent: Trentham Books.

O'Toole, J. (1977). *Theatre in education: New objectives for theatre, new techniques in education.* London: Hodder and Stoughton.

Plato. (c.360BC). *The republic. Book 3.* Variously published.

Raffel, S. (2013). The everyday life of the self. Reworking early Goffman. *Journal of Classical Sociology, 13*, 163–178.

Rifkin, J. (2010). Empathic education: The transformation of learning in an interconnected world by empathic education. *The Chronicles of Higher Education, 57*, 6.

Schonmann, S. (1996). The drama and theatre class battlefield. In J. O'Toole & K. Donelan (Eds.), *Drama, culture and empowerment* (pp. 70–76). Brisbane: IDEA Publications.

Slade, P. (1954). *Child drama.* London: Cassell.

Spolin, V. (1963). *Improvisation for the theatre: A handbook of teaching and directing techniques.* Evanston, Ill: Northwestern University Press.

Spolin, V. (1986). *Theater games for the classroom: A teacher's handbook.* Evanston, Ill: Northwestern University Press.

Vygotsky, L. (1933/1974). Play and its role in the development of the child. In J. S. Bruner, A. Jolly & K. Sylva (Eds.), *Play: Its role in development and evolution.* London: Penguin.

Vine, C., & Jackson, A. (2013). *Learning through theatre: The changing face of theatre in education* (3rd ed.). New York: Routledge.

Ward, W. (1930). *Creative dramatics.* New York: Appleton.

Way, B. (1967). *Development through drama.* London: Longmans.

Chapter 4
Bridging the Fields of Drama and Conflict Transformation

Connecting Drama with Conflict

Introduction

The DRACON project was built on cooperation between two academic and practical fields of expertise—drama and conflict management. We hypothesised that the principles and methods of the two fields can be combined to provide a powerful medium for conflict handling in schools. The two fields emerged during the twentieth century, in the same Anglo-American countries, virtually independently of each other. They share a similar knowledge base, usually similar values and even similar methods of creative group work. Yet, the two fields mostly remain apart, their fields of operation and their literature are different and largely unknown to each other, and even though they seem to borrow some practical procedures from each other, they seldom recognise one another.

In this chapter, we construct a conceptual bridge between the two fields of drama and conflict transformation. The general aim is to make the two fields mutually intelligible. In the central section, we highlight areas of convergence, divergence and complementarities. We have also made an effort to lay the foundation of a synthesised theoretical model, as well as to explore in what ways the practical procedures can be integrated.

Drama and Conflict

As we have seen, conflict has been central to drama throughout its history, both in the West and the East. To explore the Natya Shastra further, drama's primary characteristic is a representation of the state of the Three Worlds. In it there is reference to...fight, sometimes lovemaking and sometimes killing.

The Origin of Drama: 108. (Tr. Ghosh, 1959, p. 15)

Drama and approaches to conflict share keywords and concepts. To summarise briefly from the last chapter, not only are the words *protagonist* and *antagonist* used for the main parties in a conflict but the classic dramaturgical curve mirrors how mediators describe the classic phases of conflict. Tension is an important element of both, and how the release of tension is handled creates learning both in drama and approaches to conflict. Furthermore, all of the situations and relationships that are explored by dramatic action are central to real-life relationships and to all those typologies of conflict we have identified in the last two chapters.

The dramatic pedagogy we used in DRACON sets out to define and diagnose the nature of conflict, by exploring the circumstances that motivate adversaries to take particular action. We examined conflict situations by re-enacting in fictionalised contexts the dynamics of human needs, interactions and motivations that lead to the escalation of conflict, and we tried out ways of de-escalating them. The intention of our dramatic pedagogy was to deconstruct the simplistic classifications and stereotypes that tend to dominate antagonists' perceptions of and attitudes towards the nature and interests of 'the other'. This is similar to the narrative approaches to mediation described in Chap. 2.

Drama provides the participants, in the safe space of being characters in a reconstructed fiction, with a range of opportunities:

- to feel and articulate the conflict subjectively by playing the protagonist
- to deconstruct the enemy image by playing the antagonist
- to view the conflict situation more objectively by playing the third party.

Drama as a Holistic Model

Drama, as we have seen in Chap. 3, centrally depends on an emotion that is equally central to conflict resolution: *empathy*, the ability to identify not only cognitively but also affectively with others, and its complement, *emotional distance*. Drama actually works through the simultaneous operation of both empathy and distance that conflict mediators are seeking. Vygotsky's 'dual affect' (1933) simultaneously creates both emotional identification and closeness to the conflict, and dispassionate awareness of the elements of that conflict, as many writers on drama have pointed out. Concomitant with this, drama permits the point of view (and the accompanying emotional orientation) to be changed or switched back and forth from protagonist to antagonist, to the interested third parties and bystanders, to the disinterested spectators (in drama the audience, in conflict transformation the mediator).

Drama works as a holistic model to explore the interaction of all these aspects of personality and society, the cognitive and affective domain, the personal and the social need. Drama is in fact a very ancient and a very effective model of human behaviour and human relationships. It simplifies the contours of a conflict so that the important components can be seen as a whole. Drama is able to expose the skeletal aspects of conflict and subject it to analysis, simply by having control over its re-enactment. Since drama is at least one step removed from real life, the concept of aesthetic distance enables us to examine the components of the conflict, such as the roles the participants are playing, their motivation, behaviour, perspectives, and the dynamics of how the conflict is escalating.

In drama, the different phases in the conflict can be separated, explored and reassembled, and at the same time, the emotional content and the subjective meaning attached to the conflict can be made visible. Drama's deepest purpose is to animate the model, letting us see the structure of the conflict clearly, while acknowledging and retaining all the emotional and subjective factors that have shaped the conflict in the first place.

A Conceptual Integration of the Fields

In Chaps. 2 and 3, we explored basic definitions and typologies, as well as the basic procedures used, in the discrete fields of conflict transformation and drama. Our intention in this chapter is to highlight areas of convergence and divergence and to look for complementarity and the possibility of synthesis. We construct an analytical model that encompasses the fundamentals of each field and explore the ways our practices and procedures can be integrated.

Similarities

Both fields deal with conflict and transformation. In the public mind—and even official definitions—drama and conflict have always been directly related. We have mentioned the Natya Shastra's account of drama's origins in real and legendary conflict. One recent Australian drama syllabus had as a major part of its definition of drama 'the dynamic embodiment of a conflict situation involving two or more parties' (Queensland BSSS, 1991: 1). While this quotation is an oversimplification (as is the first), it is a useful working definition, accurate for most of the drama that most people come across most of the time. In this definition, people agree to be other than themselves and to enact a conflict—real, imagined or adapted—in a fictional or fictionalised context.

Drama in schools often focuses on the pedagogical benefits of involving young participants in exploring personal and social conflicts. Drama democratises the theatre-making process by handing it over to the participants. The TIE and DIE movements have developed participatory and intervention techniques that replace the notion of a passive audience receiving drama from 'actors', with that of joint participants invited into the dramatic fiction to negotiate ways of dealing with crisis or conflict.

Of the several approaches to conflict handling, cooperative approaches such as mediation, in particular problem-solving, interest-based, narrative and transformative mediation, seem to share the most similarity with DIE. The two fields have much in common in terms of philosophy, values, goals and processes. Both fields, for instance, have emerged contemporaneously as components of a broader 'progressive' and humanistic approach to building a more humane world. Both carry with them the promise of a more egalitarian and democratic society. Both emphasise a participatory approach in which people are empowered to explore or resolve human problems according to their own understanding. Both work on the assumption that the structures of society, cultures and relationships are alterable. Both are based on group work with voluntary participation plus skilled facilitation, normally without an external audience. Unlike their conventional predecessors in both fields, both narrative and transformative mediation and DIE are associated with process more than with outcome, with negotiation more than with decision-making.

Dispute resolution processes such as mediation developed as a reaction against the adversarial nature of the formal legal system and are based on a more communitarian and restorative view of justice. Mediation assumes that mutually satisfying solutions to conflicts can be found when parties voluntarily come together to identify disputed issues and explore their mutual needs in order to find new creative options. Thus, both mediation and drama are concerned with ownership—there is a structure and a process, but the right to initiate these and to participate lies in the hands of the participants, who also own the right to change them as they go along and to make their own decisions.

Most of the terminology used to express the conflict components in the two fields is different, but a few keywords, significantly, are not: the names given to the two main parties in a conflict: 'protagonist' and 'antagonist' both derive from Greek drama, and obviously words such as 'role' and 'drama' often crop up in real conflict situations. More than this, some terms have usage in common, and where the terminology *is* different, it is often possible to give a direct translation from one to another, or even to use a simile, as may be seen in Table 4.1.

Many other definitions are also shared. Narrative mediation views conflict in terms of an emerging narrative—just as drama is expressed through narrative. In latent or emerging real-life conflict, much of the underlying attitudes and motivations and some of the action are still hidden from the participants, and for others these form a revealing subtext, just as it is in the early stages of a drama, before the crisis.

Among several theories of conflict, the general theory of escalation, which integrates dispute resolution, social–psychological and communication theories, aptly explains the dynamics of interpersonal conflict, and this is often mirrored in the fictional conflicts enacted in drama. The action/reaction processes which lead to conflict escalation, and the stages of that escalation: debate or discussion > polarisation > destruction > outcome (that may be resolution or further destruction) correspond to the model of dynamics provided by the classic dramaturgical curve of the 'well-made play', in terms of *tension*—with one important difference. Table 4.2, along with the diagram of tension, shows the correspondences in structure and nomenclature that characterise the two fields.

Connecting Drama with Conflict

Table 4.1 Terms for components of conflict and drama

Conflict terms	Drama terms
Tension	Dramatic tension
Party or participant	Character
Content/issue	Theme/issue
Attitudes	Attitudes
Behaviour/conflict styles/strategies	Dramatic action
Negotiation/mediation	Argument[a]
Escalation	Building to crisis
Crisis	Crisis
Resolution/transformation	Resolution/denouement

[a] As the exception that proves the rule, this ambiguous word of course means quite the opposite in conflict situations!

Table 4.2 Terms for the escalation of conflict and drama

Conflict terms	Drama terms
Incipient tension	Expectant tension
Latent conflict & discussion	Exposition
Rising tension	Rising tension
Emerging conflict	Emerging dramatic action
Crisis: polarisation into manifest conflict	Peripateia—the crisis revealed
Escalating tension peaks	Climax—the tension peaks
Breakdown and destruction > regret or realisation	Tragic denouement > catharsis
De-escalation, resolution or transformation—happy ending	Comic denouement—happy ending
Compromise	Open ending
Debriefing	Reflection, deroling

In conflict theory and theatre dramaturgy, 'tension' means the escalating intensity of emotions, attitude, behaviour and content. In both, tension is uncomfortable, discomforting. In real conflict, this is involuntary and malign; in any dramatic conflict, whether formal theatre or educational process drama, tension is indispensable, a major factor in the very pleasure of the audience or the participants (Fig. 4.1).

This model also ties in loosely with the three-stage analysis of conflict in terms of latent, emerging and manifest conflict. The climactic plot of a play, as first mapped by Aristotle in his *Art of Poetry* (c. BCE 330) in terms of its effect on the audience, has an *exposition* phase, roughly corresponding to the *discussion* phase in conflict analysis, where background information is revealed to the audience. The parties are introduced, and the *latent* conflict content is hinted at. There follows a period of *rising action* where the protagonist and antagonist take increasing action against each other—the *emerging* conflict—to a point explored in detail by Aristotle that he labelled

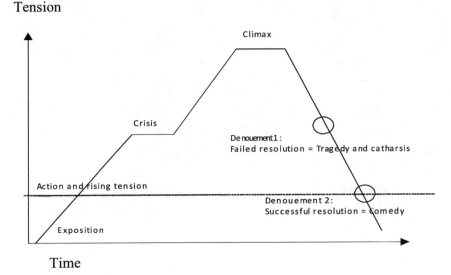

Fig. 4.1 Dynamics of the classic structure of Western drama

peripateia. This word has been variously translated as 'crisis' and 'discovery' and incorporates the meanings of both words. Though it does not have a specific label in formal conflict analysis, in common parlance this is the *point of no return* where the emerging conflict becomes manifest and without some kind of change or intervention will inevitably become destructive. In both real life and theatre, the *manifest* conflict reaches a peak, then it is either *resolved* with the tension released, or the destructive dynamic is completed, leaving the tensions unresolved, but replaced by *breakdown* or *tragedy*. There is a reflective sense of finality that Aristotle interpreted as purgation (*catharsis*), which Boal (1979) points out is an egotistical state that is in itself satisfying and discourages further action. Sometimes the tensions are eventually entirely resolved in the dénouement of comedy, or 'win–win' as mediators put it. This was also invariably the endpoint of the classic Indian drama, as the Natya Shastra describes it. As defined by Aristotle and other commentators right up to the middle of the twentieth century, 'comedy' is not necessarily a humorous play but is one with a happy ending.

In real life, complete resolution of conflict can be achieved but not without hardship. In drama, as classic comedy often shows, perfect resolution can only be achieved by divine intervention—the *deus ex machina* that real-life antagonists and mediators long to find. It is not surprising that in the pragmatic and sceptical twentieth-century theatre that began with the *realism* movement, this kind of total *denouement* became rarer; it was largely replaced with problematic compromises and open endings more reflective of the outcomes of most real-life conflicts. As conflict specialists agree, there is no complete solution in human affairs, and this reminds us that conflict resolution is a relative, not an absolute concept.

Differences

Between drama practice and Western dispute resolution approaches such as mediation, there are some striking differences, which define their specific nature and purposes. While both may be about creating new states of understanding through experience of conflict, and participants can only engage in both of them voluntarily, one is for the purpose of giving pleasure or learning, while the other is to relieve pain.

In general, the playwright and the DIE leader concentrate on the first part of the tension graph—making the problem more interesting and dramatic by escalating the conflict—while the conflict mediator must deal with the tension that has become manifest conflict, and seek to de-escalate it. In that way, their purposes are the obverse of each other: one problematises the conflict, heating up (escalating) the tension in order to learn more about it; the other seeks to de-problematise it, by cooling (de-escalating) the tension, in order to transform or resolve it. Moreover, DIE does not work exactly like either the well-made classic play or the real-life conflict mediation, though one can see the similarities.

In the case of conflict handling, the aim is to manage, resolve or transform the conflict into a less costly form of interaction. The aim and tasks are therefore to terminate, reconcile, transform or reach a settlement. One or more of the participants may initiate outcome-oriented approaches to mediation, such as problem-solving, with the aim of reaching an agreement on substantive issues in dispute. However, narrative and transformative mediation approaches are more focused on the process.

In DIE, the process is always much more important than the product. The facilitator or teacher takes the initiative for starting the process and does not necessarily demand a solution. A satisfactory denouement cannot be achieved without maximising the tension within the situation of conflict. Often there is no clear-cut resolution, the outcome is ambiguous, with each individual participant left to draw their own conclusions. This much can also be true for narrative and transformative mediation, but for the mediator it is often not the preferred outcome, while the drama teacher will frequently deliberately contrive such problematic conclusions.

In DRACON drama, we created and enacted each fictional conflict to explore and flesh out a generic understanding of conflict by particularising it through experiential enactment and reflection; not necessarily to resolve it, but to give greater insight into how it *might* be resolved. In other words, to give the participants a range of understandings about conflict that might offer them choices in real-life conflicts. Our broader aim was for the participants at the same time to learn more about human nature, human relationships, social issues and themselves.

The twin and almost contradictory components of human relationships, *empathy* and *emotional distance*, are central to both mediation and drama-in-education, but they are used differently. In a real interpersonal conflict, there is often neither empathy for one's antagonist, nor distance from the relationship. One of the main purposes of the mediator is to seek to achieve enough of either for the combatants to be able to de-escalate or transform the conflict. In drama, empathy and emotional distance can be invoked, suspended and played with at will. The participants identify empathically by entering the situation in the shoes of their fictional character. In this role, they can fine-tune empathy and antagonism at will, to 'play' with the situation. They can move from empathy to varying levels of emotional distance from the conflict by varying the form of dramatic activity used in order to reflect on the situation from outside the role, or from a range of levels of engagement and empathy. Having said that, we will return to this crucial factor of emotional distance shortly, as it is actually more complex than this.

There is an interesting, subtler difference in the levels of emotional and cognitive engagement that operate in drama-in-education and mediation that probably relate to their historical origins in late twentieth-century Western society. Such approaches to conflict as mediation emerged as reaction against adversarial legal systems and other power-based methods of conflict handling, and until the emergence of new models such as *narrative mediation* and *transformative mediation*, they were still coloured by the rationalist and outcome-oriented approach of the Western legal mind. In some models of mediation, there is a preference for 'left-brain' solutions that may be seen in the long-standing popularity of idioms such as 'conflict analysis' and 'problem-solving'. Generally, the tendency is to cool down overheated conflicts so that they become amenable to 'rational talk'. Problem-solving mediation still adheres to a rationalist and cognitive approach. The more recent approaches to mediation take a constructivist approach, such as narrative mediation (drawn from narrative therapy—White & Epston, 1990), based on Michel Foucault's ideas (McHoul & Grace, 1993) and focus more on assisting participants to deconstruct and reconstruct the narratives or 'truths' that are contributing to the conflict.

DIE arose as part of the movement in progressive schooling, and more recently in constructivist education, in part also as a reaction against the rationalistic, cognition-centred and emotionally impoverishing schooling provided by Western education systems, and seeking to incorporate an educational aesthetic. However, drama education pioneers, heavily influenced by Bertolt Brecht's 'alienation' theory (1964), were also reacting against the passive values of conventional 'naturalistic' theatre, where audiences are given a rich and deeply empathic experience. As we have seen in Chap. 2, they sought to recreate the theatrical aesthetic as a holistic experience, recreating the students as 'percipients'—participants in making, performing and reflecting on drama, through the reintegration of cognition with emotional, sensory, kinaesthetic and spiritual understanding. The processes of making drama—playing with conflict, building a group dynamic and an ensemble, physically and emotionally embodying the conflict through role-play and other forms of enactment—are to help participants understand and reflect on the nature and structures of conflict, and, more broadly, on themselves, human nature, relationships and social structures. Drama-in-education's intention is to integrate the cognitive and the affective, the personal and the social, the physical and the abstract in understanding.

Towards an Integrated Model

Both drama and cooperative conflict-handling practices such as mediation can deal with two types of reality: *everyday reality* and an *alternative reality*, which in some ways mirrors real life, but are not identical to it. Both fields are working with the interplay between the two realities but in different ways.

Drama work focuses on the alternative reality of the enacted drama—a *safe space* for role-play and improvisation. All participants know that they are not the characters they play, but they also know that the fiction has some basis in real-life 'drama'. During their dramatic activities, the participants observe themselves and the others, and after each session (and sometimes within it) their observations are shared and reflected on. The learning that happens is relevant and close to real life, but the drama has no real-life consequences.

Narrative mediation also focuses on developing an alternative reality, for example through reframing or deconstructing a dominant discourse, but with a more consequential aim of redefining or reconstructing the real-life situation. Another strategy to create an alternative reality is providing a *safe space* (safe here meaning physically and emotionally protected) in which the parties can process the conflict constructively by listening to each other, treating each other with respect and focusing on mutual interests and needs instead of taking strong positions and fighting it out. In adjudication, the alternative reality is set up as a *meta-conflict*, which takes the form of a notional legal trial where people take a strong position and argue their case in the theatricality (meta-theatricality, anyway) of the court.

When it comes to mediation, it may sound strange to talk about a *meta-conflict* as so much emphasis is placed on *cooperation* between the parties in exploring the original conflict. However, every mediator knows that cooperation is only one aspect of what happens in the mediation theatre. The meta-conflict represents another type of reality because it requires that the parties mentally step out of their original conflict positions and enter into a new type of game. Mediation cannot happen if the parties do not accept a collective new fiction or story: 'Now we will act as if we will be able to find a solution that satisfies both of us'. The real outcome is not always in accord with the fiction or story.

If we examine in more detail those two complementary/contradictory conditions for drama and conflict transformation to work: *emotional closeness* and *distance*, we may see a closer correspondence. Closeness within the meta-conflict (if not actual empathy) seems to be a major factor in conflict transformation. The meta-conflict must be close enough to everyday reality for it not to be discarded as being utopian, unrealistic or irrelevant to the original conflict. This is accomplished in mediation by letting the parties represent themselves in the mediation process. In difficult conflicts, the mediator sometimes meets with representatives or allows a support person or advocate to participate with a weaker party, but there is always a risk that the parties will feel alienated from the whole process. The risk is even bigger in a courtroom, where professionals take over most of the process in *roles* such as the 'judge', 'prosecutor', 'attorney', and/or 'counsel for the defence'.

In drama, closeness to real-life conflicts can be achieved in many ways. How close, depends on how safe the 'safe space' is. A group that likes and trusts each other will be able to work much more closely to real-life conflict than one where real conflicts or tensions between and among individuals and groups exist. DRACON has used a diversity of approaches of varying distance levels to create fictional or fictionalised conflicts to play with. For an untrusting or disunited group, it may be safer to work from distanced stories, where the generic or archetypal structures of conflict can be visible, recognised and seen to be relevant, but they will not intrude with consequences for the real relationships of the participants. Mostly, DRACON has started with the participants identifying conflicts from their own or their peer groups' lives and devising the drama work from those. Always, however, those real-life stories of conflict have been fictionalised, the real being woven together with the imaginary to provide the 'safe space' where the conflict may be played with and reflected upon with emotional distance, even by the originator of the story. Metaxis, the collision of the real and fictional worlds, is not the same thing as meta-conflict.

Taking the time and care to create the 'safe space' is equally important for the drama facilitator and the mediator. Perhaps even more crucial is the underlying attitude of both, and their relationship with their participants—the children or adult clients. The drama will not work if the teacher behaves in the traditional way as the one who knows the right answers and is therefore constantly judging and assessing. The teacher, as explained in the Drama chapter, has to be a co-learner, together with the participants raising and exploring relevant questions, making decisions and engaging in a genuine dialogue. Swedish educators use the word 'förhållningssätt´ (for which there isn't an English equivalent). The Swedish DRACON team explains this word as describing the 'willingness of the facilitator in an open and tolerant atmosphere to look at every child, with eyes of acceptance, as being capable of choosing for her or himself when to participate and how'. This would also be a good description of an effective conflict mediator.

Furthermore, to establish and sustain the safe space, the drama facilitator almost never works with the real, raw conflicts of the participants, though the basis in the recognisable and the real is crucial. Unless the participants are able to touch base with some aspect of everyday reality, neither performance nor narrative will be believable nor able to convey what may be called 'dramatic truth'—and so not useful for authentic learning about real-life conflicts. It is a paradox of dramatic fiction vis-à-vis reality that for the safe space to be achieved, from the moment when the participants step into their alternative reality the drama facilitator works to permit emotional distance. From that dual position, the participants can choose—consciously or instinctively—to engage in empathic closeness and move out again, in a controlled oscillation.

The mediator is sometimes in a similar, but not identical, situation to the drama leader, in particular when the disputants know each other too well and have a 'negative intimacy' or know their opponent´s Achilles' heel. The mediator needs to establish a measure of emotional distance between those disputants for them to engage in rational conflict handling. In other situations where the disputants are relative strangers, the mediator works to increase empathy and understanding.

If a conflict surfaces during drama sessions, the two parties are not encouraged to work together on the real conflict, because in order to understand conflict, it is often necessary in drama to work *unilaterally,* from the point of view of one protagonist. The mediator working on symmetric conflicts must be impartial—bilateral or multilateral—working with all parties at the same time. That makes drama particularly relevant to the investigation of asymmetric conflicts, where gross power imbalances mean the conflict-handling needs to be unilateral; this was affirmed in the Brisbane 'Acting Against Bullying' subproject. That is also the very underpinning of *Theatre of the Oppressed*, which seeks only to change the situation and behaviour of the oppressed protagonist, not the oppressor (see Chap. 3, Section "DRACON's Central Drama Strategies"). Some other forms of Theatre for Development, DIE and TIE also take a unilateral conflict management approach as a guiding principle—to raise awareness of the nature of oppression and the possibility of liberation, for training in advocacy and to give a voice to the disempowered. When participants are offered the opportunity to take part in the dramatic fictions in order to try out what it feels like to be powerful and experiment with the most effective ways of dealing with misuse of power, they are being given valuable instruments to use in their real-life struggles.

When a drama has been derived from a real situation, there is another reason why participants are discouraged from playing their own characters, or characters in situations like their own—it underlines the importance in drama of emotional distancing. If a participant plays himself or herself, she/he naturally identifies with that character in the drama, and the freedom to explore different pathways of action and reaction is diminished or closed. Even if their egocentric needs and defences do not undermine their willingness to engage openly in the drama, the close identification with 'themselves' robs them of the ability to think afresh.

Similarly, the success of mediation is partly dependent on the capacity of the parties to step out of their ongoing real-life conflict into a safe space where they can enact a more cooperative meta-conflict. In the new game, the parties are still playing themselves, but the rules are different. The safe space may permit the revelation of more realistic understandings of the nature of the conflict and their own behaviour than in the real-life battle, when they are usually engaged in defensive behaviour. When processing their perceptions and emotions, parties can sometimes feel their sympathies shift and develop empathy or deconstruct their 'truths' and recognise that the original conflict was an illusion, evaporating like a nightmare on waking.

In drama too, the interplay of distance and closeness often creates dream-like situations where participants appear to observers (and themselves) to demonstrate greater knowledge and insight of human behaviour than they could reasonably be expected to have, or a psychological depth of understanding about the characters they are playing that is far beyond their everyday awareness and knowledge. The drama weaves together the memories of their real experiences, their observations, the stories they have read and shared, and the products of their imagination, into an integrated 'lived-through' experience.

Innovative Pedagogies

Transformative Learning

In considering how an individual's understanding of the dimensions of conflict might be developed towards understanding the possibility of conflict transformation, we must explore more deeply the nature of effective learning. If we accept that changes in behaviour and action are driven by changes—transformations—in thinking and attitude, transformative learning practices must be found to drive such shifts.

The importance of learning through shared social experience and critical reflection is central to much learning theory and has been from the time of Socrates, with his public questioning sessions in the Athens marketplace. Expanding opportunities for dialogue to influence wider social and democratic exchange is the task that Paulo Freire sees as central to effective education. The significance of transformation in learning is clearly articulated in his argument that one of the most important tasks of educational practice is to:

> ...make possible the conditions in which the learners, in their interactions with one another and with their teachers, engage in the experience of assuming themselves as social, historical, thinking, communicating, transformative, creative persons. (1998 p. 45)

For Freire, this process of consciously assuming the power to transform enables individuals to deepen their awareness of the sociocultural reality, which shapes their lives. This then makes it possible for them to transform reality through action.

Indeed, progressive educational theorists and practitioners have long argued that transformation is central to all learning. Bruner (2005) believes that active learning involves three simultaneous processes: the acquisition of new information, the transformation of knowledge to make it relevant to new tasks, and evaluation. This transformation of knowledge is crucial at every stage of development. It is through transformation that very young children develop a perception of their environment as an objective reality. The use of transitional objects by infants enables them to move away from an egocentric view of the world to acceptance of others and a recognition that part of the world is outside themselves (Winnicott, 1971). Through acts of transformation children create symbols and repeat and ritualise everyday experience, thereby becoming initiated into the culture of our society (Erikson, 1977). It is partly through these forms of transformation that a fundamental aim of education is realised—the transmission of the society's culture from one generation to the next.

The concept we label 'transformative learning' can be attributed to Mezirow (1978). Writing in the field of adult education, he argued that we need to better recognise and acknowledge the importance of different frames of reference or what he called 'meaning perspectives' in shaping learners' thinking, feelings and actions. In drawing attention to the importance of transformative learning, Mezirow acknowledged that this concept was founded upon the distinction Habermas (1981) makes between instrumental learning and communicative learning. Instrumental learning focuses on the skills necessary to manipulate and control, and it utilises deductive

Innovative Pedagogies

reasoning. Communicative learning involves discourse and exchange (dialogue, as we call it in Chap. 3), requiring intellectual and empathic perception to shape new understanding. In fleshing out the importance of this more socially constructed form of learning, Mezirow offers the following definition:

> Transformative learning is the process by which we transform problematic frames of reference (mindsets, habits of mind, meaning perspectives)—sets of assumptions and expectations—to make them more inclusive, discriminating, open, reflective and emotionally able to change. (2009, p. 92)

Clearly, an approach to learning that acknowledges a role for affective experience—sensory, emotional and embodied—in the development of cognition is important to consider in relation to transforming behaviour and attitudes in conflict. As we argued in the last chapter, drama is ideally placed for this to happen.

Central to transformative learning theory is the notion that habits of mind are shaped by sets of assumptions. Among other things, these assumptions are informed by those differences in the learner's particular cultural, social, political and psychological frames of reference. Mezirow suggests two key components of transformative learning—critical reflection and self-reflection—which give the learner an opportunity to deconstruct tacitly held beliefs and assumptions.

Critical reflection allows individuals to understand and evaluate internal and external realities and to transform their personal perspectives and reference frameworks. This idea of a fundamental change in perspective is identified also by King (2002) as the heart of transformative learning. When individuals undergo such a change, they have in essence transformed their view of themselves or of the world, and so too they have transformed how they interact with others in their environment.

How this transformation can take place is described by Mezirow as following a common set of phases, which we have listed chronologically:

- *A disorienting dilemma*
- *Self-examination of feelings, e.g. guilt, shame or anger*
- *A critical assessment of assumptions*
- *Recognition that one's discontent and the process of transformation are shared*
- *Exploration of options for new roles, relationships and action*
- *Planning new action*
- *Acquiring the knowledge and skills for implementing one's plans*
- *Provisional trying of new roles*
- *Building competence and self-confidence in new roles and relationships*
- *A reintegration into one's life on the basis of conditions dictated by one's new perspective.*

(2009, p. 94).

It is interesting to consider these phases in terms of the role educators can play in facilitating the conditions for them to take place. Readers will have noted how many resonate strongly with the role drama can play in the provision of transformative learning experiences. Drama can stimulate the 'disorienting dilemma' within socially shared contexts, explore options for new roles, relationships and actions and provide opportunities for the provisional trying out of those new roles and the building of confidence in them.

The action of assuming a different perspective is central to all drama activity and is fundamental to the way a process or performance is experienced. Transformation involves the creation and manipulation of symbols. Symbolic transformation occurs when a specific meaning or subjective importance is assigned to a person, object or activity, which extends significance beyond the nature of the thing itself. The symbolic act of transformation is illustrated most graphically by Jung's (1956) theory of the collective unconscious, which expresses itself through the realisation of archetypal symbols—in his phrase, symbols of transformation. This ritualising function of transformation has been extensively exploited as a functional tool by major drama practitioners, such as Heathcote and Bolton, whose practice and that of their followers has been deeply concerned with generating social learning, and an understanding of the operation of the society in which their students live. The major purpose of the 'shift of appraisal' that drama provides, as Bolton defines it (1979, p. 41), is to create 'change of insight' with its implications for social action.

Transformative Mediation

Transformative mediation provides a unique approach to conflict intervention and has been the subject of much study, research and development. The approach was first articulated in 1994 by Robert A. Baruch Bush and Joseph P. Folger in *The Promise of Mediation*, and is an approach to conflict intervention that places the principles of empowerment and recognition at the core of helping people who are in conflict to change how they interact with each other. The transformative framework is based on and reflects relational ideology, in which human beings are assumed to be fundamentally social, that is, formed in and through their relations with other human beings, essentially connected to others, and motivated by a desire for both personal autonomy and constructive social interaction (Bush & Folger, 1994).

As summarised by Della Noce, Bush, and Folger (2002), the transformative approach to mediation practice takes an essentially social/communicative view of human conflict. According to this model, a conflict represents a crisis in some human interaction—an interactional crisis with a somewhat common and predictable character. Specifically, the occurrence of conflict tends to destabilise the parties' experience of both self and other, so that the parties interact in ways that are both more vulnerable and more self-absorbed than how they behaved before the conflict. Further, these negative dynamics often feed into each other on all sides as the parties interact, in a vicious circle that intensifies each party's sense of weakness and self-absorption. As a result, the interaction between the parties quickly degenerates and assumes a mutually destructive, alienating and dehumanising character. According to transformative theory, being caught in this kind of destructive interaction is the most significant negative impact of conflict for most people. The transformative model posits that despite conflict's potentially destructive impact on interaction, people have the capacity to change the quality of their interactions to reflect relative personal strength or self-confidence (the empowerment shift) and relative openness or responsiveness to the other (the recognition shift). Moreover, as these positive dynamics feed into each other, the interaction can regenerate and assume a constructive, connecting and humanising character. The model assumes that the transformation of the interaction itself is what matters most to parties in conflict—even more than a settlement on favourable terms. Therefore, the theory defines the mediator's goal as helping the parties to identify opportunities for empowerment and recognition shifts as they arise in the parties' conversation, to choose whether and how to act upon these opportunities, and thus to change their interaction from destructive to constructive (Bush & Pope, 2002).

In transformative mediation, success is not measured by the settlement or outcome of the mediation, but by party shifts towards personal strength, interpersonal responsiveness and constructive interaction in the process. As parties talk together and listen to each other, they build new understandings of themselves and their situation, critically examining the possibilities and making their own decisions. Those decisions can include settlement agreements; however, no-one is coerced into any decision or agreement. The outcomes are entirely in the parties' own hands and subject to their own choices. Effective mediator practice is focused on supporting empowerment and recognition shifts by allowing and encouraging each party to deliberate and make decisions, and take inter-party perspectives, in various ways. A competent transformative mediator practises with a focus on communication, identifying opportunities for empowerment and recognition as those opportunities appear in the parties' own conversations, and responding in ways that provide an opening for parties to choose a way forward.

Peer Teaching

'To teach is to learn twice over.' Joseph Joubert. (eighteenth Century French philosopher)

One very powerful strategy emerged during the evolution of DRACON research: the use of peer teaching to support the development of participants' understanding of conflict, and foster transformative learning through a more democratic approach. In Australia, Sweden, and in later work in the UK, peer teaching was centrally used in the DRACON projects with young people in schools. It served to deepen engagement and develop conceptual learning. Although the cultural contexts and participants were different, in each sphere the strategy was supporting the same central DRACON goal, i.e. to develop an understanding of conflict, and through this personal and relational insight and transformation.

Peer teaching as a learning medium operates on a number of levels, and it is a powerful tool for learning for a variety of reasons. Although the procedural details of how it was used in each DRACON context will be detailed in later chapters, it is worth exploring at this point why the strategy was so valuable. Peer teaching can be defined as learners of one social group taking on the role of 'teacher' to help other learners within the same social group. In the process of this activity, both peer teacher and learner develop insight and understanding. Empathy, motivation and agency, all central to engagement and transformational learning, are fundamental features of the peer teaching experience.

How Peer Teaching Operates

Bene and Bergus (2014) remind us that peer teaching is not a new strategy and has been used in a number of educational contexts and fields—from elementary level schooling through to postgraduate programs and beyond, for example in medical training. How and why peer teaching became a central tool is not surprising, given the core elements it shares with both drama and conflict theory.

Peer teaching is normally used in one-on-one situations, with one student teaching another. We used it more uncommonly as a group strategy in the Brisbane and Swedish DRACON projects—a group co-teaching a whole class of their peers. In Brisbane, this was expanded to a relay approach, where the older students passed the baton to their younger peers, who having learned the conflict concepts through the drama, were able to use them to teach their own younger peers, and so on. We found that peer teaching developed not only conceptual understanding in the learner, but metacognitive opportunities for the peer teacher, through its ability to foster reflective knowledge and self-efficacy. Simply put, we found that peer teaching had as much to offer the peer teacher as their tutee, if not more.

Peer teaching as a strategy requires very direct social engagement. In their roles as teachers, pupils have a dual responsibility. Firstly, they have to organise and structure the learning of others, and secondly, as teachers in a classroom, they have to communicate on a social and emotional level with their peers if they wish to maximise the engagement of their learners. Although peer teaching has traditionally been a strategy more commonly used to transmit and support subject content learning, in the DRACON projects there were two goals—the development of understanding in the learner, and reflective opportunities for the peer teachers to deepen their own understanding about the content and about themselves.

Motivation, Agency and Democratic Learning

In all three DRACON contexts, students from ten to eighteen years old carried out the peer teaching, and the leaders were not always the most highly motivated or engaged learners. This bears out Ford and Nichols's simple and insightful formula from their own research into adolescent motivation: 'Motivation = Goals × Emotions × Personal agency' (Ford, 1992, p. 130), and their accompanying comment:

> Experiences that explicitly attempt to link caring behaviour (e.g. the intrinsic pleasure of helping others; positive feelings about one's self; a sense of connectedness with other people; a sense of task accomplishment) are likely to produce more initial and enduring interest and more meaningful engagement in pro-social activities than programs that fail to make these connection. (p. 149)

Linked to this are ideas from Flutter and Rudduck's research into 'Pupil Voice'. They suggest that the way to look at problems in schools is 'to learn through the eyes of those most closely involved' (2004, p. 2), namely to actually ask the pupils and teachers. They found clear evidence that consulting young learners enhances self-esteem and confidence and promotes stronger engagement and motivation to learn. So did we in all our projects, some examples of which are detailed in the Swedish and Brisbane chapters. This provided clear evidence of what Moos (2004, p. 9) proposes, that it is only through giving pupils real power that participation and responsibility will increase, and once pupils begin to see themselves as peer teachers, their commitment can deepen.

Fostering Trust and Responsibility

Bene and Bergus (2014) identify two ways in which peer teaching is effective for the learners too: cognitive and social congruence. We would add a third: emotional congruence. Peer teachers of the same age as their tutees, or nearly, sometimes have a better understanding of their peers' prior knowledge and can better read their emotional states than the teachers. They may therefore be better able to fine-tune their teaching to respond accurately to those needs. This is what we found in DRACON. The peer learners too appreciated the benefits and understood why. As one Sydney interviewee put it: 'They were in Year 9 only two years ago and they survived, so they know what we need better than the teacher!' Moreover, peer teachers have closer social congruence with their peer learners, and this can foster a more comfortable environment in which to learn. We noted this not only in the classroom itself, but in the ambience that the peer teaching created among groups of students who were normally widely separated in the school environment; they formed new cross-age social relationships in the schoolyard, based on more caring attitudes from the older students and more confidence and trust from the younger. In some schools, this actually led to an effect on the whole school with fewer reported instances of cross-age bullying.

Personal and Imaginative Development

Increasingly, peer and cross-age mentoring have been shown to provide benefits to personal and social development. Judging by the lack of published work on this subject, formal peer teaching, where older students teach classes or groups of younger ones in specific subject areas, was relatively uncommon until the time of DRACON. However, some research of the period (e.g. Rubin and Herbert, 1998; Goodlad and Hirst, 1989) supported our observations in the project that the self-reflective opportunities offered through formal peer teaching are a particularly potent learning strategy—especially for the peer teachers themselves. Over and over again, our data showed that pupils who had been peer tutors, particularly those lacking self-esteem, gained increased self-confidence and improved self-image.

The use of drama and peer teaching as an integrated combination of discipline and pedagogy can also empower students through creative engagement. It is worth reflecting on how peer teaching is, of itself, a creative activity and how schools have a role to play in developing experience through creative processes—particularly through drama.

Our ability to imagine 'what if' scenarios—or as Elliot Eisner describes it, our ability to 'imagine possibilities we have not yet encountered' (2002, p.3)—is an important part of how humans formulate concepts. Through them, the imagination plays a central role in offering concrete possibilities for understanding and experience—and for problem-solving. Maxine Greene takes the argument further, noting that an individual can through such imaginings 'break with what is supposedly fixed and finished, objectively and independently real', to look at situations from multiple perspectives, which can lead to 'intensified realisation' (1995, p. 19). Although both Eisner and Greene are considering the role of all the arts in fostering imagination, the concepts they describe can be seen in any approach to teaching and learning that seeks empowerment and change. Peer teaching offers students the opportunity to operate from a different vantage point—that of teacher. Furthermore, in that role it makes challenging demands that expand their ability to imagine possibilities.

Integration in the DRACON Project

The goal of the transformative education that is embedded in dramatic pedagogy—to create change of insight and action—was widened by the addition of peer teaching in the Brisbane and Swedish projects and the follow-up theatre-in-education approaches in the Malaysian and Brisbane projects. Each has provided another dimension for indirectly dealing with real conflict, through the increased sense of agency generated in the project. These extensions sought to reach beyond the individual student, and beyond the joint understanding of the participant group or class, into the wider community of the whole school and the local community.

Drama in the DRACON project has not been used as a replacement for conflict transformation procedures such as mediation, nor as a direct aid in providing additional techniques for the resolution of real-life conflicts. At the inception of the project, this was seen as one of the intentions by some of the conflict resolution specialists in the team, but not by the drama specialists. The initial theoretical negotiations between the two specialised disciplines resulted in a mutually agreed purpose for drama vis-à-vis conflict—as a strategy and set of techniques and instruments for *indirect* conflict resolution, management and transformation. All four of the projects have pursued this investigation of drama as a way of assisting young people to deal with conflict for themselves, by providing them with knowledge and understanding of the structures and processes of conflict, not by intervening directly with drama in their own conflicts. Certainly, all four of the projects have invited and encouraged the students to use their own conflicts, and their emotional engagement with those conflicts, as integral parts of the drama work, but as the raw material only. Real-life conflicts were processed into metaphor through the aesthetic of dramatic fiction and, particularly in the case of the Malaysian project, through other transformational art forms such as dance, music, visual arts and creative writing. Each narrative was an embodied metaphor, lived-through in the moment by the students, but framed and reflected-on through discussion and distanced action, both simultaneously and after the event. The students' real stories have guaranteed a measure of authenticity and emotional engagement in the drama. The fiction and the framing provided the distance necessary for usable understanding. This understanding could then be transferred from the fictions to illuminate real-life conflicts with the cool light of cognitive understanding. Evidence from the project clearly demonstrated that participants used their DRACON understandings, and the tools for transformation that the project had provided, to help them both in transforming and in resolving subsequent conflicts.

It has been our hypothesis that, armed with this knowledge, adolescents will themselves have the tools to address and even prevent the conflicts that do arise in their lives. Within the project, we described this as 'conflict-handling competence' and 'conflict literacy', a competence and literacy that emerges from and infuses the whole participant group or class and is processed by each student into a personal understanding and a sense of agency or empowerment: 'I no longer feel so helpless in the face of conflict, because now I understand how and why conflicts happen and what I can do to de-escalate them', as a thoroughly conflict-literate interviewee explained.

DRACON was at least a first step towards changing the culture of the schools. The students shared their understanding of 'self' and 'other' through an artistic experience that created both conflict literacy and transformative learning. They also shared a new familiarity, empathy and respect for that 'other', based on a stronger understanding of the selves within the 'self' and what those selves together can achieve.

References

Aristotle. (c. BCE330). *The art of poetry*. Variously translated and published.
Bene, K., & Bergus, G. (2014). 'When learners become teachers: A review of peer teaching in medical student education. *Family Medicine, 46*(10), 783–787.
Boal, A. (1979). *Theatre of the oppressed*. London: Pluto Press.
Bolton, G. (1979). *Towards a theory of drama in education*. London: Longmans.
Brecht, B. (1964). *Brecht on theatre: The development of an aesthetic* (John Willett, Trans.). London: Methuen.
Bruner, J. (2005). *In search of pedagogy: The selected works of Jerome Brunner 1957–1978*. London: Routledge.
Bush, R. A. B., & Folger, J. P. (1994). *The promise of mediation*. San Francisco: Jossey-Bass.

Bush, R. A. B., & Pope, S. G. (2002). Changing the quality of conflict interaction: The principles and practice of transformative mediation. *Pepperdine Dispute Resolution Law Journal, 3*(1), 67–96.

Della Noce, D. J., Bush, R. A. B., & Folger, J. P. (2002). Clarifying the theoretical underpinnings of mediation: Implications for practice and policy. *Pepperdine Dispute Resolution Law Journal, 3*(1), 39–65.

Eisner, E. (2002). *The arts and the creation of mind*. New Haven: Yale University Press.

Erikson, E. (1977). *Childhood and society*. London: Paladin.

Flutter, J., & Rudduck, J. (2004). *How to improve your school: Giving pupils a voice*. London: Continuum.

Ford, M. E. (1992). *Motivating humans: Goals, emotions and personal agency beliefs*. Newbury Pk, Cal: Sage.

Freire, P. (1998). *Teachers as cultural workers: Letters to those who dare teach*. Boulder, Col.: Westview Press.

Ghosh, M. (Tr. 1959). *The NatyaShastra of Bharata Muni: A treatise on Hindu dramaturgy and histrionics*. Book 1. Calcutta: The Royal Asiatic Society of Bengal. https://archive.org/details/NatyaShastraOfBharataMuniVolume1. Accessed 13 June 2018.

Goodlad, S., & Hirst, B. (1989). *Peer tutoring: A guide to learning by teaching*. London: Kogan Page.

Greene, M. (1995). *Releasing the imagination: Essays in education, the arts and social change*. San Francisco: Jossey-Bass.

Habermas, J. (1981). *The theory of communicative action*. Tr. Thomas McCarthy. Boston: Beacon Press.

Jung, C. (1956). *Symbols of transformation* (p. 36). London: Routledge and Kegan Paul.

King, K. P. (2002). 'A journey of transformation: A model of educators' learning experiences in educational technology'. In J. Pettit & R. Francis (Eds.), *Proceedings of the 43rd Annual Adult Education Research Conference* (pp. 195–200). http://www.adulterc.org/Proceedings/2002/papers/King.pdf (NB Not accessible).

McHoul, A., & Grace, W. (1993). *The Foucault primer: Discourse, power and the subject*. Melbourne: Melbourne University Press.

Mezirow, J., Taylor, E.W. & Associates. (2009). *Transformative learning in practice: Insights from community, workplace, and higher education*. San Francisco: Wiley.

Mezirow, J. (1978). *Transformational dimensions of adult learning*. San Francisco: Jossey-Bass.

Moos, L. (2004). 'How do schools bridge the gap between external demands for accountability and the need for internal trust?' *Journal of Educational Change, 6/4*.

Queensland BSSS (Board of Secondary School Studies). (1991). *Senior Drama syllabus*. Brisbane: BSSS.

Rubin, J., & Herbert, M. (1998). Peer teaching: Model for active learning. *College Teaching, 48*(1), 26–30.

Vygotsky, L. (1933/1974). 'Play and its role in the development of the child'. In J. S. Bruner, A. Jolly & K. Sylva (Eds.), *Play: Its role in development and evolution*. London: Penguin.

White, M., & Epston, D. (1990). *Narrative means to therapeutic ends*. New York: Norton.

Winnicott, D. W. (1971). *Playing and reality*. London: Tavistock.

Part II
The Research Projects

Chapter 5
Malaysia—Creative Arts in Conflict Exploration

This chapter outlines the Malaysian DRACON project carried out in schools in Penang, Malaysia from 1995 to 1998. The chapter opens by providing a background to the Malaysian cultural context and school system, then explains the various action research cycles and ensuing results.

The focus of research of the Malaysian DRACON team was to examine the potential of existing process-oriented creative arts methodology to test and develop new modes of conflict exploration and conflict education. The Malaysian project was interdisciplinary and brought together specialists with competence in two fields: educational drama and conflict handling. Both are relatively new fields in Malaysia, educational drama emerging in the 1970s and conflict studies emerging as late as the mid-1990s.

Background

The Malaysian Cultural Context

Malaysia is both multicultural and multi-ethnic with a predominantly Malay population of 55%, Chinese 23%, indigenous 14%, Indian 7%, others 1%. The majority of the Chinese and Indian populations are second and third generation settlers, many descendants of migrant workers brought into Malaya by the British between the eighteenth and twentieth centuries to meet the demands of the expanding colonial economy.

When Malaysia gained independence from Britain in 1957, the status of its migrant settlers was resolved by way of a constitutional social agreement which gave citizenship rights to migrant groups and political privileges to the indigenous Malays. The newly formed independent government retained the colonial practice of pluralism (where the ethnic groups maintain their cultural identities and special interests). As a result of this, communal-orientated thinking persists in the field of political management, economy and education. The complicated and uneven association between ethnicity, economic and political power among the different ethnic groups resulted in racial clashes in 1969 which were subdued by the introduction of policies on national culture, national unity and affirmative action.

To navigate its culturally diverse society, Malaysians have over time developed an aggregate of values and attitudes framed by national policies and their shared environment. In this collectivist Malaysian culture, the 'we' orientation supersedes the 'I' orientation, emphasising accommodation, compromise and consensus in an attempt to sustain unity. However, within their own ethnic groups, individuals are socialised to fit into their own cultural and religious moulds, and they even feel safe and secure doing so. Accommodation and loyalty to the larger Malaysian collective as well as the smaller member group assure security. However, trying to adhere to ethnic or religious norms while adapting to the Malaysian collectivist culture exerts pressure on individuals and remains a difficult and unpredictable journey that all Malaysians have to navigate.

Despite independence, the Malaysian culture retained hierarchical practices inherited from its early feudal history. Malaysians are brought up in a culture that is vertical and places a high premium on high power distance. This has resulted in a social, institutional and political milieu that is authority-centred, seniority-based and paternalistic. Dominant values include vertical loyalty bonds, consciousness and respect for authority, low individualism, group orientation and avoidance of conflict situations.

Barnes (2007) observes that the complexity of multi-ethnicity and subcultures in Malaysia results in a wide variety of conflict behaviours and mechanisms for managing, preventing and mediating conflicts within the diverse cultures in Malaysia. Cultural indices developed by Hofstede (1980) have been adapted and used by the

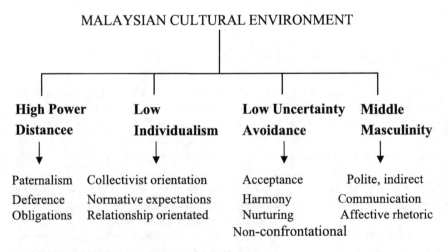

Fig. 5.1 Cultural values and attitudes in a Malaysian context

Malaysian DRACON team researcher to summarise Malaysian cultural values and attitudes (Fig. 5.1).

The Education System in Malaysian Schools

The earliest schools in Malaysia were non-formal Islamic religious schools dating back to the sixteenth century. From the early nineteenth to the mid-twentieth centuries, private vernacular schools (using the native languages of communities) were set up by philanthropists and clan associations from among Chinese and Indian settler groups as well as Muslim missionaries. Modern education (using English instruction) was introduced by British colonisers and Christian missionaries in the 1800s. In the 1900s, Chinese vernacular schools also adopted a modern education system (using Mandarin). By the mid-1920s, as the British opened the doors in Malaya to increasing numbers of foreign labour, more private Chinese and Tamil language schools were established to support the migrant population.

As part of the movement to independence in 1957, the education system was nationalised and existing private or missionary schools were given the option of becoming national-type schools. However, some vernacular language schools chose to remain independent of government. All curriculum and examinations of national-type schools came under federal jurisdiction. In 1970, all national-type schools were required to use the national language (Malay) as a medium of instruction except for those independent vernacular schools which retained the use of native languages as their medium of instruction.

Today, the range of privately managed schools in Malaysia is wide and includes not just independent Chinese and Tamil vernacular schools and Islamic religious schools, but also English-medium private schools that follow the national curriculum and those that follow international curriculum. The complex division of public education by language and curricular content has been criticised for allegedly creating cultural polarisation among Malaysians at an early age.

Malaysia has 12 years of compulsory education consisting of 7 years (age 6–12) of primary schooling and 5 years (age 13–17) of secondary schooling. Academically inclined students proceed to one or two years of high school education before going to university. All missionary schools and some vernacular language schools are single gender schools, while the newer national schools, private schools and tertiary institutions are mixed gender.

Management of Conflict in Malaysian Schools

School guidance or counselling services in Malaysian schools were professionalised only after 2000 with the appointment of one counsellor per school, the training of peer counsellors, and the upgrading of counselling services to include enrichment activities, crisis counselling, etc.

During the time of the Malaysian research (1995–1998), the school counsellor was a subject teacher who received some in-service training in counselling. The mandate of the part-time counsellor was mainly associated with vocational guidance and discipline management. Students' utilisation of counsellors was not very encouraging as counselling generally carried a stigma of someone having either personal or disciplinary problems. The school generally avoided providing helping relationships for personal problems that involve conflict related to parties outside the school such as family, community or friends. The cultural socialisation of children in national schools was left to parents and their ethnic communities outside of school.

In the area of conflict handling, there has been almost an absence of mediation in Malaysia, until very recently. Rather than working with all parties of the conflict simultaneously, most efforts depend on an individualised, problem-solving, counselling approach that places a high premium on relationship building. The conventional counselling model usually employed, whether religious or secular, tends to be based on saving the face of the one party and advising that party on acceptance, sharing and group harmony.

Educational Drama in Malaysia

The British, through extra-curricular activities such as drama clubs and literary societies, introduced the modern concept of drama in schools. While visual art and more recently music are offered as a legitimate subject at primary level and as options at secondary level, drama has never been given a place in the official curriculum. As a consequence of this neglect, drama only functions outside the official curriculum in what is termed 'school drama', (drama as extra-curricular activity or drama competitions as instrumental to language enhancement).

Young people's theatre in Malaysia is a relatively new phenomenon spanning about 40 years. As a reaction to 'school drama' that never ventured beyond the staid conventional staging of scripted works, young people's theatre (outside of schools) has experimented widely, devising new forms, working in unconventional spaces and adopting new creative pedagogy.

Its early beginnings can be traced to the 1970s when Malaysian school educators had the opportunity to further their studies in Britain in the teaching of language, art and literature. They returned home to develop courses in local universities which introduced educational drama and advocated the use of creative dramatics, drama as pedagogy, playwriting and theatre for young audiences. In the late 1970s, university students who graduated from these courses began to organise non-formal arts programs outside of school in partnership with arts groups, arts institutions or libraries and began to experiment with arts by and for children.

New process-oriented approaches such as creative dramatics and Theatre for Development were introduced to Malaysian practitioners in the late 1980s and early

1990s by regional groups such as Philippine Educational Theatre Association (PETA) and the Thai group MAYA. These approaches were inspired by Freire's principles of empowerment and the liberal educational tenets of Dewey and Rousseau, drawing heavily upon theories of play, child development and learning styles. The approaches were not just limited to drama, but incorporated games, video, drawing, music, sculpture, role-play, puppetry, etc.

In the 1990s, Augusto Boal's (1987) interactive techniques of forum theatre and image theatre, and other forms such as theatre-in-education (TIE) were incorporated into the repertoire of educational theatre practice in Malaysia by arts educators who became acquainted with these forms through international conferences, workshops or research. The first forum theatre production by children was produced by Five Arts Centre in 1991.

Five Arts Centres in Kuala Lumpur and Young Theatre Penang are two examples of private theatre companies in Malaysia which conducted creative arts programs for a period of 10 years starting in the 1990s. Five Arts Centre's creative arts program for young people called *Teater Muda* (Young Theatre) was conducted in Kuala Lumpur from 1992 to 2002 and also in Penang from 1995 to 2000. A similar-type creative arts program was conducted in Penang from 1998 to 2006 by Young Theatre Penang. Both companies also worked with older youth to tour theatre-in-education productions to schools between 1996 and 2005. The creative arts programs by Five Arts Centre and Young Theatre Penang focused on the aesthetic, personal and social development of young people aged 10–17. Both employed artists from the field of drama, visual arts, dance and music and combined educational methods and techniques in a hybrid manner. Programs were orientated more towards creativity and the process of art-making rather than product.

Research Incorporating Conflict Handling and Processual Creative Arts

In 1993, Swedish researchers involved in a previous collaborative study with Malaysians on 'culturally conditioned models of conflict resolution' expressed a desire to start a new project to study educational drama as a potential method for conflict handling in different cultures. As described in Chap. 1, the Swedes were invited to observe *Teater Muda* which was led by arts educator Janet Pillai and other collaborating artists in Kuala Lumpur. The idea was mooted as to whether this processual creative arts program which used a hybrid of educational drama approaches could serve as a pedagogical model to study, test and develop new modes of conflict handling and conflict literacy. In 1994, after further discussion, Pillai was invited to join the DRACON project. She formed a research team in Penang in 1995 made up of artists who had been conducting creative arts programs since the 1990s and who were enthusiastic to use their pedagogical approach to examine the subject of conflict.

Aims and Rationale of the Research

The main aim of the Malaysian research was to test the potential of using multi-arts exercises and process-orientated creative arts (as used in the *Teater Muda* program) for the purpose of exploring conflict and enhancing conflict literacy among school-going adolescents. The Malaysian DRACON team felt that attempts at handling conflict needed to go beyond the culturally and religiously divisive approach used in schools. The team hoped to encourage schools to take a more studied approach to conflict and conflict handling that would work across all ethnic and religious groups, yet take into account the cultural sensitivity of all Malaysians as a collective. Also, counsellors in schools, who functioned within the high power distance common to the Malaysian school culture, tended to simply deliver 'proper advice' or use a top–down regulatory mode as a means to resolve student conflicts. The team believed that processual creative arts could offer a more participatory and creative approach for young people to locate, investigate and negotiate a personal topography of conflict in a manner which would be emancipating and empowering and yet non-confrontational to the existing school counselling system.

Research Team and Participants

The research team was led by two lecturers from Universiti Sains Malaysia in Penang: Janet Pillai from the Department of Performing Arts who served as team leader and drama facilitator, and peace researcher Latiff Kamaluddin from the Department of Research and Education for Peace who served as observer-researcher (henceforth referred to as the researcher). Three artists from the field of dance, music and visual arts served as arts facilitators in the project. In addition, a clinical psychologist joined the team for Phase 2 of the research.

The sample population consisted of three separate groups of students, generally between 10- and 17-years old, who attended national schools in an urban setting in Georgetown, Penang. Each group comprised a mix of students from various ethnicities (Indian, Chinese and Malay) and income groups (lower to middle income).

Research Design

The methodology and techniques from the *Teater Muda* program were used as a base to test the potential of processual creative arts for conflict handling. *Teater Muda* employs a combination of process drama techniques and multi-arts exercises. The program uses a processual creative arts approach, where young participants acquire and use arts vocabulary to explore issues and problems related to self or

Table 5.1 Shape and timescale of Malaysian DRACON project

Research cycles	Activities	Research methods	Duration	Participant age and gender
Cycle 1: 1995 Testing the potential of process-oriented creative arts for exploring conflict	Collective exploration of school conflicts	Observation, reflective writing by researcher	24 sessions	Age: 10–16 10M; 10F
	Collective devising of performance based on school conflicts	Observation and reflective writing		
Cycle 2: 1996–97 Applying process-oriented creative arts exercises and procedure as conflict intervention tools	Assessing conflict understanding among adolescents	Baseline survey	1 day	Age: 16 30M; 30F
	Workshop 1: Introduction to arts vocabulary	Reflective writing by research team	2 day	30M; 30F
	Workshop 2: Exploring personal conflicts	Time-based questionnaires	2 day	Reduced to 17M; 17F
		Summary stage questionnaire		Reduced to 12M; 14F
	Transfer of promising creative arts exercises to school counsellors	Nil	10 sessions	20 counsellors Age: 30–50
Cycle 3: 1998 Testing theatre-in-education as a means to enhance conflict literacy	Identification of adolescent conflicts	Baseline survey	1 day	Age: 16–17 300 students
	Devising of TIE performance from survey findings	Multi-arts enquiry on focus group	2.5 days	45 students
	Pre/post-performance survey	Nil	4 weeks	Four adult actors and director
	Administration of conflict literacy kit	Nil	1 day	Age: 16–17 300 students Mixed gender
	TIE performance	Post-performance survey	Half day	Age: 16–17 300 students

community, then use the information and the acquired arts vocabulary to compose creative outputs that are reflective of or interpretive of the themes explored.

The Malaysian DRACON project was structured into three-research cycles which spanned the period from 1995 to 1998 (See Table 5.1). The first cycle tested the potential of using processual creative arts as used in *Teater Muda* to collectively explore conflict; the second cycle used processual creative arts procedure and exercises to explore personal conflicts; and the third cycle used processual creative arts to devise and perform a theatre-in-education piece to enhance conflict literacy among adolescents.

As practitioners, the research team (artist-facilitators, peace researcher Kamaluddin and team leader Pillai) decided it was appropriate to use 'practice-led research' as the main methodology, supported by some empirical methods. This creative and qualitative approach refers to research which is initiated in practice where questions, problems and challenges are identified and informed by the needs of practice and practitioners and the research strategy is carried out using specific methods familiar to the practitioners (Gray, 1996). Using practice as a method of inquiry, the research team worked creatively to incorporate conflict handling into process-oriented arts methodology while simultaneously reflecting on their own practice through critical journalistic reflections.

In all three cycles, Kamaluddin was involved in open observation, qualitative data gathering, debriefing and analysis. He used a multi-modal approach to data gathering, relying on observation of non-verbal signals, expressive variations in the process of creating artworks and analysis of discernible patterns arising from both process and product. He recorded meanings and intuitive feelings and new ideas as they emerged and reflected on this information in relation to his own knowledge as a peace researcher. From the analysis of this data, he attempted to highlight some of the fundamental aspects of process-oriented creative arts that could make a potential contribution to the field of conflict exploration. Kamaluddin, together with other members of the International DRACON team, also served as a resource person guiding the facilitators on matters relating to conflict-handling concepts and procedures.

Research Cycle 1: Testing Potential

The main task for the research team in the first cycle was to test if the existing processes and creative arts exercises used in the *Teater Muda* program could be applied to engage students in the exploration of conflict.

Design of Research Cycle 1

A processual creative arts program was carried out with the sample group of 20 students over a total of 24 sessions (3-hour sessions held twice every weekend, over a duration of 3 months). The participant group, aged between 10 and 16 years, consisted of a balanced mix of gender, ethnic and income groups. Three artist-facilitators (in the field of drama, dance and visual arts) worked with the small group of participants on social and personal conflict issues related to school.

A processual arts procedure and multi-arts exercises were used as the format to explore and map conflict situations in school experienced by the participants. The arts procedure was matched closely with conflict-handling procedures:

- Building familiarity and trust
- Introduction of arts as expressive vocabulary
- Disclosure of conflict situations
- Articulation of emotions and behaviour related to conflict
- Mapping the conflict journey
- Communicating, i.e. representing the problem in performance
- Feedback on the experience.

Participants then used the data collected from their exploration of conflict to devise a dance-drama performance for an audience.

In Research Cycle 1, the artist-facilitators applied a heuristic approach (a practical problem-solving process which may not necessarily produce optimal results) to test whether procedures in process-oriented art-making coincided with specific procedures in conflict handling and if a multi-arts approach could help students articulate conflict. Kamaluddin acted as external auditor, relying on close observation of the process and on feedback and discussion with the artist-facilitators to produce an analysis of the efficacy of process drama and arts for conflict exploration.

Implementation of Research Cycle 1

The program began with warm-ups, ice-breakers, and interactive and collaborative games, in order to build an atmosphere of cooperation and trust. The participants were then introduced to some very basic vocabulary in movement, drama, sound and visuals as forms of expression. Participants were then encouraged to brainstorm the types of conflicts experienced in relation to school, using creative techniques such as memory recall, imaging, improvisation, simulation, role-play, storyboarding and problem posing. The young participants were then asked to articulate emotions related to their conflict, using object/material manipulation, soundscapes and physical movement. They were encouraged to use exaggeration or abstraction to express strong emotions.

Next, facilitators led the group through a process of play-building and composition, helping participants to reconfigure their fragmented personal experiences into a fictionalised collective narrative. As a final step in the creative arts process, participants showcased their collective creative piece on school-based conflicts to an audience of parents and peers. In articulating school conflicts, their chosen medium was a dramatically structured movement performance incorporating music and the manipulation of objects. The performance depicted a typical school day and traced the collective conflicts they faced, such as the trauma of waking up late for school, struggling with homework, reprimands by prefects and teachers, dealing with bullies and the tension of examinations.

In this fictionalised narrative dance-drama, characters used highly exaggerated and repetitive signature movements and gestures (such as dragging feet, pointing, and falling) to express their conflict status, attitudes and emotional states. Objects such as desks were constantly manipulated and rearranged in the dance to depict the atmosphere of chaos, confusion or rigidity which was plaguing the students in the classroom. Characters also used body sounds (clapping, stamping, slapping body parts) and pulsating music as a powerful way to express emotional states such as fear, anxiety, and frustration.

Insights Gained

The participants responded well to the primacy of the artistic media such as movement, sound, dramatisation and manipulation of objects, giving them a new vocabulary. The use of this multi-arts vocabulary opened up a large range of expressive media (besides language) for the participants to articulate the components and dynamics of conflict. For example, the participants chose comic storyboard to narrate the development of their conflicts, body sculpting and exaggerated movement to display the attitudes of conflicting parties, atmospheric music to paint moods, and dramatic manipulation of sets and props to depict intensity of emotions. It seems that a multi-arts approach might be more advantageous than a single-art approach when exploring the intricacies of different conflict components.

Participants aged between 10 and 13 years were able to release themselves physically and emotionally better than the 14–16 year olds, who showed some concern with 'self-image'. The younger children were quite comfortable with 'fragmented' articulation of their conflict situation, while the older group were more concerned with the logic of cause and effect. Both groups displayed an aversion to dealing with their emotions directly in a confrontational manner. This could be related to the general Malaysian cultural tendency to avoid direct confrontation of emotions or persons in conflict situations.

The participants opted for various forms of displacement by using:

- manipulation of objects to display strong emotions
- aural, physical, visual or dramatic exaggeration
- abstraction in the form of symbolic visuals or movements.

Certain strategies and techniques used in the process of eliciting creativity worked better than others. In the vocabulary building process, the dance facilitator discovered that task-orientated or problem-solving methods were more successful than demonstration in engaging most participants. Demonstration, such as how to use the limbs for expression, tended to encourage imitation. More open-ended tasks, such as finding five exaggerated means to express emotions with the limbs, encouraged subjects to interpret the task more openly and to explore action more creatively. Spontaneous exercises were able to harmonise the subconscious and the conscious feelings. This was obvious from the depth of expression achieved in some exercises, such as newspaper sculpting, object manipulation, and body sculpting. In newspaper sculpting, participants worked in an intensely quiet atmosphere and used memory recall to picture the details of their conflict situation, then spontaneously proceeded to tear, twist, roll and crush piles of newspaper to create a sculpture to express their deep emotional state.

Working on real-life conflict situations motivated participants to go beyond the stereotype and to explore tense relationships and emotions in depth. This was in sharp contrast to the stock situations and characters, and the melodramatic emotions enacted by the participants in earlier *Teater Muda* programs who had been asked to work with imaginary conflicts. The performance of their final creative piece using the metaphoric language of art provided the participants with a safe yet powerful way of projecting and ventilating their experiences of conflict situations in school. While they found it difficult to verbally articulate their understanding of the conflict in the final question-and-answer session, their engagement in the artistic reconstruction and representation of the shared conflict revealed clearly enough their grasp of the components of conflict.

Conclusions from Research Cycle 1

Research Cycle 1 revealed effective learning of conflict-handling constructs through the overlapping of dramatic and real tensions, where conflict was represented through movement metaphors. The successful integration of process-drama and conflict-handling procedures, from identification to articulation of the conflict, indicated that the process drama procedure—used initially for play-building—was easily applied to exploration and mapping of real conflicts. The process drama when adapted for this purpose managed to help participants indirectly and subconsciously to reflect on conflict and its components. The composition process allowed the participants to share, reconstruct and map real experiences using a safe fictional platform.

Pedagogically, intervention styles that were facilitative or spontaneous empowered the participants to make their own inquiries into conflict and to be informed by their own making (experiential learning). The problem-solving approach also encouraged the participants to inquire deeper and motivated them to process the information. These intervention styles seemed better able to engage the participants (perhaps because they are young?) than the instructional or demonstrative intervention styles conventionally used in counselling or conflict handling.

The spontaneous displacement and articulation of intense emotions through physical enactment and other artistic modes also allowed the 'affect' (inner unexpressed feelings) to break through consciousness and become realised. This sets up a dialectical dynamic between cognition and affect and allows for a harmonising between the subconscious and conscious minds. This dynamic is lacking in those forms of conflict handling which are limited to verbal conversation, where focus on the affective is often repressed. In Research Cycle 1, participants were able to use the expressive, the metaphorical, the fictional and the embodied aspects of the art experience to reflect on their generalised conflict situations from a safe entry point.

Research Cycle 2: Testing Effectiveness

Research Cycle 2, carried out in 1996, aimed to test the use of multi-arts exercises as potential exploratory tools for conflict intervention and to measure the effectiveness of these tools in explicating personal conflict when combined with conflict-handling procedures.

Design of Research Cycle 2

The sample population consisted of 60 students, from 3 schools, whose mean age was 16 years. They were of mixed ethnicity and gender and from the lower income bracket. Four artist-facilitators (dance, music, drama and visual arts) were involved, together with a clinical psychologist and Kamaluddin as observer-researcher.

The procedure from Research Cycle 1 combining processual creative arts with conflict handling was adopted and implemented with the sample group, this time only in relation to their personal conflicts:

- Identification of conflict
- Exercises to build familiarity and trust
- Introduction to expressive vocabulary
- Definition and elaboration of conflict using learnt vocabulary (situation, emotions, behaviour, etc.)
- Mapping and reporting on the conflict journey using compositional skills.

In this cycle, the four artist-facilitators took on the role of co-researchers and used an autobiographical mode of writing to reflect on participants' responses as well as their own. These critical narratives were summarised by the team leader Pillai, and handed over to researcher Kamaluddin who then combined the data with his own observations and reflections to come up with the theoretical insights. Empirical inquiry methods were also employed in this cycle by a clinical psychologist who used survey questionnaires to quantitatively verify the outcomes of the subjective data recorded by the artist-facilitators and the researcher.

Implementation of Research Cycle 2

At the start, the researcher administered a baseline survey to a sample population of 60 students that asked them to determine what conflict meant to them, describe a current conflict situation and response, and explain how they handled the conflict situation. Students who identified an ongoing conflict were briefed on the research—that they would be using a creative arts approach to explore their conflicts—and given a choice to participate or to withdraw from the project.

Two types of workshop were conducted over a period of 4 days in each of the 3 schools; the first 2-day workshop was to acquaint all students with a range of expressive and communicative vocabulary in drama, visual arts, dance and music. In the second 2-day workshop, students were encouraged to choose exercises from this repertoire to explore their personal conflict. All participants underwent a short session on trust and alliance building before each workshop.

a. *Expressive vocabulary workshop (2 days)*

In this workshop, specific forms of drama, visual arts, creative movement and music were introduced to the students as expressive vocabulary. Students were introduced to the basic elements of the art forms, then taught a few simple creative arts exercises that could be applied as potential intervention tools to explore the components of conflict. Students were coached on how they could use this arts vocabulary in that exploration:

- In the visual arts session, students were introduced to body portrait drawing as a means to identify conflict; comic drawing as a way to sequence the conflict; speech bubbles to express inner thoughts; and sculpting with newspapers as a way to express intrapersonal feelings.
- In the drama session image theatre, storytelling and scripting were taught as a way to sequence the conflict dynamics, and forum theatre was taught as a means to explore the viewpoints of all parties.
- In the creative movement session, students were introduced to solo exercises such as moving personal body parts to express intrapersonal feelings and duet movement exercises to express interpersonal communication—such as imitating a partner face to face (mirroring), moving to the instructions of a partner (whispering), etc.
- In the music session, students learned to express feelings by producing sounds using body parts, objects and voice or to express inner thoughts by chanting short phrases, etc.

b. *Conflict exploration workshop (2 days)*

Only 34 of 60 participants completed this workshop. In the workshop, participants were expected to identify and work on their personal conflicts individually with the artist-facilitators. Participants could choose any one or a combination of the arts exercises they had been taught in order to methodically explore their personal conflicts in the following order:

- Define the characters, situation, feelings and attitudes from the protagonist's viewpoint.
- Elaborate and ventilate their feelings, attitudes and behaviour.
- Map and replay the conflict from the protagonist/antagonist's viewpoint.

The final presentation revealed to the adolescent participants the general contours of their own conflict topography (its components and dynamics); helped them ventilate; and assisted them to reflect upon the nature of conflict-generating situations and on their positions as actors in the conflict.

Insights Gained

Observations by the researcher and the artist-facilitators highlighted that specific art-forms and exercises lend themselves better to different aspects of conflict exploration. The most popular mediums chosen by the 34 adolescent participants for exploring their conflicts were visual arts (24) and drama (12). Music was less popular (9), and movement the least popular (7).

Specific findings for each creative arts exercise procedure

- Creative arts exercises as tools for warm-up and alliance building:

Many creative arts exercises that are routinely used for warm-up and for alliance and trust building in drama and movement proved to be useful as preparation for the conflict exploration process. These preliminary exercises brought to light the reality of the body and its connections to thoughts, emotions and feelings. In terms of conflict, this relates to inventory-building, i.e. identifying the mental and emotional baggage that one carries around with oneself and its physical manifestations.

- Creative arts exercises as intervention tools for disclosure, articulation and ventilation of conflict:

- MEMORY RECALL: This mental recollection exercise was mostly used in combination with and prior to other exercises. It helped each participant to uncover more detailed aspects of the conflict that were private in nature.
- STORYTELLING: Storytelling allowed participants to identify the problem and the central actors, i.e. the protagonist and antagonist. In introducing storytelling, students were allowed to become the 'owner' of their own conflict stories—an important stage in the endeavour for empowerment in conflict resolution.
- IMAGE THEATRE: Image theatre or postcard drama (presenting conflict scenarios in dramatised still sequences) facilitated the construction of a storyboard or plot in picture form. It served as a conflict map, allowing for a chronological enactment of real-life conflict scenarios. Since role-taking and role-reversal were involved, participants were allowed an insight into what could be termed as subjective and objective image building, a crucial ingredient in conflict resolution with regards to the formation of 'enemy' images.
- CHARACTER IMPROVISATIONS: Through solo improvisations, the elaboration of feelings, attitudes and behaviour of the 'protagonist' (i.e. the adolescent) were explored. In order to ensure a certain degree of empathy, role reversal was introduced where the adolescent participant played the 'antagonist' as well. The researcher commented that these improvisation exercises with body language and minimal text were geared towards enabling the participant to consciously perceive the reactions to conflict of both protagonist and antagonist. Through this, he had been able to accurately gauge the intensity of engagement on the conflict spiral and the type of intervention that could be employed in the helping relationship.

- SCRIPTING: Scripting provided a useful opportunity for participants to uncover information about conflict, such as the escalation process, or to explore the relationships within a conflict from a distance. Joint scripting exercises sometimes helped participants explore the dynamics of action and the reactions between protagonist and antagonist. Role reversal exercises in scripting were attempted, but the participants generally met any exploration of the antagonist point of view with resistance.
- FORUM THEATRE: This technique, which allowed spectators to become actors in role, was skilfully utilised to explore conflicts in the context of specific relationship dynamics. The researcher was alerted to the possibility of a multiplicity of roles ('the party dimension') that actors may take on in a conflict. These included real participants, apparent participants and focal participants, 'advocates' and 'representatives', 'advisors', 'scriptwriters', 'cheer-leaders' 'supporters' and the general audience. Moreover, forum theatre also emerged as an effective conflict exploration tool that sensitises us to the fact that actors can move in and out of role—a fact that often leads to changes in the dynamics of conflict resolution. Forum theatre also enabled the participants to present the characters in the conflict with more experiential, emotional and psychological depth.
- COMIC DRAWINGS: Kamaluddin reported that 'comic drawings' served well to identify the problem and also as a projective technique where the comic strip characters represented the self and other parties. The frame-by-frame narrative aspect of the comic strip allowed for a sequential recall of the conflict journey from the inciting incident to its escalation. The art of using lines to express action and emotional states helped participants express how a conflict became amplified. Thought and speech bubbles allowed them to articulate key thoughts and feelings and to become self-aware. They expressed that they felt safe drawing for themselves.
- BODY PORTRAIT DRAWING: This technique involved the tracing of the body outline of one partner by another and filling the portrait with icons, images or words reflecting needs, fears, etc.—a powerful exploration/brainstorming tool for identifying problems and prioritising the issues involved.
- NEWSPAPER SCULPTING: 'Newspaper sculpting', according to Kamaluddin's observations, was a therapeutic projective technique. Some participants used the process of tearing, crushing and folding to vent suppressed emotions, and the process of sculpting the paper to express their perceptions of the conflict. While some created symbolic sculptures, others created more literal images and scenarios. The visual arts facilitator commented that although newspaper sculpting was not a popular choice, the few who used this form experienced a sort of catharsis through intra-personal disclosure, displacement and ventilation of negative feelings.
- MOVEMENT: The movement facilitator led participants through a 'memory recall' then moved to 'posturing exercises' where they enacted postures that helped them express and embody the attitudes and emotions of protagonist and antagonist. The facilitator then encouraged participants to use spontaneous 'improvised movement' to choreograph an entire conflict scene, in solo, duet or group. However, participants displayed some reluctance to move owing to inhibitions about dance or expressive movement. When participants did express their emotions, they

tended intuitively to use mime, pedestrian gestures or stylised movements. Despite their hesitation, some of them managed the journey through movement to identify their problem and to ventilate emotions and find a moment of truth for themselves.
- The final phase in the movement section involved the re-choreographing of an entire scene, highlighting the beginning, middle and end of the conflict. Even bearing in mind the pitfalls of linear conflict projection, the researcher still supported the use of this sequencing in that it permitted fluid movement along a conflict spiral, with deliberate stops for microanalysis and in-depth exploration. Choreography sessions such as these might prove to be a useful method in structuring 'play-back' moments in an emerging or manifest conflict scenario.
- LYRIC WRITING: The researcher and the music facilitator both observed that lyric-writing and music-making exercises were useful aids in identifying problems, characters and moods. The music facilitator noted that metaphors, hazy references and imagery used in the lyrics allowed for a certain amount of distancing and the release of 'secret' or private information. Extended pleas, advice or blame were often voiced through repetition of lines, and seemed to serve as a means of amplification as well.
- MUSIC MAKING: In the music making session, the participants expressed their feelings through percussion instruments, by manipulating tone, pitch, rhythm, dynamics and tempo. In addition, they were asked for keywords and phrases related to conflict which were then superimposed over short rhythmic patterns played on instruments. The music facilitator commented that many participants treated playing music as ventilation, where feelings and emotions were displaced via instruments and voice. It was also clear that participants felt more comfortable resorting to known or familiar musical forms.

Problems and Recommendations

The participants found working on the disclosure, articulation and ventilation of their personal ongoing conflicts difficult without a fictional interface. Participant numbers reduced significantly from 60 to 34 when the conflict exploration workshop began and reduced further to 26 students by the fourth day. It can only be speculated that this was perhaps due to discomfort or fear of disclosure. More time should have been taken to create an atmosphere of safety and trust between facilitators and participants before moving into conflict disclosure.

The researchers commented that working through an art-form could prove to be very frustrating if not counterproductive for participants who did not have a prior leaning towards it, natural or learnt. Some participants were unable to express themselves intuitively in the art form because of feelings of uncertainty, their perceived lack of skills and self-consciousness. It was, therefore, important to work with forms that were already familiar to participants and popular with them.

The conflict exploration workshop became uncomfortable for the artists, too, when disclosure was not forthcoming or alternatively when it became too intense. The artist-facilitators expressed that helping participants to maintain aesthetic distance was difficult and they felt unsure about where to draw the line so as not to drift into the area of therapy; they were also unsure how to work on closure. The artist-facilitators expressed the need to understand the theory and scope of conflict handling better.

Empirical Survey and Results

In this cycle, the project's clinical psychologist also employed empirical methods using questionnaires to measure the effectiveness of the creative arts in handling personal conflict. The survey analysis was derived from the responses of the 26 participants (12 females and 14 males) who were able to complete the 4-day workshop.

In the initial baseline survey (conducted on 70 students) to determine adolescent understanding of conflict, participants had indicated that they perceived conflict as 'a composite of feelings experienced while in a conflict situation'. The clinical psychologist decided to use this functional definition of conflict to test the effectiveness of the creative arts in handling conflict. To do this, it was necessary to measure the changes in participants' feelings of conflict and their levels of understanding of the conflict before, during and after intervention.

Twenty-six participants who completed the creative intervention (Workshop 2) were administered a survey questionnaire at three points in time: before Workshop 2, after Workshop 2 and after the summary stage questionnaire. The questionnaire required them to report feelings associated with the conflict, then use a graded scale to indicate the intensity of each feeling. They also had to indicate the level of understanding of the conflict.

The overall generalised intensity of conflict that participants experienced was derived from a composite score on their reported individual intensities of feelings experienced over time (see Table 5.2). We initially hypothesised that the results would show an increase between phases Time 1 and Time 2 since this period dealt with identification of conflict, magnification and intensification. However, the results went in the other direction. This could be due to the fact that identification, magnification and intensification might in themselves have been therapeutic: i.e. they assist in ventilating feelings, resulting in a decrease of the intensity levels of feelings related to conflict.

As can be seen from the table, there was a highly significant decrease in self-reported intensities of feelings between Time 1 and Time 3, after the subjects combined the creative arts process with their subjective evaluation of the workshop (i.e. the summary Stage Questionnaire). A comparison of Time 2 and Time 3 also indicated

Table 5.2 Changes in intensity of feeling across time

Time 1 (prior to creative intervention)	Time 2 (immediately after creative intervention)	Summary Stage Questionnaire	Time 3 (after summary stage questionnaire)
6.41	5.75	–	4.50

a decrease in intensity of feelings. This clarifies that the combination of creative arts and the summary questionnaire is more effective than simply using the creative arts alone for conflict handling. We can say that the processual creative arts experience seems to have much more impact when reflected upon.

No statistically significant changes were recorded in subjects' understanding of their own feelings and their ability to express their feelings. No differences were found between the sexes in terms of changes in the intensity of feelings or in their levels of understanding of conflict. The results suggest that males and females were equal to the tasks demanded by the creative arts process in terms of applying the arts tools they had learnt to conflict exploration.

The research hypothesised that intensity of feelings and levels of understanding of conflict would be negatively correlated, but no such statistical correlation was found. Most participants reported that they felt a significant decrease in conflict feelings and were able to better understand their conflict.

A summary stage questionnaire (or evaluation) was administered to all participants before termination of the project, to facilitate personal reflection upon their conflict and their understanding of the situation, the process and facilitators and learning points. Below is a summary of salient points derived from this questionnaire.

1. Analysis of the areas of conflict showed a higher rate of reports by girls regarding conflict situations involving family (such as communication, divorce, alcoholism, etc.). Male and female participants reported an equal number of conflict situations, but fewer, involving friends and school (such as academic problems, problems with teachers, and bullying).
2. When participants were asked if they felt they understood their conflict better after the conflict exploration process, 16 of 26 participants answered affirmatively, citing the following as helpful factors:

   - working and rehearsing on the details of the conflict
   - thinking deeply and in sequence
   - the ability to express their feelings.

   Five participants answered negatively, citing as obstructions discomfort with the approach and their inability to express.
3. When asked what they gained from the process, the most common answers were:

   - an increased sense of calm
   - the ability to express their feelings
   - they could focus and think clearly.
4. When asked how they would handle their problems, only a very few answered the question, with replies including:

   - seek counselling
   - use creative arts
   - analyse the situation
   - avoid the problem.

5. When asked what caused the change (if any) in their overall feeling of conflict, among the main reasons cited were:

- the intensity of the exercises
- intervention by the facilitators
- increased understanding and clarity of the problem
- expression and reduced feelings.

The above summaries are very much in keeping with the findings in the empirical study. Although the rigour of quantitative methods is not in question here, there may be a strong case for using a qualitative methodology as more efficacious in research of this nature. It may be that qualitative analysis (rather than quantitative scores) is more suited to measuring feelings. The qualitative questionnaire enables reflection and fosters more cognitive processing and self-evaluation.

Conclusions from Research Cycle 2

Findings from Research Cycle 2 indicated that a head-on and direct approach to handling of real conflicts is not necessarily suited to the Malaysian cultural context. Exploration of conflict needs to be distanced somewhat in order to be viewed as a non-threatening experience. This can be achieved through the conscious and knowledgeable selection and use of artistic forms and exercises.

An important consideration when applying arts exercises for conflict intervention is an understanding of the concept of distancing as a safeguarding strategy: knowing which exercises encourage emotional connectivity with the problem and which allow for reflection and making sure that the correct degree of aesthetic distance is achieved in relation to the intention and depth of intervention. Aesthetic distance is achieved when the individual manages to simultaneously maintain closeness and separateness to the experience, and re-experience emotions but not be overwhelmed by them (Bullough, 1964). Scheff (1981) used the terms 'under-distancing' and 'over-distancing': under-distancing to mean bringing oneself closer to the real experience, and over-distancing to refer to the separating of oneself from the real experience.

Creative arts procedures provide valuable opportunities for the practitioner to delve into a range of mechanisms for problem and party identification, articulation and ventilation of emotions and mapping the conflict journey. Using a multi-arts approach affords a new look and expanded approach in the area of helping skills and coping skills in conflict handling. These include perceptual skills (problem identification and exploration), emotional skills (articulation and ventilation of feelings) and stress management skills (tension reduction).

Transfer to School Counsellors

In 1997, the research team organised a 10-day intensive course for 20 full-time school counsellors. This was based on feedback from school counsellors who were observing research cycle 2, which suggested that a processual creative arts approach to conflict handling could be a valuable counselling asset in schools.

Counsellor training began with warm-up exercises focused on relationship building and reorientation to the subject of conflict handling by the researcher. One artist-facilitator acted as a trainer to transfer the more promising drama and visual arts techniques from Research Cycle 2 to counsellors. The counsellors also participated in a workshop led by a clinical psychologist to help them make the link between counselling strategies, processual creative arts and problem-solving models of conflict handling. At the end of this workshop, counsellors were set the task of using any of the techniques they had learnt as part of their counselling strategy when they returned to the school situation.

All 20 counsellors participated for the entire duration of the workshop. However, approximately half of them found it very difficult to take a critical re-look at basic assumptions and standard techniques of school counselling and to put aside their set ideas about a helping relationship. Many counsellors enjoyed the warm-up and alliance building games but became very self-conscious about expressing themselves through the art-forms of drama or visual arts. This was despite the fact that those counsellors who observed Research Cycle 2 had rated drama and visual arts exercises positively.

Disappointingly, a month after the completion of the training, all the counsellors reported that they had not applied any of the techniques and were not interested to return for a feedback session. The research team concluded that at the level of practice, school counsellors were not receptive to the action-orientated creative-arts approach to conflict handling.

The research team was unable to question the counsellors on their failure to apply the techniques learnt and could only speculate on the possible reasons. Counsellors probably found the levels of sharing and participation awkward when they returned to the school context, where a teacher–student hierarchy was prevalent. Another reason could be that they were not used to the collective and creative methods of working, and were more comfortable with one-to-one counselling and an advisory rather than an empowering role.

It seems that any attempt to introduce new pedagogical working methods within an institutional setting would require long-term stakeholder engagement. This is because the ideology, agenda and aims of the working method would need be clarified, discussed and accepted by all parties. Test sessions as well as adaptations of the method might be needed for parties to develop a sense of ownership and confidence before applying it to their school situation.

Research Cycle 3: Enhancing Conflict Literacy

The final phase of the Malaysian DRACON research project was carried out in 1998 and focused on using TIE and an accompanying educational kit to enhance conflict literacy among an adolescent population (16–17 years). The intention was to help adolescents reflect both cognitively (through conflict theory) and affectively (through drama) on their emotional involvement in and management of conflict.

Design of Research Cycle 3

The research was undertaken collaboratively by a team once again consisting of Pillai as team leader, who also developed the resource kit and directed the TIE performance, with Kamaluddin acting as observer-researcher and four adult actor-facilitators. The sample population for the research involved 300 school-going adolescents aged 16–17 years of age, of mixed ethnicity and from low-income backgrounds.

The research cycle spanned five-months and consisted of several stages of development and implementation.

- Enquiry into adolescent conflicts
- Devising the TIE performance
- Developing a conflict literacy kit and transmitting the contents prior to performance
- Interactive performances
- Surveys.

A baseline enquiry was carried out with a focus group to identify the types of conflicts adolescents experienced. The actors used this data to devise a performance about adolescent conflicts. Teachers administered a conflict literacy kit (introducing the components and dynamics of conflict) to the 300 students in their classrooms prior to their viewing the interactive TIE performance.

The 300 students completed questionnaires after the program to discern the effectiveness of the TIE performance (and the accompanying educational kit) in raising awareness about conflict and conflict handling. Video-recordings were also made to document audience response to the TIE performances. The researcher observed all processes and made field notes.

Implementation of Research Cycle 3

Enquiry into Adolescent Conflicts

A simple pre-program baseline survey was administered to the 300 students to gather information on adolescent conflict issues. Of the 300 students, 45 were also involved in 2½ days of focus group enquiry led by the adult actors using creative drama techniques. These techniques included storytelling, improvisation, theatre games, role-play, forum theatre and writing exercises. The information gathered from the survey and focus group enquiry was used to devise the TIE performance.

Questions directing this enquiry were:

1. What were the values, needs and interests of the target audience?
2. What were the conflict issues and conflict types experienced by the target audience at school workplace and home?
3. Who were the parties involved?
4. How did their conflicts escalate and what sort of conflict behaviour did they display?
5. What were the common ways in which these adolescents managed emotions or dealt with conflicts?

The results from the survey questionnaire, though not rich, did confirm the main findings derived from the focus group enquiry. We employed several drama techniques to gather the information needed. These included story-telling, image theatre (a series of still scenes), improvisation and role-play to demonstrate the dynamics of their conflict situations. Drama methods, moreover, were able to reveal nuanced and embodied information on adolescent conflict behaviour, attitudes and feelings. Drama methods were also able to reveal the types of allies, bystanders and victims who figure strongly in adolescent conflicts, and in addition, to make evident the dynamics of conflict.

Using a combination of drama methods proved useful in verifying and cross-checking information. For example, through storytelling technique participants revealed how they faced conflicts in the work place when they took on part-time jobs that they believed required no particular skills. Using image theatre to illustrate the situations made concrete those who were parties in that conflict. Role play and improvisation revealed that the respondents often lost their jobs due to lack of work know-how or communication skills. In focus group discussions, they further revealed that they did not derive pleasure from their jobs, but more from the money earned 'for personal spending'.

Devising the TIE Performance

The information elicited from the two enquiry methods helped the actors prepare the four fictional conflict scenarios for a TIE performance relevant to an adolescent audience. The drama enquiry also helped the actors prepare their characters with greater accuracy. The scenarios incorporated information such as the source of conflict (poor communication, adult expectations, need for recognition, etc.); the parties involved (peers, parents, teachers, employers); the feelings associated with conflict (anger, revenge, unease, dissatisfaction, etc.); the dynamics of escalation (rapid or drawn out); and the type of action taken to deal with the conflict (calm, restraint, aggression, etc.).

Developing the Conflict Literacy Kit

The kit provided theoretical information on the components of conflict (parties, attitudes, behaviour and contradictions); the types of conflict (latent, emerging and manifest); and the dynamics of conflict escalation. There was information on how to manage emotions, particularly introducing the concept of 'emotional intelligence'. The kit also highlighted the impact of perceptions and emotions on conflict escalation. All this information was provided in accessible forms such as illustrated drawings, word games, worksheets and discussions.

The teacher in moral education and religion was expected to apply the kit over three 40-min lessons, a week before the TIE performance. Teachers were guided on how to apply the kit. It was hoped that the students would be able to apply information learned from the kit when making interventions within the interactive performance of the TIE.

The Interactive Performance

Ten performances of the TIE performance *Stop! Look! Go!* were played to a total of 1300 teenagers aged 16–17 years (including the original 300 sample population). Interactive drama techniques were incorporated into the performance, offering audiences several opportunities to intervene and improve on the conflict situations. Audiences carried three cards which they could raise up at any point during the drama to indicate if they agreed with the characters' actions (green card), disagreed (red card), or were unsure about them (orange card). A mediator would ask the audience member to explain their intervention and to propose an alternative action. This method alerted audiences to pay attention to characters in the performance, and to predict the consequences of their actions and reactions, before deciding to intervene.

During the performance, the actors used under-distancing techniques such as emotive songs to portray their feelings; they sat on a 'hot chair' to reveal their hidden thoughts or motives; or they addressed audiences directly, to try and convince them of their respective standpoints and intended actions. These under-distancing techniques led audiences to empathise with the characters. Over-distancing (or alienation as it is known in theatre) techniques were also used in the performance to help audiences distance themselves from the affective experience and engage cognitively in conflict analysis. One example is when audiences raised their cards to interrupt the performance and gave suggestions for intervention.

Post-program Survey

A questionnaire was administered to the 300 sample population to discern the effectiveness of the TIE performance and the accompanying educational kit, in raising awareness about conflict and conflict handling. The questions posed were on identifying the types of conflict in the drama, the audience member's understanding of the phrase 'Stop, Look, Go' (i.e. stop to think before reacting), and whether they would apply it in managing their own conflict situations.

Results of TIE Performance and Post-program Survey

The TIE *Stop! Look! Go!* played out scenes of adolescent conflicts through intelligently constructed, dramatised roles and situations. The play was able to create authentic moments of conflict, thereby codifying day-to-day conflicts on the level of the audience's perceived reality. During the TIE performance, audiences found it easy to identify with the characters during the dramatic and interactive scenes. However, they were less inclined to support the character's point of view and instead held on to their own points of view.

Being sensitive to the affective dimension, the adolescent audience members were able to spontaneously react to the situations of conflict, based on the differing 'needs, values, and interests' of the characters introduced in the scenes. At the end of each scenario, the characters barraged the audience with problem-posing questions. This over-distancing technique encouraged the spectators to switch to a cognitive state of mind and offer the actors their perspective.

The performance provided an active platform for participatory intervention where audiences became actively involved in taking responsibility for their views, values and positions. However, although the audience members raised their coloured cards to show their agreement or disagreement with characters' actions, they scored lower on the cognitive intervention techniques that required them to provide verbal opinions regarding their intervention.

Stop! Look! Go! successfully reintroduced a conflict language via dramatic and forum-like interactions that made the conventional DASIE model (develop, analyse, support, intervene and evaluate) come alive in a simulated setting.

The post-program survey revealed that 55% of respondents understood the performance to be about the components of conflict and about how to handle responses in conflict situations. However, they could not name the different styles used in the drama to handle conflicts (competing, avoiding, compromising, collaborating, etc.). 78% of respondents displayed a moderate awareness of the various components of conflict (attitude, behaviour, contradiction) displayed in the performance, but only 45% of respondents understood how to reflect on this information sufficiently to use it in their own conflict situations.

Of the respondents, 45% displayed high awareness and 36% displayed moderate awareness of the 'Stop! Look! Go!' method of managing emotions that were used in the performance. 38% of respondents understood how they could apply the method to their own conflict situation.

Problems and Recommendations

Some school teachers missed the briefing on how to use the educational kit or were unmotivated to teach the kit in their classroom. In schools where the kit was handed out to students without guidance from the teacher, audiences tended to react spontaneously at the interactive sections, rather than actually applying knowledge from the kit. They reacted affectively rather than cognitively. More advocacy should have been done in advance by the team to draw teachers into the project, and also more time should have been allocated for both teachers and students to assimilate the topic and the materials in the kit.

Kamaluddin was critical of the pre- and post-program surveys, pointing out that the different questions used in the two surveys resulted in a loss of opportunity to measure the level of change in audience knowledge before and after the performance.

In addition, the post-program survey questions did not use reliable methods to accurately measure the level of audience engagement in the performance or learning from the conflict literacy kit. Parts of the survey that used open-ended questions proved especially unpopular with male respondents and resulted in a distortion in the data analysis. The researcher recommended that conflict literacy should be measured via a post-program problem-posing questionnaire similar to that designed by Cornelius and Faire (1989).

Outcomes and Implications

The Malaysian DRACON project managed to identify contact points between processual creative arts and conflict exploration and to evolve an integrated creative arts-cum-conflict exploration process through action research. Findings revealed that the combination of creative arts and conflict exploration added an experiential and instinctive dimension to the overtly rational and cognitive approach used in counselling or conflict education. Bringing in arts procedures and instruments led to the engagement of both the cognitive and affective domains, through the integration of experiential and reflective tasks:

- experiential tasks—when key elements in drama-making or art-making were employed for the purpose of examining conflict
- reflective tasks—when the key elements of composition, presentation and interpretation were employed for mapping the journey, building empathy or problem solving.

The metaphoric nature of the arts and the processual orientation of art-making provided a safe platform for participants to examine and reflect on conflict. We observed that the model contributed well to the enhancement of coping skills, including perceptual skills (problem identification and exploration), emotional ventilation skills (expression of feelings) and stress management (tension reduction).

These findings have implications for practitioners in the fields of educational drama, counselling and conflict handling, as well as educators who wish to promote conflict education.

Cultural Implications

In this limited project with Malaysian school-going students of 10–17 years, we discovered that there are some crucial dimensions of conflict handling that need to be broached in a way relevant to the Malaysian cultural norms of collectivism, high power distance and high tolerance. The dimensions include modes of self-disclosure, communication and handling of conflict situations. The Malaysian participants tended to be uncomfortable with self-disclosure and methods that encouraged introspection and self-analysis, as this was seen as an encroachment on the realm of the private and sensitive. They were more comfortable retracing a real conflict in a fictional setting and expressing feelings via metaphor and symbols.

When imparting skills, sufficient care had to be taken by the artist-facilitators to avoid assertive communication and to maintain the polite system of communication, emphasising the maintaining of face, respect for hierarchy, linguistic nuances, a gentle pace, etc. Forthright verbal communication did not go down well with Malaysian participants. Coded messages, modesty, even shyness were dominant over assertive person-centred positioning, role clarification and clearly defined disclosure. There was a tendency towards controlled disclosure clothed in generalities and guarded phraseology, as communication in the Malaysian context is usually indirect, subtle and polite. Even the term 'conflict' was not translatable into any single term. Instead the project participants preferred affective, indirect rhetoric, describing conflict via a list of feelings experienced during conflict.

In the Malaysian school context, the adolescents' personal and family conflicts often remained at the latent level. The manifest and latent aspects of conflict may be compared to the *text* and the *subtext* of drama or other art forms. Text, which refers to overt expression, is usually congruent with the concealed subtext that motivates certain communication patterns and actions. However, for the adolescent Malaysian participants, the text of their behaviour on the social level was often incongruent with their subtext (Fig. 5.2).

As a result, the most appropriate communication model for conflict exploration among Malaysian adolescents appears to be one that favours indirect modes of expression. For this reason, the integrated multi-arts approach was most productive because it gave wide scope to participants to bring to the surface their subtext (latent conflict) using the metaphorical language of music, drama, visual images and movement.

In conflict-handling styles among participants, there appeared often to be a predisposition towards avoidance and compromise and even suppression. Handling of conflict often occurred in a non-confrontational manner. Positional power and authority-centred relationships tended to predominate over personal. Paternalistic

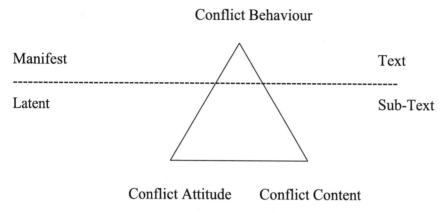

Fig. 5.2 Revealed and concealed in drama and conflict

consensus-seeking postures also tended to prevail. The needs for maintaining face and for honourable reciprocity that the participants felt tended to be overwhelming.

Given the society's collectivist orientation, the preferred approaches to conflict handling are collaborative consensus-building activities and the compromise mode of problem-solving. This being the case, it was, therefore, imperative for conflict-handling practitioners in Malaysia to avoid 'head on' modes of exploring conflict. On the other hand, while there is a need to be sensitive to socio-cultural conditioning, it must be remembered that it should not be romanticised. Conflict exploration is about self-confrontation where and when necessary. Culture is learned behaviour and can and should be adaptable where and when personal volition might have to outweigh group affiliations. This is particularly the case in situations where the skills to create affective change might sometime have to work in combination with the skills for cognitive change, when working towards re-patterning intra- or inter-relationship structures.

Implications for the School Counselling System

The conventional counsellor-client setting in Malaysia appears to be unpopular with students, as authority and power relationships make self-disclosure difficult and only lead to the enforcement of norms and rules. There is, therefore, a need to provide an alternative to the conventional counselling system in schools. The introduction of the peer counselling model has at least begun to favour group-oriented and collective situations. These run counter to the conventional conflict resolution models, which aim to satisfy the individual's needs and expectations rather than addressing the whole context of a problem or conflict.

The integrated conflict exploration process used in this research can help expand the counselling continuum in schools beyond providing outsider advice or a helping hand into an action-orientated exploratory process. This would provide a welcome alternative to the situation of having to 'talk', which many of our subjects found to be too confrontational; being able to 'act' provided them with a more comfortable forum for conflict exploration.

In order to successfully provide a workable context for using integrated conflict exploration in schools, there must be more openness on the part of school authorities to try out experimental conflict-handling modes. Far too often their perception has been that such empowerment exercises 'threaten' school stability and they need to reappraise this attitude.

Exposure of the students to training alone is hardly enough. Both practitioners and clients have to be knowledgeable and confident in the processual creative arts themselves, and how these work in conflict transformation and resolution. This is best done via long-term education, training and practice. That will demand a holistic, integrated conflict exploration model, incorporating elements of conflict exploration, communication, therapy-oriented disciplines and process-oriented drama, creative movement, visual arts and music.

Conclusions

The whole Malaysian study revealed that combining a process-oriented creative arts approach with the conventional conflict-handling model provided a possible interface between the affective and cognitive modes of conflict recognition. We visualise that this interface might broaden the boundaries of conventional conflict exploration, making it more participatory (less 'talk' more 'action-orientation'); more empowering (exploring projected needs and interests); more comfortable (moving from personal to group space); and safer (moving from real to fictional).

These insights led the Malaysian team to postulate a process-oriented model of conflict exploration that engages the participant in various experiential, in-role and reflective tasks in order to facilitate the exploration of conflict. The model draws from the process-oriented arts, where participants are given the opportunity to bring their experiences from the real world and explore them in the safety of the fictional context of art-making.

The interrelated use of art-forms such as drama, music, movement and visual arts provides space for a more deeply integrated examination of the participants' conflicts, with the safety of distance provided by metaphor. Simulating events through metaphoric expressions provide a safe distance for participants to deconstruct and objectively re-examine a problem. This creative process allows personally satisfying meanings to be constructed through deconstruction and reinterpretation of experiences drawn from reality. Those meanings may then be brought back into transactions, interactions and negotiations in the real world.

The model has without doubt enabled conflict exploration to oscillate comfortably between the dichotomised realities of personal and group space, narrated and real-time, metaphorical and actual expressions, fictional and real experiences, symbolic and literal meanings, in a manner that is comfortable for those experiencing it. This stems primarily from the processual and self-empowered orientation that the creative arts lend to conflict exploration.

Outcomes and Implications 117

All photographs: Janet Pillai

Malaysia 1: Cycle 1: Students explore feelings through movement in school-related conflicts

Malaysia 2: Cycle 1: Student-devised dance performance of school related conflict

Malaysia 3: Cycle 2: Introduction to postcard theatre for exploring conflict situations

Outcomes and Implications 119

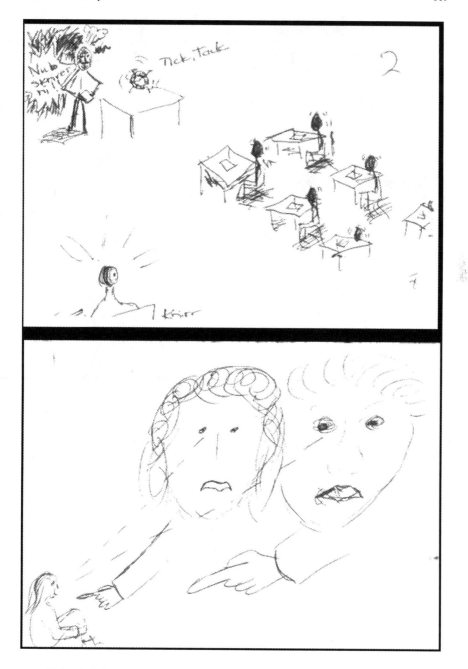

Malaysia 4: Cycle 2: Using visual arts (comic drawing) to explore personal conflicts

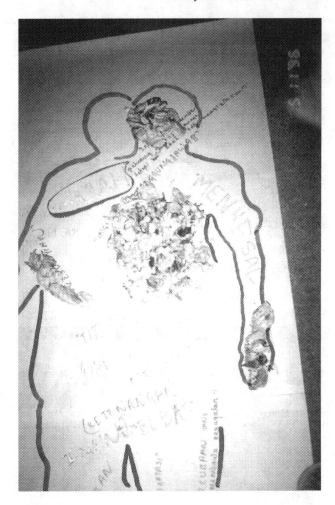

Malaysia 5: Cycle 2: Using visual arts (self-portrait) to explore individual conflicts

Outcomes and Implications 121

Malaysia 6: Cycle 2: Participant explains her newspaper sculpture to her colleagues

Malaysia 7: Cycle 3: Actors use a spin wheel of types of conflict in 'Stop! Look! Go!' TIE

Malaysia 8: Cycle 3: An actor solicits opinions from students in 'Stop! Look! Go!' TIE

References

Barnes, B. (2007). *Culture, conflict and mediation in Asian Pacific*. Lanham: University Press of America.
Boal, A. (1987). *Theatre of the oppressed*. London: Pluto Press.
Bullough, E. (1964). 'Psychical distance' as a factor in art and as an aesthetic principle'. In M. Rader (Ed.), *A modern book of aesthetics: An anthology* (3rd ed.). New York: Holt, Rinehart and Winston.
Cornelius, H., & Faire, S. (1989). *Everyone can win—How to resolve conflict*. NSW Australia: Brookvale.
Gray, C. (1996). *Inquiry through practice: Developing appropriate research strategies*. http://carolegray.net/Papers%20PDFs/ngnm.pdf. Accessed July 8, 2018.
Hofstede, G. (1980). *Culture's consequences: International differences in work related values*. Newbury Park CA: Sage.
Scheff, T. (1981). The distancing of emotion in psychotherapy. *Psychology and Psychotherapy: Theory Research and Practice, 18*(1), 46–53.

Chapter 6
Sweden—Teenagers as Third-Party Mediators

Introduction

The Swedish DRACON Project shares the same general research questions with the other country projects. Our aim has been to study how teenagers usually handle conflicts and to test whether a combination of educational drama and conflict theories can enhance the understanding of conflicts and conflict handling among Grade 8 students. However, there are some characteristics specific to the Swedish approach. Here the focus has been on third-party roles, in particular the role of the mediator. Ultimately, our aim has been to find out whether or not Grade 8 students would be able to take on the role of peer mediators in real-life conflicts by applying the drama methods they learnt during the program.

In the Swedish project, we have addressed the following overriding questions:

- Are there basic styles for handling conflicts among teenagers?
- Is it possible to develop a drama program that combines conflict theory with practical exercises in classes as developmental aids for learning?
- How can the program be implemented in schools?
- Can teenagers learn to act as impartial mediators in conflicts?
- What kinds of measurements can be developed for studying the effects of conflict-handling programs?

By addressing the above issues, we hope to contribute to further theory development within the field.

Historical and Cultural Background

Sweden is a technologically advanced country with a population of ten million inhabitants on the northern periphery of Europe. It is one of the oldest States in Europe and emerged as a Lutheran nation-state in the sixteenth century. There have been almost no religious, ethnic, linguistic or regional divisions until the recent wave of immigration. In 2018, about 20% of the population was born outside the country.

Sweden has a long history of peaceful solutions to internal and external conflicts. Sweden belongs to the Nordic community—together with Norway, Denmark, Iceland and Finland—which has developed a strong tradition of mutual co-operation and negotiation between sovereign States that is almost unique in the world. Since 1995, Sweden has also been a member of the European Union (EU).

The present era in the political life of Sweden originated in the 1930s when the Labour Party began its long period of political governance. Capital, State, labour and land entered into a 'historic compromise', and the foundation was laid for the building of an industrial welfare state.

Industrial Sweden was at its peak around the year 1960 when measured by the percentage of the labour-force working in the industrial sector (45%). Many indicators today point to Sweden as being one of the most post-industrial nations in the world. The bulk of the population, 70%, work in the service sector, and only 27% remain in the industrial sector.

The psychological dispositions of the Swedes have been listed by Daun (1989). Among others the list includes shyness, independence, conflict avoidance, honesty and emotional self-control. A positive interpretation of Swedish egalitarianism would be that people pay attention to the needs of others; that they feel certain empathy with their fellow citizens and particularly with the weak. Thus, they are reluctant to put their own needs above the needs of others. This interpretation gets some support from Hofstede's finding that Sweden is the most 'feminine' country in a worldwide sample of fifty countries (1997). Swedish culture promotes the 'feminine' value of nurturing rather than the 'masculine' value of achievement. Feminine values such as taking care of people and nature, and helpfulness, have been institutionalised in the Swedish welfare state, in government aid to poor countries, in high standards of environmental conservation and in the belief that 'small is beautiful'. It is also a fact that Swedish women have a strong position in Swedish society and culture, particularly in politics where female representation has reached almost 50%.

Sweden is also a 'low-anxiety country' (Daun, 1989: 119). Levels of inner tension and stress are relatively low. Therefore, there is less need to express strong emotions and aggressiveness. This finding is in harmony with the findings of Hofstede that Sweden is low on 'avoidance of uncertainty'. The value of safety from the cradle to the grave has been institutionalised in the Swedish system, to such a degree that Swedes are able to tolerate quite a lot of uncertainty, ambiguity, deviance and dissent. There is a basic belief that conflict and competition can be dealt with constructively through direct negotiations and democratic procedures. A word with many positive connotations in the Swedish language is 'compromise'.

Introduction

The Swedish School System

The Swedish school system comprises compulsory as well as various types of voluntary schooling. The compulsory school program is directed at all children between the ages of 6 and 16 years. Public education is free; parents and students are not required to pay for meals, transport, teaching materials or health services related to schooling.

The Swedish Parliament and government determine the guidelines, national objectives and curriculum for the public education system. The Swedish School Act stipulates that all children and youths have equal access to education, regardless of social status, economical situation or gender. Consideration is also given to students with special needs.

In 1991, Swedish municipalities were given total responsibility for the administration of schools in their own areas. Statutory directives such as curricula, timetables and criteria of assessment provide a framework within which municipalities and schools can develop their own profiles and modes of practice. Local school plans (with descriptions of organisation, funding, development and assessment) are thus adopted in the different municipalities. These, together with the statutory objectives mentioned above, constitute the local work plan, which is drawn up by the principal in consultation with teachers and other school personnel. Among other responsibilities, the principal has the specific task of drawing up, implementing and evaluating a work plan condemning all forms of abuse among students and staff.

Schools and preschools in Sweden are aligned to three main democratic assignments. Firstly, as an integral part of conventional schooling, the student should be taught basic democratic values. Secondly, students and staff in the schools themselves should also actively participate in a democratic process, encouraging participation and enhancing empowerment. Thirdly, it is the responsibility of the schools and pre-schools, in co-operation with the home, to foster students to become democratic citizens and to function as responsible members of society where values such as solidarity, equal opportunity and equal rights are fundamental. It is their task to actively counteract all types of deviant behaviours such as racism and bullying. According to a study in Sweden, approximately 10% of students in the comprehensive school reported that they were bullied, half of them by schoolmates and half of them by teachers (Eriksson, Lindberg, Flygare, & Daneback, 2002; Skolverket, 2002). Fifteen years later, the number had risen to 16% of the students being exposed to bullying a couple of times every month (OECD, 2015).

Regarded as a whole, these three assignments should be able to enhance an overall democratic awareness among students. In schools, where daily relations are complex and dynamic, learning to treat others with respect and showing empathy becomes part of an ongoing process of learning to apply democratic values in practice. Focusing on and learning how to prevent bullying and other forms of violence at an early age should in the long run also be of benefit to society as a whole. Schools and preschools thus have an important task to help to counteract all types of abusive treatment.

Drama and Conflict Handling in Swedish Schools

Theatre has been used to enhance learning in Swedish schools since the sixteenth century. In 1571, the first curriculum stipulating the use of theatre in both Latin and Swedish was introduced to a small elite of boys (Lindvåg, 1988). However, it was not until the beginning of the twentieth century—'the Century of the Child' (Key, 1996)—that the modern history of educational drama started to take form.

Drama in Sweden has developed along two significant lines. One has its origins in folk literature, children's literature and children's theatre. The other can be found within the school system, where ideas of equality and the right of every child to develop and express him/herself through 'learning by doing' has been inspired by Dewey's reform pedagogy. Recent research has shown that reform pedagogy and drama in a modern sense was already used in girls' schools at the beginning of the twentieth century (Hägglund, 2001).

Extending storytelling into pantomimes and dramatised folk tales and books for children was introduced by Elsa Olenius, a librarian in Stockholm. During the period 1942–1961, she developed and organised 'Our Theatre', which comprised 14 municipal children's theatres in the Stockholm area. Here children could perform for each other. Many of these theatres still exist within the framework of the Stockholm School of the Arts. Olenius also started an education course for children's theatre leaders, the forerunner of contemporary education of drama pedagogues. In addition, she introduced creative dramatics at a girls' school in Stockholm and at several summer courses for teachers during the 1950s. The teachers who participated in these courses were those who later continued to develop drama in schools and influence curriculum planning (Lindvåg, 1988).

The democratic potential of drama, and its different perspectives in relation to four national curricula, have been analysed by Sternudd (2000). The value of drama pedagogy is generally connected to the *artistically oriented perspective*, i.e. supporting the development of dramatic creativity, language learning and bringing literature to life. The 1962 curriculum stipulates a *personal development perspective* for educational drama, i.e. understanding the relationships between individuals, groups and society, and of dynamic processes and decision-making in human interactions. In the 1980 curriculum, there is a strong support for the use of drama pedagogy as an additional perspective—*the holistic learning perspective*. Here dramatic imagination is used as a learning tool for attempting human problem-solving with universal significance.

The interest among teachers in drama methods connected to conflict handling has been influenced by different kinds of social needs in schools. Drama has been used in primary and secondary schools for preventive conflict work since the 1970s. Variations of forum theatre—focusing on the *critically liberating* perspective—can be said to be the drama method most widely used (see Chap. 3, Section "Theatre of the Oppressed"). Katrin Byréus (2010) has adapted Boal's method to suit work with Swedish teenagers, combining values clarification and forum theatre in what she terms Forum play. In the middle of the 1990s, gender research resulted in a focus on the need to create space for the silent girls. As a consequence of the normative problems in schools, a new subject—'life knowledge'—has been introduced; each school produces its own curriculum and may choose drama as an activating method within this new subject.

Most drama methods used to prevent conflicts in schools work on an indirect and generalised level, although some teachers have developed and used direct interventions. Lelkes (1996), starting with the aim of relieving conflicts through puppet theatre, tried out a creative conflict-solving method among students aged 9–12 years. Actual conflicts among the students were dramatised and acted out in front of a video camera. While looking at the film, the students raised ideas about how to solve the conflict. A small group of trained teachers use psychodramatic techniques in direct conflict handling. One of them, Monica Westblad-Dicks (2000), has described how such work may be carried out among young students in conflict with each other. A study of Peace Education in Grades 4–6 *Violence Prevention and Conflict Resolution* (Utas Carlsson, 1999) gives basic theoretical and practical knowledge for teachers in drama as well as for any teacher with interest in life knowledge.

Lennart Wiechel (1983) emphasises an interdisciplinary view of drama and has constantly advocated the use of drama as a multi-medial language in education. Drama in Sweden is looked upon as being a total integration of progressive pedagogy and dramatic art form, as a pedagogy of experience involving the whole human being in the learning process.

Swedish upper secondary school has been compulsory since 1994 and comprises a range of programs. The aesthetic program, including theatre, has proved to be popular among the students. Sweden has a reputation for good municipal Schools of the Arts that provide opportunities for interested children and youths to develop and enhance their cultural abilities. These schools always offer music and sometimes drama, theatre and dance as well.

In teacher education where drama courses are available, there is an increasing interest in Forum play and other drama methods that can help conflict handling in schools. Almost everyone involved in preschool, in preparatory work among six-year-olds, or in leisure-time activities has some kind of education in drama. Within ordinary teacher education programs, students of other age groups are given little education about or in drama.

Further education in drama for teachers can be obtained at several regional universities. The national teacher training program offers opportunities for future teachers to choose drama as a subject. Some Folk High Schools (a Scandinavian form of adult education) have offered a biannual program for Education of Drama Pedagogues since 1974. This program was the only avenue to becoming a drama specialist until 2016. A three-year education program for teachers in drama and theatre started at Stockholm University in 2016. Although the body of professional drama pedagogues and drama teachers is small, it has had a widespread and significant influence on drama activities in and outside schools in Sweden.

The use of drama in nursing education, by other health care professionals and among social workers and psychologists has increased due to research in the field.

Preliminary Student Survey

Basic Strategies for Handling Conflicts

As described in Chap. 1, the DRACON International Project has used the following primary research questions as a guide for all four DRACON teams:

- What are the most common types of conflicts among adolescents?
- How do they perceive their conflicts?
- How do they behave in typical conflict situations?

In order, therefore, to learn more about typical conflict situations among Swedish school children prior to designing specific drama exercises, the Swedish team carried out a first study in Grade 7 of the compulsory comprehensive school. Students were interviewed about how they understood conflicts and about typical conflicts they experienced at school, at home and in their leisure time. They were also asked how they usually tried to solve conflicts with schoolmates, teachers, parents and friends. On the basis of these interviews, we designed a questionnaire with open-ended questions as well as questions with fixed alternatives.

Aim

Our main aim in the survey study was to study general, basic ways of handling conflicts among Swedish students at the higher levels of comprehensive school. A subsidiary aim was also to study differences between boys and girls in both the structure of their strategies and their frequency of using these strategies. In a follow-up study, we used a causal model to test the relationships between teacher competence, school attitudes and self-esteem on the one hand (independent variables) and conflict-handling strategies on the other (dependent variables).

Method

Lantieri, Roderick and Ray (1990) have developed a conflict tree in order to show different ways of handling conflicts. Taking this model as a starting point, our purpose was to construct items on every branch of the tree, collect new data from a sample of students and through factor analysis try to get a better understanding of basic strategies for handling conflicts. This study was carried out in April 1998.

Students were asked to answer how they usually handled a conflict with classmates in school or with friends in their leisure time. We collected data from 13 schools and from 48 different classes. Over 1200 students answered the questionnaire, approximately 900 from Grade 8. The statements were presented in a Likert-survey form with the alternatives 'almost never', 'seldom', 'sometimes', 'often' and 'almost always'. At the same time another questionnaire was distributed to the same students, in which questions were asked about the teaching and learning situation at school and the students' school adjustment. This was done in order relate students' conflict-handling strategies to teacher competence, social relationships and school adjustment.

Factor analysis (principal component analysis) was carried out and on the basis of the outcome a second-order factor analysis was done. Finally, we carried out an alternative factor analysis using LISREL (Jöreskog & Sörbom, 1999) in order to deepen perspectives on some of the conflict-handling factors.

In October 1998, we carried out a new study. The most appropriate items from every factor in the previous study were kept and some new ones were added—61 statements in all. A study by Thomas and Kilmann (1975, 1977) inspired some new items. We collected data from 5 schools and from 30 different classes. A total of 674 students out of 721 were present the day data were collected; thus, only 6.5 per cent were absent, with few internal missing responses. Although only five schools were chosen, we consider this to be a fairly representative sample of Grade 8 students in Sweden. Should the results be similar to that of the previous study, this would be an indication that the results were reliable and that we would have a good understanding of Grade 8 students' self-assessed conflict-handling strategies.

Results—How Students Handle Conflicts

Analysis of the statements about conflict handling in the two studies showed very similar results. We identified three factors which all showed variations of aggressive behaviour: *physical aggression, psychological aggression*, and *displaced aggression*. These three factors could be labelled **confronting** alternatives. We were also able to identify three variations of **avoidance**: *wait/ignore/withdraw, hide/mask* and *postpone/avoid person*. Four **fronting** factors were found: *give up, win–win/co-operate/compromise, assistance seeking/third party* and *self-blame*. A second-order factor analysis showed these three components very clearly: confronting, avoidance and fronting (see Chap. 2, Section "The Components of Conflict" for detailed definitions of these terms).

In the second study, we used an improved questionnaire and thus the reliabilities of the different factors have also increased if the instrument is used to form scales.

In order to gain a better understanding of the relationships between the items in the questionnaire, LISREL analyses were carried out to test the measurement model in the three main factors. The analyses showed that the instrument could be reduced to 38 items and still maintain acceptable reliability when measuring the 10 factors (Fig. 6.1).

Under confronting behaviour we found, besides the general aggression factor, three specific factors as in the earlier test: *physical aggression, psychological aggression* and *displaced aggression*. The reliabilities were fairly high: 0.89, 0.72 and 0.78, respectively. If all items are used to measure the general confronting factor, Cronbach's alpha coefficient appears to be 0.86.

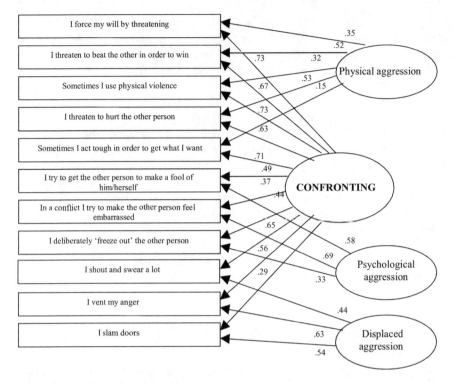

Fig. 6.1 *Confronting* measurement model (Chi-square = 44; d*f* = 32; *p* < 0.08; RMSEA = 0.030; GFI = 0.98)

Under the general avoidance factor, three specific factors could also be identified. The first specific factor is defined by the words *wait, ignore* and *withdraw* and consists of six items. The alpha turned out to be 0.81.

The second specific factor can be understood by the words *hide or mask*. In Study 2, hide and mask appeared as two different factors. Three items are found here with a scale reliability of 0.72 (Fig. 6.2).

The third specific factor is called *postpone or avoid person* and includes three items. The reliability analysis showed an alpha coefficient of only 0.60. If all items are put together into an avoidance scale, the alpha is 0.84.

The third main factor in how students handle conflicts is called Fronting. It is a way of acting, but not aggressively. Also here we found three specific factors. These three factors are called *give up* (alpha = 0.70), *assistance seeking/third party* (alpha = 0.72) and *self-blame* (alpha = 0.67). The fourth specific factor in the model in Fig. 6.3, *win–win/co-operate/compromise* (alpha = 0.88), did not turn up as a specific factor. Instead, items belonging to this domain define for the most part the general factor. If all the 15 items are summarised into a scale, the reliability coefficient (Cronbach's alpha) is 0.85.

Preliminary Student Survey

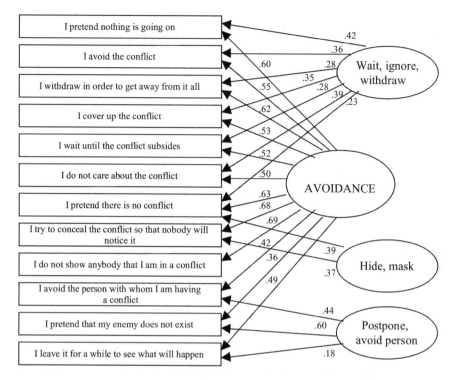

Fig. 6.2 *Avoiding* measurement model (chi-square = 68; df = 40; RMSEA = 0.032; GFI = 0.98)

Frequencies of Different Conflict-Handling Strategies

One of the aims was also to study differences between boys and girls in both the structure of their strategies and their frequency of using these strategies. No differences could be found regarding the structure of strategies. Some differences could be found, however, when frequency was studied.

There are three differences between boys and girls that are fairly large. A big difference becomes evident, as expected, concerning physical aggression and threats. Girls more seldom use this kind of strategy. As many as one-third of all girls say that they never use any of these kinds of aggression mentioned in the test items. Instead, girls more often use some kind of fronting behaviour. The difference is big on items measuring win–win/co-operative/compromising behaviour. Another difference worth observing is that of psychological aggression. Girls do not use this strategy as much as boys do.

All other differences are rather small. Within the DRACON project, we wanted to improve adolescents' strategies in conflict situations, try to further reduce the frequency of confronting behaviour and stimulate the use of win–win/compromising strategies and third-party solutions.

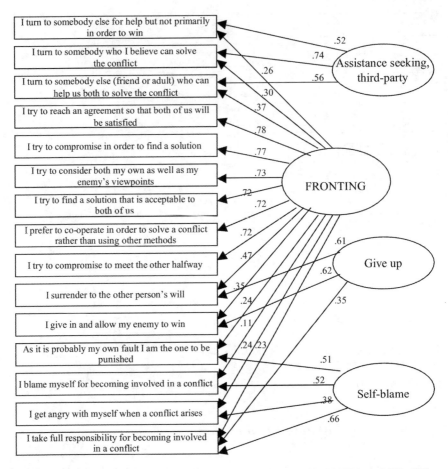

Fig. 6.3 Fronting measurement model (chi-square = 130; d*f* = 78; RMSEA = 0.032; GFI = 0.97)

In a follow-up study, we were interested in studying the relationships between teacher competence, school attitudes and self-esteem as determining factors in conflict-handling strategies. We were especially interested in studying the relationships between these three school factors on the one hand and the three styles of confronting and two styles of fronting behaviour on the other hand. Gender is also included as an independent factor. We summarised a number of indicators of teacher competence into seven subscales: (1) discipline and structured learning, (2) subject knowledge, (3) teaching skills, (4) social competence, (5) positive attitudes to students, (6) feedback and individualised teaching and (7) fairness. We measured attitudes to schooling using four indicators. There are clear causal relationships between teacher competence, school attitudes, self-esteem, gender and ways of handling conflicts.

The more positive students' attitudes to schooling and teacher competence are, the less likely they are to display aggressive behaviour. In the same way, highly rated teacher competence and positive self-esteem among students result in more compromising behaviour. Obviously, there is a negative relationship between confronting and fronting, and girls display less confronting behaviour. When they act aggressively, this takes the form of frustration. Girls are more willing to compromise. Boys display greater self-confidence. Both boys and girls with low self-esteem tend to act with frustration in conflict situations. The three factors of teacher competence, school attitudes and self-esteem are highly correlated.

Students' Basic Strategies for Handling Conflicts

In Swedish culture, conflict handling where violence is used to reach one's goals is regarded negatively. As avoidance does not solve a conflict, that is also regarded negatively. This evaluation of conflict handling is, however, culture related (Allwood & Friberg, 1997). Contrary to Swedish culture, in Malaysia avoidance is accepted as a proper way of handling conflicts. In Sweden, we prefer compromise-oriented strategies. However, avoidance is still quite frequently used.

Within the **fronting** domain, two of the specific factors, *give up* and *self-blame*, cannot be considered as adequate ways of handling conflicts, at least from a Swedish perspective. Swedish adolescents rarely use assistance seeking and third-party solutions. It may appear strange that self-blame shows up together with items measuring compromising behaviour. However, it is a way of acting in a conflict situation and bearing that in mind, it is understandable that the factor shows up in this context. Boys and girls have somewhat different preferences when they find themselves in a conflict. Boys display more aggressive behaviour while girls more often use compromising alternatives.

The consistency in the study's results indicates that the project team adequately covered the main ways of handling conflicts. The questionnaire we developed seems to be a very useful measuring instrument to study the frequency of adolescents' conflict-handling strategies. It is also useful as an evaluation instrument in experimental settings with programs aimed at improving adolescents' conflict-handling strategies and at developing third-party and other solutions involving compromise and negotiation. The follow-up study has subsequently shown that students' conflict-handling strategies are related to teacher competence, school attitudes and self-esteem (see Löfgren & Malm, 2007).

The above survey study is based on self-reported data, i.e. the students' answers in writing, not on observations of real conflict situations. We consider our results consistent enough to be reliable.

Developing a Classroom Program

Third-Party and Mediator Roles

The Swedish DRACON Project focused on third-party roles, in particular the role of the mediator. Our ultimate aim has been to find out whether or not Grade 8 students, with no previous training in drama or conflict handling, would be able to take on the role of peer mediators in real-life conflicts by applying the drama methods learnt during the program.

Constructing this type of program for the training of mediators takes time. It has to be developed through an evolutionary process whereby each new trial needs to be corrected in view of errors made in previous trials. We performed six such studies before a final program was developed.

Action research involves taking action to improve practice and systematically studying the effects of the action taken. In the practice setting, problems are described, possible solutions are identified and implemented, and then the process and outcomes of change are evaluated (Streubert & Carpenter, 1999). The goal is to generate practical knowledge relating directly to the problems specific to a setting. Practitioners are then able to learn about their practice in that setting and implement change in order to improve their practice.

For DRACON, each study consisted of a program integrating drama and conflict work in a comprehensive classroom process. The program aimed to accomplish the following pedagogical tasks in a logical sequence:

1. To teach drama literacy, i.e. getting the students involved in and familiar with the language and ways of drama
2. To use drama as a way of teaching conflict literacy, i.e. the basic concepts of conflict theory
3. To use drama and conflict literacy to provide the students with opportunities to learn constructive ways of conflict handling both as direct parties as well as third parties (enhancing of the conflict competence of students)
4. To use drama and conflict literacy specifically to learn peer mediation
5. Finally, to use peer teaching as a way of learning peer mediation.

In addition to developing and implementing a program, the aim was also to study the pedagogical process by using different kinds of measurements. We wanted to know how the students' involvement and understanding of the languages of drama and conflict developed during the whole drama process and if there were any long-term effects of the program both at the individual level and the level of the class itself. An important research question was to discern whether or not there were any critical moments in the pedagogical process at the group level. We were also interested in getting information about typical student conflicts and the ways these are handled by the students. Would the students themselves develop more constructive ways of handling conflicts simply by exploring a number of different strategies in conflict role-plays? Would the results of the classroom studies correspond to the findings of the survey study presented above?

It is important to realise that in our iterative approach with six research cycles everything evolved gradually, the program as well as our research questions and our measurement techniques. As the six cycles spanned a period of four years (1996–2000), the evolutionary process was also significantly affected by parallel processes in Malaysia and Australia.

The six studies that were aimed at the development of a class program constitute only the first phase (Phase I) of the action research study. That was followed by a second phase (Phase II) starting in 2001, in which efforts were made to implement the program in two schools. We wanted to know if the program worked well when made compulsory and taken over by the schools themselves. This phase required much more attention in regard to decision-making structures and selection of schools and classes. Under what conditions would it be possible to create a long-term commitment to the DRACON program in the school and would it work well under the new conditions (Table 6.1).

Table 6.1 Steps in developing and implementing the program

Study	Focus and content
Phase I. Developing a classroom program	
1	Designing and trying out a preliminary program (including forum theatre and self-confrontation)
2	Adding teaching of conflict literacy by lecturing
3	Developing conflict literacy by reflecting on the role-play
4	Adding peer mediation training
5	Studying if and how the program worked with teachers
6	Further developing the program with teachers and relating drama exercises more explicitly to conflict management
Phase II. Efforts to implement the program in schools	
7	First step in implementing the program at 'Linden'[a] School (one class)
8	First step in implementing the program at 'Birch' School (one class)
9	Second step in implementing the program with the teachers involved from Linden School and Birch School

[a]The names of the schools have been changed for anonymity

Phase I: Six Classroom Studies

The first phase in our study was to design a program for dealing with conflicts through drama work and to test if the program worked in a few school classes. This resulted, as has been mentioned, in six studies.

The first study was a single-day workshop with university students in 1996, supervised by five researchers within the field of conflict management, drama and education.

The next study (Study 2) was extended into a three-day program with Grade 8 students. This program was carried out in 1998, under the supervision of three researchers. Here the teaching of conflict literacy was introduced into the program.

Six months later, Study 3 was carried out at Linden School, in a town with a predominantly middle-class population. At this newly built school, the environment seemed positive and pleasant. The group consisted of volunteers from Grade 8, ten girls and two boys, some of whom had experience of drama.

Study 4 was conducted at the same school as in Study 3 (Linden), with five boys and four girls as volunteers. A presentation about the program had been given to the students two weeks prior to the study. The five-day workshop, with the weekend in between, made the process less stressful for the participants. The fifth day focused on the training of peer mediation.

For future development and use of the program, it was essential to involve adult participants (Study 5). The participants, mainly drama pedagogues and teachers, took part in the same program as the 8th Grade teenagers in Study 4. The main aim was to study how the program worked with teachers, as they would be responsible for managing the program if it became integrated in the school system. The program proved a great success—on a professional as well as personal level. However, our impression was that the students learned the content of the program even more quickly than the teachers. Teenagers tend to simplify the theories and grasp the underlying structure more easily. The program was applied a second time with other adult participants over a period of five (whole) days. Study 6 was carried out in the same way as Study 5, with only minor changes. The program showed itself to be applicable to both teenagers and adults.

The Classroom Program

The DRACON classroom program consists of the following stages:

1. Stage I—Building a positive working environment
2. Stage II—Learning the languages of drama and conflict
3. Stage III—Constructing and performing conflict role-plays
4. Stage IV—Interventions in role-plays (video-recorded)
5. Stage V—Self-confrontation and analysis of video-recordings
6. Stage VI—Role-playing peer mediation
7. Stage VII—Peer teaching (added in Phase II, Implementation of the program)
8. Stage VIII—Evaluation.

Developing a Classroom Program

The program starts by building a working environment and recreates this context every morning by different warming-up exercises (Stage I). Each day is similarly structured—starting by sitting on chairs in a circle so that everyone can see each other. The day ends in the same way by writing diaries and listening to each individual describing his/her experiences of the day. A verbal working contract concerning work principles has to be agreed upon early in the program. As personal conflict experiences are disclosed, the participants need to feel reassured that their conflicts will not be discussed outside the group.

As a starting point for learning conflict literacy (Stage II), the students, in groups of four or five, are asked to describe a conflict they have personally been involved in. When the conflicts are described, everyone in each group paints something related to what they remember about the conflicts of the others. These paintings are exhibited and used for analysing the kinds of roles different parties take in a conflict situation, as well as to ascertain the power balance in conflicts—i.e. symmetric or asymmetric conflicts. (These phrases and other specialised conflict terminology used in this section, including the ABC conflict model described below, are defined in detail in Chap. 2).

At the end of the first day the students, in groups of four or five, plan and act out conflict situations concerning school, family, leisure time or other kinds of conflicts. They are asked to change names and not to play themselves in order to distance themselves from real life. The material provided by the improvisations is used with the aim of enhancing their understanding of conflicts (Stage III).

On the second day, one painting from each group is chosen and analysed in detail, so that different levels of conflict can be revealed. The ABC theory is introduced. The students enact several short role-plays in pairs about typical conflicts that teenagers experience to focus on how conflicts escalate. From the basic instinctive reactions of fight, freeze and flee (FFF), they gain additional perspectives by relating the work to five different conflict-handling styles symbolised by five animals: lion, camel, tortoise, fox and owl. A sequence of role-plays exemplifying the different conflict styles are acted out and discussed.

During the third day, the concept of third party is introduced by a non-verbal 'Sculptures' exercise in groups of three. A modified form of forum theatre is introduced. Instead of focusing on the oppressed person in the play, third-party interventions are applied. Groups of four or five students construct a role-play where the conflict escalates from contradictions about the content (C) via negative attitude (A) towards negative behaviour (B), stopping when the situation is at its worst. The role-play is rehearsed and performed in front of the class.

On the fourth day, the experiment with third-party interventions starts and each intervention is video-recorded (Stage IV). The rules for the interventions are that everyone in the audience can stop the play at any time, take the role of one of the subsidiary actors or outsiders, or of an invented but possible character (e.g. a neighbour) and act in the conflict in order to de-escalate it.

The other parties in the play react or respond in the way they believe the character they are playing would have done in real life. As long as the students have ideas about third-party interventions, they are encouraged to act them out and each intervention is video-recorded.

The next step is the analysis of all the interventions. By examining one intervention at a time, a kind of self-confrontation becomes apparent to the students (Stage V). The aim of self-confrontation is to enable the students to understand, through reference to their own experiences, what kinds of third-party intervention promote a win–win solution. As a problem-solving conflict style does not come easily to teenagers, many interventions are necessary before the students realise that the third party needs to be neutral and not allied to one of the principal actors, provided the conflict is a symmetric one.

The fifth day is devoted to mediation (Stage VI). It starts with exercises about status in relationships, effects of body language and training in active listening. These are followed by two dramatic situations played by the researchers about two neighbours in a dispute about a garage building. In groups of three, the students try out a mediation session, taking on the parts of the two neighbours and a neutral mediator. Lose–win, win–lose and win–win solutions are discussed.

The last session is devoted to different forms of evaluation such as diaries and paintings. Proper closure of the program is important (Stage VIII).

As described earlier, we developed the final program during the six studies carried out in 1996–2000. Stage VII peer teaching was inspired by the Brisbane team and added in Phase II; it was not tried in Phase I.

The program was expanded from one day to five days. In Phase II, we wanted to implement the program in schools during a whole-school term: it therefore seemed suitable to divide the program into 12 sessions with each session lasting for 100 min.

Analysis and Discussion

During Phase I, video-recordings of role performances turned out to be the major source of data for drawing conclusions about the nature of teenager's conflict handling, and diaries the major source for analysing students' involvement in the process.

Analysis of Diaries

The aim of using diaries was to describe how 'drama in training' was individually experienced by students in Grade 8. The analysis of data was based on student diaries written during their participation in the drama program. Ten minutes were set aside for diary writing, and the diaries were collected after each day's training session. All the student diaries were carefully documented in Studies 2, 3 and 4.

Diary instructions were used to encourage the students to write about their thoughts, reactions, feelings and experiences from the drama experiences throughout the day. Our reasoning was based upon positive experiences from a previous study in nursing education, as well as our desire for an openness that would capture the participants' direct, spontaneous and immediate experiences. In the DRACON project, the motivation to use diaries was to get the students to work through different experiences, develop a reflective standpoint, develop their ability to document events and also learn to share the data material with others.

Three different categories of content emerged: *positive expression, negative expression* and *reflection*. Within these categories, subcategories were constructed that represented qualitatively different ways of experiencing the drama program. The contents of the diaries indicated the ways in which the researchers succeeded in building up a functioning classroom context. By reading the diaries after each drama session, the drama pedagogue was given important information, knowledge and indications as to how the students had experienced the content. This information was used in planning for the next session. Sometimes students disclosed feelings and thoughts that were not evident during the drama session. This possibly gave the teacher a greater understanding of a specific student's motives and behaviour; it might also have given the teacher ideas of how to alter some of the content of the program. Some students wrote quite personal thoughts as well as drawing pictures and sending greetings to the teacher. Generally, girls wrote more in their diaries than boys.

Analysis of the diaries from Study 4 indicated that it is possible to integrate the languages of drama and conflict and that co-operation between the researchers from drama and those from conflict handling is a requisite for this.

Based on the diary analysis from the three studies, the pedagogical implications can be described as follows:

- Most students enjoyed the warm-up exercises, the games, constructing the plays, theatre, video-recordings and performance, but they found conflict theory difficult, sometimes boring, of less interest and therefore harder to concentrate on.
- The students preferred working in small groups and choosing their own participants. Working within friendship groups gave them more courage.
- Three days was a very short period for the process; some students never found time to understand the program fully. Five (half) days including a weekend break proved better for developing the process satisfactorily.

Analysis of Video-Recordings

At that point of Phase I, video-recordings constituted our main source of data. As indicated above, they gave us a lot of information about the spontaneous conflict behaviour of Grade 8 students as well as whether or not the students learned something from participation in the drama program. The video-recordings were able to illuminate questions such as:

- What are the typical parties in students' conflicts?
- What are the conflicts about?
- How do they escalate?

- What are the most common conflict-handling strategies?
- Do students learn more constructive ways of handling conflicts by trying different types of interventions in conflict role-plays?

We found drama to be an excellent method of eliciting information about teenager's conflicts. When a safe space had been created, the students were more than willing to report on their conflicts in a drama context and to display properties of the conflicts in role-plays. However, we had strong reasons to believe that they were still censoring some of their most sensitive conflicts. Despite this they were willing to disclose information about fairly serious conflicts, for instance violent conflicts between teachers and students, provided the class teacher was not present in the room.

Two conflict-handling styles were dominant: the *lion*, which is concerned only with reaching its own goals in a conflict situation, and the *turtle*, which avoids conflict. The styles of the *camel* (adapting to the other), the *fox* (compromising) and the *owl* (searching for win–win solutions) were not as common. Even those who chose and behaved like camels would have liked to be lions! This also seemed to hold for some girls: 'We have to fight in order to be respected!'

The socially favoured style of conflict handling in Sweden, as we have mentioned earlier, is compromise, which is generally believed to be an ideal way of handling conflicts among adults. Grade 8 students seem to be at a critical turning point in their lives. They are at the point of discovering the limits of an egocentric approach in social relations, focusing mainly on their own interests, which leads to power struggles in conflicts. At this point, a tremendous increase in social competence is possible. We had discovered that the DRACON program could speed up this process by letting the students experiment with the lion style, playing the lion against all the other styles and studying the outcomes.

To the extent that the role-plays chosen by the students reflected real-life conflicts, the video-recordings showed that anger, violence and name-calling were common in adolescent conflicts. The conflicts were of two kinds: symmetric and asymmetric. In an asymmetric conflict, there is a power imbalance between the top dog and the underdog, e.g. teacher–student or parent–child relationships.

Phase I Conclusions

In Phase I, our intentions were to develop a well-functioning program in order to increase teenagers' capacities for handling conflicts, to examine what kinds of conflicts they usually have and whether or not drama can be used in order to help them understand the nature of conflicts.

In our studies, we observed that this age group rarely experienced theoretical studies as fun. However, the DRACON classroom process engaged the students in direct drama work as well as in reflections about conflicts presented through drama. The drama work was fun, and it permitted learning by having fun. In one week, an

Developing a Classroom Program

ordinary class was able to reach such a high level of understanding of the nature of conflicts that some students were able to perform well as peer mediators in conflict role-plays. We found the involvement of the students usually increased over time. Also, students who had low status in the class might turn out to be good at drama. When that happened, drama offered them the unexpected opportunity to become more visible in the class and more appreciated by their classmates.

Another relevant discovery was finding out whether or not drama can be used as a method of learning skills that students can apply to real-life conflicts. If a student participated in the DRACON program, would it change the way he/she dealt with his/her own conflicts after the program? Would it transform the student's class or even the school?

The conclusions we drew and lessons we learned from Phase I can be summarised as follows:

- During the first phase (Studies 1–6), we developed and tested a step-by-step program, aimed at teaching teenagers about conflicts and conflict handling through the use of drama. When critical moments in the classroom process became evident, we made changes in the content or in the order of exercises.
- The students became increasingly satisfied as the different studies progressed. The program was elaborated until mediation was concluded in Study 4. The post-interview (Study 4) indicated that the students expressed a very positive picture of the drama experience. When asked to tell about their experiences, they exclusively mentioned positive ones. Their bodily expressions during the interview supported this, as they all looked bright and alert when talking about the drama meetings. It is worth noting that the students were free to choose between participating in Studies 3 and 4 or doing ordinary schoolwork. That this choice was voluntary seems to have influenced the positive outcome.
- We were able to register great congruence between the kinds of conflicts the teenagers chose to dramatise and those frequently represented in the survey study.
- The students succeeded in becoming familiar with the drama language, enhancing their interest in dealing with different ways of de-escalating conflicts. They learnt from their own experimentation with interventions in conflict plays.
- The students showed an increasing understanding of conflicts and a growing awareness of constructive conflict handling and peer mediation. To a limited degree, it was possible to prove long-term effects on an individual level. This was not possible on the group level, due to lack of relevant measurements and the small number of students participating in the voluntary program.
- The program proved to be advanced enough to succeed in teaching teachers and drama pedagogues about conflict handling in a satisfactory way.

Phase II: Implementing the Program in Two Schools

The possibility of testing and implementing the program in schools appeared at the beginning of 2002 (Phase II of the action research study, see Table 6.2). Two schools were chosen: Linden School (Study 7), the school used in the Phase I study, and Birch School (Study 8). Study 9 involved running the program with teachers at these schools. The aims of Phase II were:

- To make the program a whole-class approach spread over a whole-school term (compulsory attendance of students).
- To add peer teaching to the program.
- To evaluate the effects of the program by pre- and post-testing on an individual, class and school level (questionnaires, interviews, sociometric data, etc.).
- To identify some conditions for successful implementation of the program in schools (by comparison and reference to how implementation was carried out in the two fairly different schools in our study).
- To implement the program in a whole school, making the school responsible for the management of the DRACON process after introduction of the program in one class.

Table 6.2 Description of the program, sessions 1–12

DRACON session	Content	Stage
1	Getting to know one another. Verbal contract Painting a conflict Different parties in a conflict	I, II
2	ABC model—escalation (of conflict) and de-escalation symmetric and asymmetric conflicts	I, II
3	Continuing the ABC model. FFF-theory Role-plays in couples related to Basic Strategies for Handling Conflicts	I, II
4	Conflict styles: lion, turtle, camel, fox and owl	I, II
5	Third-party sculptures Role-plays: escalated conflicts—videotaped	I, II, III
6	Interventions in the conflicts—videotaped	I, II, IV
7	Analysis of video-recorded interventions in conflicts	I, II, V
8	Analysis of four different third parties. Preparation for mediation	I, II, V
9	Training in mediation in a fictional conflict	I, II, VI
10	Preparation for peer teaching in Grade 7	I, II, VII
11	Peer teaching in Grade 7	I, II, VII
12	Evaluation—closure	I, II, VIII

Developing a Classroom Program 143

It should be emphasised that the program differs from the earlier ones (Phase I) in several important ways. First, it was spread over three months during a school term. Second, peer teaching was included at the end of the program. Third and most important, participation was intended to be compulsory for all the students in the selected class.

The program was re-organised to be taught during 12 sessions of 100 min, including one session to prepare and one to implement peer teaching. As mentioned earlier, the program consists of eight (VIII) stages. As peer teaching in Brisbane, implemented from Cycle 2 of that project onwards (see Chap. 8), had proved so successful, it was added in Phase II as an additional tool.

In the earlier studies (Phase I), students had been recruited more or less on a self-selected base. Would the positive results obtained during conditions of voluntary participation be maintained during conditions of compulsory participation? The reader is reminded that we were here working with students who had little or no previous training in drama and conflict handling.

The Two Chosen Schools

Linden School seemed at first to be a fairly successful school with a good working climate. We chose this school due to our previous positive experience in Phase I; the headmaster, who had some training in drama, supported the DRACON program strongly. The school was situated in a town with a predominantly middle-class population.

In a northern province of Sweden, twenty-six schools were invited to take part in the project. Only two schools were seriously interested and willing to accept the conditions for participation. Birch School was chosen as it included Swedish students and students from recent immigrant families. The two class teachers and the headmaster strongly supported the DRACON project. The population of the catchment area was predominantly working class. We expected the implementation of the program at Birch School to be more difficult than at Linden School (Table 6.3).

Table 6.3 Participants involved in Phase II

Study school		Year	Time	Participants	Female/male
7	Linden	2002	12 × 100 min	Grade 8 stud.	9/15
8	Birch	2002	12 × 80 min	Grade 8 stud.	4/11
9	Linden + Birch	2002	5 days	Teachers	11/5

Phase II Analysis and Discussion

We conjectured that it would be more valuable for the students to get the DRACON program spread over most of a term rather than compressing it as in the earlier phase. Extension in time would give many natural opportunities to reiterate the conflict theory. On the other hand, several weeks without DRACON lessons might disturb the continuity of the program and affect the teaching and learning situation negatively. The Swedish program could effectively be carried out during 12 sessions of 100 min as planned. Smaller changes due to the situation in the class might be necessary, for example the need to use different kinds of games.

During the first three sessions at Birch School, the students had much to learn about the rules for the DRACON work. Although they were amiably disposed, there was a lot of physical restlessness in the classroom, which gave rise to different kinds of challenges expressed by some of the boys (both immigrants and Swedish-born). It took more time here than at Linden School to clarify the rules (listen to each other and speak one at a time) and, because participation was compulsory, it took longer to establish the class as a safe space than in the voluntary groups of students in our earlier studies.

At Linden School, the headmaster expressed a strong commitment to the DRACON project and decided which of the two Grade 8 classes would participate. Unfortunately, because of this, the class teacher and the students expressed that they were forced into the project. In spite of several meetings with parents and teachers, a negative attitude and several logistical problems (with the schedule and in the classroom) persisted. These problems were not solved until participation in DRACON became voluntary.

However, most of the students in all our studies enjoyed planning and performing conflict plays, especially in front of the camera. With one or two exceptions, the students at Birch School appreciated the lessons as fun. The students at Linden School valued the program more from a utilitarian point of view than Birch School.

Adding Peer Teaching

The peer teaching session appeared to be a successful way of finishing the program in both classes. The students had to recapitulate the content of the whole program before they could choose what they wanted to teach the Grade 7 students. This challenge stimulated them while they were planning and carrying out their program of peer teaching. They freely chose mediation and thereby were able to reinforce their own learning about mediation via peer teaching. One student at Linden School was acting like a trained teacher while leading the peer teaching. In a way that amazed the researchers, while teaching his Grade 7 peers he used dialogue, demonstrations, drama activities and examples of conflicts between himself and his siblings. At Birch School, one girl and one boy particularly surprised the class teachers by assuming the responsibility for leadership.

Third-Party Interventions

One of the aims of the Swedish DRACON program was to focus on students as third parties in conflict situations, as a starting point for learning about the role of the mediator. One of our hypotheses was that as teenagers are normally self-centred, they have limited possibilities of seeing themselves as helping third parties in conflicts. By experiencing new role behaviour in conflict plays, ideas about how to handle conflicts in real life may be evoked. Another hypothesis was that students learn about conflicts more easily when they study conflicts from the safe distance that third-party roles provide. A third hypothesis was that increased civil courage might develop parallel to a growing understanding of the importance of impartial third party interventions.

At Linden School, the students constructed four conflict plays with several interventions. For example, two girls verbally abused each other, and the second intervention was able to demonstrate a win–win solution. Another play showed a conflict between a teacher and a student in the classroom. In the third play, boys from Grades 8 and 9 were standing in a lunch queue. A few of the older and bigger boys started pushing forward in the queue. The first intervention showed up who supported whom, and led to more physical fights with the older boys. Then several authority figures were tried, a teacher and finally impartial interventions. The fourth and last play was about girls betraying and changing friends. After several interventions, a boy made a successful intervention as an impartial friend.

At Birch School, the students made a total of 10 interventions in three conflict plays. The most common type of intervention was as authorities (2) or as powerful allies to one of the parties (3). A couple of interventions were made as supporting peers or a teacher trying to stop the conflict before it erupted (2); one demonstrated a totally surprising solution, and two students made impartial interventions. For example, in a fictional conflict between two Palestinians in an aggressive dispute with a Jewish person, the last intervention was made by one of the immigrant boys. He clearly demonstrated impartial mediation by separating the parties and questioning them one at a time. This intervention was an example of standard mediation procedure and may be looked upon as an example of growing awareness.

In all the nine studies, there are examples of participants making non-authoritarian impartial interventions. After several attempts at third-party interventions as an authority figure (teacher, headmaster, etc.), as supporter or as ally, the students started to understand the dynamics of third-party interventions and experienced the fact that impartial mediation often resulted in win–win solutions. We want to emphasise that this was a crucial part of the students' learning process. They had themselves discovered the possibility and importance of mediating in conflict handling in order to come closer to a win–win solution.

These patterns of impartial interventions appearing after several attempts by the students were clearly evident in both schools and had also been observed in our earlier studies.

What Students Remembered 6 Months Later

After about six months, project members not actively involved in the program conducted follow-up interviews with the students. The interviews consisted of 12 open-ended questions, thus providing room for discussion. The students at Birch School (15) and Linden School (9) were asked to recount what they remembered about the lessons they had participated in, whether they had learnt anything new and if they had been able to utilise these experiences afterwards. They were also asked about specific content matter in the lessons and what their reactions to these had been.

Most of the students at Birch School remembered quite a lot from the DRACON lessons, even though they did not always remember why they had done certain exercises. Some said they had got new ideas and mentioned that after the project they thought more before they reacted.

Although most of the students experienced the sequences of exercises as enjoyable, they were not very interested in theoretical explanations. Most of them had not noticed any new changes in the way in which the class functioned now compared to before the DRACON program. However, a few said that things were calmer now and that one could speak out more about problems that arose.

They gave many examples of what they had enjoyed during the lessons. Peer teaching, although at times difficult, was mentioned by most of the students as the aspect they had enjoyed the most. Other examples of what they had experienced as difficult were performing in front of others and unruliness in the class.

At the end of the interview at Birch School, each student was asked whether he/she had anything to add. Those who did were positive.

> I've been able to use it. It's somewhere in my brain and one uses it, although one isn't really aware of it. I used to be really nasty before. (Student D)

At Linden School, the interviews were conducted with the nine students who completed the program. Analysis of the interviews indicated that seven out of the nine students had an astonishingly good comprehension of the cognitive aspects of the program. They remembered the conflict theories that had been presented, and three of them could describe them in detail. They showed a good understanding of mediation and five reflected on conflict styles and what kind of animal style they themselves mostly used. Four of the students were able to discuss in a more complex way which kinds of conflict might be difficult to manage.

The students specifically mentioned mediation between neighbours as fun, and also peer teaching. Two girls expressed themselves fairly positively, and one boy was extremely positive about the cognitive content as well as the drama method. One student was able to explain in detail how he had been able to use this new knowledge when mediating between a younger brother and sister.

Interesting differences in the outcome were evident between the two schools. In spite of all the problems at Linden School, the interviews clarified that the students who voluntarily chose to participate in the project gained a good cognitive understanding of all the aspects of conflict management they had studied during the project. At Birch School, where the program ran smoothly, the cognitive outcomes were more

Developing a Classroom Program

uncertain. The difference might to some degree be explained by the social and intellectual differences between the two classes. The students at Linden School were motivated towards theoretical studies, while the students at Birch School worked hard to pass exams in order to be accepted for upper secondary programs. The outcome at Birch School connected more easily to social and emotional development than to cognitive. The fact that students tried to solve conflicts by talking instead of fighting (Study 8) indicated a kind of social learning that influenced their conflict handling.

Training the Teachers

In addition to the eight studies, the program was introduced to the teachers for their training. We found that it took twice as long to go through the whole process with the teachers as it had with the Grade 8 students. Obviously, adults needed more time for discussing conflicts, conflict theories and role-playing. Some of the teachers had difficulties with deroling and with distancing themselves from real-life situations. Feelings of anxiety were expressed when conflicts were dramatised. One year after the teachers from Birch School participated in the DRACON program, they had not started to implement the program in a Grade 8 class as had been agreed to. Several of the teachers wished that their training had preceded the training of the class.

Phase II Conclusions

The first two aims of Phase II were fulfilled: making the program a whole class approach spread over a 3- to 4-month period with compulsory attendance of students. Adding peer teaching to the program turned out to be a success. Our ambition to evaluate the effects of the program by pre- and post-testing gave useful information only to a limited extent, due to the relatively small sample. The data-gathering tools used in Phases I and II (classroom observations, diaries, pictures, videos and interviews) still appeared to be entirely adequate.

Our aim of implementing the program in a whole school and making the school responsible for the continuing management of the DRACON process after the introduction of the program in one class turned out to be the most problematic part. At Linden School, we had to finish the project due to organisational problems. At Birch School, one of the teachers trained in the DRACON program gave an introduction to a group of interested students in Grade 8 one year after the original project. That same class was invited to participate in a rehearsal of the program during the summer vacation. Glimpses of the program were used for a video which was added to the Swedish handbook about DRACON in school (see Chap. 9, Section "Persistence: What Happened In The Dracon Schools?").

We concluded that teachers needed to understand and apply the theoretical as well as the practical aspects of the DRACON exercises. It would be a good idea to train the teachers before implementing the program and to involve the class teachers from the outset.

The program seemed too advanced to be fully comprehended during one single week by teachers with no education in either educational drama or conflict theories. Finding ways of implementing the DRACON program in a whole-school context still remained to be done. In order to do this, we identified that several conditions were needed, the most important of which were:

- Support from the whole school, headmaster and school staff
- A shared interest in DRACON among teachers, students and parents
- A decision from the school board as to whether or not the program should be compulsory or voluntary
- No competition between the program (12 sessions of 100 min) and other subjects
- A written agreement about the conditions for implementing the project
- Training of the teachers prior to the start of the program in the class and continual guidance of teachers during the implementation of the program.

Overall Conclusions

At the beginning of this chapter, we stated our aims and formulated some overriding questions. Here follows a brief summary of our findings and what we accomplished.

Our empirical research started by studying whether there were some general basic strategies of conflict handling among Swedish teenagers. Although our data were based on students' answers to questionnaires and not on direct observations of real conflict situations, we were and remain convinced that we did capture some typical ways of handling conflicts. It is possible that these strategies are not limited to the age groups we studied, but are valid for both younger children and adults. We were also able to show some substantial and interesting relationships between teacher competence, school attitudes, self-esteem, gender and ways of handling conflicts.

Our intention was to develop a program that combined conflict theory with drama, and to develop learning aids for implementation in schools and classes. In turn, successful implementation necessitates the need to further educate teachers to carry on this work. It was especially significant to the project to develop third-party intervention and to find out whether or not Grade 8 students, with no previous training in drama or conflict handling, would be able to take on the role of peer mediators in real-life conflicts by applying the drama methods learnt during the program.

Six stages were developed over four years and carried out before the final program was completed. The final program was then implemented in two schools and evaluated. Analyses from diaries, video-recordings and post-program interviews showed that the program has had many positive effects. The students became increasingly satisfied as the program progressed and was continually improved. They succeeded in becoming familiar with the drama language, enhancing their interest in dealing with different ways of de-escalating conflicts. Obviously, they learnt from their own experimentation with interventions in conflict plays. Moreover, the students showed an increasing understanding of conflicts and a growing awareness of constructive conflict handling and peer mediation. Adding peer teaching to the program turned out to be a success. In other words, we are satisfied with the final program, its applicability and its significance for education in our schools.

Our experiences since DRACON from weekly courses with teachers are also positive. The teachers have been very enthusiastic and have taken part with great pleasure and delight. However, it is doubtful whether or not teachers, after a course such as this, are sufficiently prepared for leading drama activities in their classes. The DRACON program can perhaps be considered too advanced to be comprehended during one single week by teachers with education in neither educational drama nor conflict theories. Hopefully, a program for further teacher education can be designed in order to stimulate teachers to use drama in conflict-handling courses in schools in the future.

Implementation of the DRACON program in schools has proved difficult due to several organisational factors. Careful planning and preparation are necessary in order to maximise the effects of the program. A genuine commitment and sense of responsibility from school leaders and teachers are essential, as are positive attitudes from parents and students.

As we were interested in mapping students' learning processes as well as evaluating the program as a whole, we developed different kinds of measuring instruments, such as questionnaires, interviews, diaries and video-recordings. The measurement instruments we developed in our studies can be useful for future research related to conflict-handling programs in schools.

What the DRACON team in Sweden has accomplished so far can be summarised as follows:

- Mapping the conflicts and conflict-handling styles of teenagers in Sweden
- Integrating conflict theories, at what is an advanced level for teenagers, with drama pedagogy within an educational program
- Creating a step-by-step program with a specific focus on third-party roles and mediation
- Demonstrating that teenagers can gain new knowledge about conflict handling by participating in the DRACON program
- Supplying adult participants with new knowledge about drama in education and conflict handling with the help of the DRACON program.

All photographs: Lukas Eisenhauer

Sweden 1: Starting the Process—In a 'drama circle', the teacher introduces the procedures

Sweden 2: Painting a conflict to share with the other students

Overall Conclusions

Sweden 3: 'Third Party Sculptures'—protagonist and antagonist in action

Sweden 4: 'Third Party Sculptures'—two mediators in action with protagonist and antagonist

Sweden 5: 'Third Party Sculptures'—mediating is difficult!

Sweden 6: 'Third Party Sculptures'—The mediator practises on a teenage-mother conflict, with interested audience

Overall Conclusions

Sweden 7: 'Third Party Sculptures'—the antagonists respond, with concentrated onlookers

Sweden 8: Peer teaching—A Year 8 student explains the ABC theory model to Year 7 peers

References

Allwood, J., & Friberg, M. (1997). *Culturally conditioned models of conflict resolution: A comparative analysis of Malaysia and Sweden*. Göteborg: Padrigu.
Byréus, K. (2010). *Du har huvudrollen i ditt liv. Om forumspel som pedagogisk metod för frigörelse och förändring [You have the leading role in your life. Forum play as an educational method for liberation and change]*. Stockholm: Utbildningsförlaget Liber.
Daun, Å. (1989). *Svensk mentalitet: ett jämförande perspektiv [Swedish mentality: A comparative perspective]*. Stockholm: Rabén & Sjögren.
Eriksson, B., Lindberg, O., Flygare, E., & Daneback, K. (2002). *Skolan en arena för mobbning [The school—An arena for bullying]*. Stockholm: Skolverket.
Hofstede, G. (1997). *Cultures and organizations: Software of the mind*. New York: MacGraw-Hill.
Hägglund, K. (2001). *Ester Boman, Tyringe Helpension och teatern. Drama på en reformpedagogisk flickskola 1909–1936 [Ester boman and theatre at the tyringe helpension. Drama at a progressive education girls' school 1909–1936]* (Studies in Educational Sciences 47). Stockholm: HLS Förlag.
Jöreskog, K-G., & Sörbom, D. (1999). *LISREL 8.30*. Lincolnwood, IL: Scientific Software International.
Key, E. (1996). *Barnets århundrade [The century of the child]*. Stockholm: Informationsförlaget.
Lantieri, L., Roderick, T., & Ray, P. (1990). *Resolving conflict creatively: A draft teaching guide for alternative high schools*. New York: Educators for Social Responsibility Metropolitan Area.

References

Lelkes, E. (1996). *Dare to ask. Dare to listen. A book about creative problem solving.* Täby: Leva Konsult, Eva Lelkes.

Lindvåg, A. (1988). *Elsa Olenius och Vår Teater [Elsa Olenius and our theatre].* Stockholm: Rabén & Sjögren.

Löfgren, H., & Malm, B. (Eds.). (2007). *DRACON international: Bridging the fields of drama and conflict management. Empowering students to handle conflicts through school-based programmes.* Malmö: University of Malmö. http://dspace.mah.se/bitstream/2043/5975/1/drac06nov.pdf.

OECD. (2015). *PISA report Results* (Volume III Chapter 7). Students' Well-Being. http://www.oecd.org/edu/pisa-2015-results-volume-iii-9789264273856-en.htm.

Skolverket. (2002). *Relationer i skolan—en utvecklande eller destruktiv kraft [Relations in school—A developing or destructive power].* Stockholm: Skolverket.

Sternudd, M. M. F. (2000). *Dramapedagogik som demokratisk fostran? Fyra dramapedagogiska perspektiv—dramapedagogik i fyra läroplaner [Educational drama as a means of fostering democratic values? four perspectives of educational drama in four curricula]* (Uppsala Studies in Education 88). Uppsala: Acta Universitatis Uppsalaiensis.

Streubert, H., & Carpenter, D. (Eds.). (1999). *Qualitative research in nursing: Advancing the humanistic imperative* (2nd ed.). Philadephia: Lippincott.

Thomas, K. W., & Kilmann, R. H. (1975). Interpersonal conflict handling behaviour as reflections of Jungian personality dimensions. *Psychological Reports, 37,* 971–980.

Thomas, K. W., & Kilmann, R. H. (1977). Developing a forced-choice measure of conflict-handling behaviour: The "MODE" instrument. *Educational and Psychological Measurement, 37,* 309–325.

Utas Carlsson, K. (1999). Violence prevention and conflict resolution. *A study of peace education in grades 4–6.* (Studia Psychologica et Pædagogica, 144). Malmö: School of Education, Department of Educational and Psychological Research.

Westblad-Dicks, M. (2000). *Hantera livet i skolan [To Handle Life in School].* Göteborg: Gothia.

Wiechel, L. (1983). *Pedagogiskt drama. En väg till social kunskapsbildning [Drama in Education. A Way of Gaining Social Knowledge].* Lund: Natur och Kultur.

Chapter 7
South Australia—Adolescent Conflicts and Educational Drama

Secondary Schooling in Australia

The largest providers of secondary education in Australia are the State governments, which operate a fairly centralised and unified system of free schools in each state, funded partly on a state and partly on a federal basis. In some States all state schools are co-educational; others provide a mix of co-educational and single-sex schools.

There are a number of separate educational management systems in each State. The 'private' educational sector is comprised of a series of smaller education systems. Some schools, including many of the most prestigious and 'academic' schools, are independent and fee-paying, though they are also subsidised by federal funds. The largest of several Christian church-based systems is the Catholic education system. The Anglican and Uniting Churches, along with many of the growing band of other churches, also operate a range of schools, many of them long established. All of these charge varying fees according to need and are also subsidised by the federal government. All of them prepare students for the Senior (Year 12) examinations run by independent boards of senior school studies in each State. Except for the most extreme Christian sects, all also take a full part in developing and teaching to the various States' Years 1–10 Curriculum.

In Australia, schooling is compulsory from Year 1 (6 years old) to Year 10 (15 years old). Some States provide a preparatory year (5 years old) and all States have well-developed preschool programs. Years 11 and 12 constitute the senior level, after which students can progress to a university or other forms of further education.

The Australian Cultural Context

There have been numerous failed attempts to define an Australian national identity. Australia is a continent comprised of multiple identities. It is one of the most multicultural countries in the world with diverse cultural values, varying from State to State, from city to city, suburb to suburb, from rural to urban areas and from indigenous to non-indigenous populations. Australia has been a pluralist society since European colonisation. It has significant cultural diversity, with differences based on class, religious heritage and gender as well as ethnic origin. Ethnic groups include the original Aboriginal and Torres Strait Islander peoples, the mainly Anglo-Celtic colonisers, Chinese who migrated to Australia in the 1800s during the gold rush, Germans who migrated in the nineteenth century and the many other ethnic groups which have arrived in Australia since the post-Second World War period.

The indigenous people in Australia—Aborigines and Torres Strait Islanders—in the main distinguish themselves from other Australians and comprise many different language groups. They are linked together by a sense of belonging to a particular locality and to extended family. On all indicators, indigenous people emerge as the most disadvantaged group in Australia, in part because of the history of colonisation. Aboriginal self-determination and the strengthening of Aboriginal identity, family and kinship are seen to be central to the survival of the Aboriginal culture.

Postmodernist thinking would see attempts to define or categorise an overall Australian cultural identity or context for this study as futile and artificial. However, in the main the dominant discourses reflected in the States' laws and policies are liberal, egalitarian, male, white, 'Western' or Anglo-Celtic, and middle class, with capitalism and economic rationalism dominating the State and Commonwealth Governments' economic agendas.

There is considerable diversity among the Government-funded State education systems in Australia, and also diversity between and within each school in each State, for example between the wealthy independent schools and the poorer State schools, or between the Catholic, Independent and State schools in different localities.

Since Federation in 1901, there have been six States in Australia and two Territories. South Australia was the only State in Australia to have been settled in the 1800s by 'free settlers' (rather than convicts), in the main from England, Ireland, Scotland and Cornwall. From the beginning of European colonisation, South Australia has enjoyed a national reputation for being 'liberal' and 'progressive' in many fields, including education and the arts.

Schools and Drama in South Australia

In Australia from the 1970s onwards, the arts became more and more a focus in national life, particularly in education. However, the pendulum of support for the arts has swung from one extreme to another as the years have gone by.

South Australia has been at the forefront of the development of the arts, especially of youth arts, in Australia. The 'Dunstan Decade' (named after the arts-loving State Premier of the 1970s) gave a particular focus to the arts and education in this State. Some of Don Dunstan's initiatives included the biennial Adelaide Festival, the complex of buildings comprising the Festival Centre, and the presence of the biennial *Come Out!* Festival for children, which has been recognised internationally as an example of best practice. At the time of our study it was recognised that the arts were of vital importance, particularly for the young, as vehicles not only for creativity, cultural and personal development but as a means of communication leading to social cohesion and understanding, crucial in a multicultural society. The establishment of an arts centre for young people and the South Australian Youth Arts Board, unique in Australia as a discrete funding body for Youth Arts, demonstrated the support given to youth arts.

South Australia was the first State in Australia to have a written drama curriculum. Both educational drama and conflict management are well-established fields in Australia, but the South Australian DRACON Project focused on something relatively new for our State—the linking of educational drama with the field of conflict management in the classroom.

The South Australian Project

Research Aims

There were two overall research aims for the Adelaide-based South Australian project:

Firstly, to ascertain the perceptions, experiences, nature, prevalence and hurtfulness of conflicts among Year 9 students in a range of metropolitan secondary schools in South Australia. This involved conducting focus groups and a survey of Year 9 students in a range of Adelaide metropolitan schools of different types (fourteen in total). Here we obtained adolescents' views of the nature of conflicts in their school and the way that they were experienced and handled. We also interviewed teachers and counsellors.

Secondly, to discover whether culturally relevant skills for dealing with conflict in a positive, constructive way can be imparted to adolescents through the active medium of educational drama. We used the research data from stage one to develop strategies to test the effectiveness of educational drama as a method for imparting conflict-handling skills to adolescents in one of the metropolitan public secondary schools surveyed.

Adolescent Conflicts in Australian Schools

When we conducted the DRACON project there was a lack of longitudinal data about the nature of conflict in Australian schools to indicate whether or not aggressive forms of conflict were increasing. However, there was anecdotal evidence to suggest that there was an increase in serious behaviour problems that teachers had to deal with, including bullying and sexual harassment. A number of Australian researchers were asserting that dominant masculine discourses were contributing to aggressive behaviours in school, in particular among adolescents (Collins, 1999; Connell, 1995; Gilbert & Gilbert, 1998). However, the only aspect of school-based conflict that had been researched in a detailed, systematic way in Australia at that stage was bullying (Rigby, 1996, 2002). Within the past two decades, extensive research has identified covert bullying by females as widespread and harmful, and Australasian research has been particularly important in this field.

When we started the project, Australian studies had suggested that destructive conflict was occurring in schools among students and between students and staff; it could be caused by and/or involve parents or other 'outside' forces not directly connected to the school. Teachers reported that they did not know what to do about the problem. Other evidence suggested that hindering others, racial abuse, sexual and sex-based harassment, verbal abuse, physical aggression and physical assault were common in Australian schools (Australian Government, 1994; Kenway, Willis, Blackmore, & Rennie, 1997).

In 1996, the South Australian DRACON Project team organised a seminar involving 30 participants from educational settings, universities and schools including representatives of the State Government, Catholic and Independent Education Departments in South Australia. Participants indicated that drama teachers in South Australian schools were often asked to deal with conflict situations through drama, but reported that there was little knowledge available to guide teachers, and teacher education and training in the South Australian universities did not adequately prepare them for this task. The same seminar participants also indicated that Year 9 was generally the most conflict-ridden year in secondary schools, which was confirmed by subsequent interviews with school counsellors in the 14 schools canvassed in our research.

What Adolescents Said About Conflict

With a small grant, Dale Bagshaw and Ken Rigby from the University of South Australia conducted some preliminary theoretical research. The research comprised two phases that directly involved a total of 798 students (652 completed the questionnaire and 146 participated in focus group discussions). Year 9 students were selected from single-sex and co-educational schools from the state, Catholic and independent secondary education sectors in South Australia. A range of types of school and socio-economic status of the student backgrounds was accommodated in the study. In total, the survey sample was composed of 197 boys and 243 girls from co-educational schools and 92 boys and 120 girls from single-sex schools. The purpose of the more structured questionnaire was to obtain additional quantitative and qualitative data about the nature, incidence and sources of conflicts at school.

The South Australian Project 161

Stage 1: Focus Group Research

Research Aim

The central research question addressed in Stage 1 of the research was 'What is the nature, incidence and the perceived sources of conflict at school for students in Year 9 in secondary schools in metropolitan Adelaide?' The overall aim of this stage of the study was to examine the prevalence of aggressive behaviours among Australian school children; the reported harmfulness of different types of peer behaviour; the styles of conflict handling used; and the similarities and differences in the behaviours and reactions of girls and boys.

Findings

The findings of the focus group research illustrated the kinds of conflict and violence involving adolescents taking place in schools in metropolitan Adelaide and the reported harmful effects of conflicts on some students. In spite of suggestions that verbal, relational and indirect forms of abuse were the most prevalent forms of abuse, especially for girls, the focus group participants focused more on discussing physical conflicts in their reports. Subsequent DRACON research identified the covert nature of much female bullying and the reluctance of teenage girls to openly reveal its occurrence.

Physical conflicts between boys and also between girls were graphically described. It was easier for them (and obviously more enjoyable) to talk about physical fights, which some suggested were fun to watch and relieved the boredom at school. Many participants admitted that they enjoyed watching a physical fight, as long as they were in control and safe from harm, although the level of physical aggression in some schools was frightening for students.

There were indications that verbal and relational forms of abuse were viewed and experienced as harmful, but for boys in particular the personal effects were much harder to discuss with a small group of adolescent peers. In later DRACON research, homophobic bullying emerged as a major issue for boys.

Aggression between students was seen as varying in seriousness according to where it took place. Focus group participants described aggressive acts in the schoolyard as more serious and unmanageable than those in the classroom. Aggression outside the school, often involving non-students as well, was seen as the most serious of all. There was evidence that conflict between students at school extended into conflicts involving relatives and friends in the wider community. Some conflicts were described as occurring along racial lines. In general, students attending schools in low socio-economic areas reported more violent responses to conflicts than those in other schools.

A recurring impression from the focus groups was that boys felt under pressure from peers to behave in a tough, aggressive manner, seen as befitting a male, and that their ways of reacting to conflict were strongly influenced by the expectations of others. This was consistent with the view that hegemonic masculine discourse encourages violent behaviour and that its impact may not be limited to the behaviour of boys.

Generally, students believed that teachers' responses to conflict were ineffective, a point supported by teachers who were interviewed, and that peer mediation was unsuitable for their age group.

Having gained a picture of the nature of the conflicts experienced by adolescents in schools from the students in the Focus Groups and from interviews with several school counsellors and teachers, the research team's attention then turned to examining in more detail the reports of aggressive acts and their consequences from individual students in a survey, using a questionnaire methodology.

Stage 2: The Survey Research

We conducted a survey of adolescent students to discover:

- the nature, frequency and reported hurtfulness of negative treatments they received from others at school
- the kinds and frequency of the conflict-handling approaches they employed at school.

The questions we used to elicit relevant information were based, in part, on what we had learned through the preliminary investigations with the Focus Groups.

The sample of students consisted of 289 boys and 363 girls from private, state, co-educational and single-sex schools. All of them were attending Year 9 classes (the second year of secondary schooling in South Australia). Their mean age was 14 years. The questionnaire was administered by teachers and the researchers in classrooms, and answered anonymously. We took care to ensure the anonymity of respondents and schools was protected.

Findings from the Survey of Negative Behaviours

The most striking thing about the information we gained from the survey of the experiences of adolescents who were targets of aggressive behaviours is the remarkable extent to which their peers were subjecting them to ill treatment. More than half the respondents had been treated badly, i.e. physically, verbally and relationally. Almost one in three reported that they had experienced bullying on a weekly basis. A minority of students appear to have been particularly vulnerable to different kinds of abuse from peers. All this suggested that, for a high proportion of students, conflicts in schools were not being handled well.

The results of the survey suggested that boys and girls had similar experiences of the main kind of ill treatment from peers, which was verbal abuse. Hence, we concluded that conflict-handling skills that prevent differences or disputes from escalating into wars of words must be given a high priority. Among boys especially, we saw a need to prevent conflicts from leading to physical confrontations; among girls, there was a particular need to prevent conflicts from taking the form of relational and manipulative forms of aggressiveness. However, we were cautious about essentialising gender or exaggerating gender differences: girls may sometimes experience and deliver direct or physical forms of attack; boys may become victims of relational aggression and find themselves excluded from groups or socially disadvantaged.

The Hurtfulness of Aggressive Acts

We were interested also in the extent to which students reported being hurt or upset by aggressive acts directed towards them. Students were asked how hurt they had been after being treated by a peer in a specified way. Being teased or sworn at was not experienced as being particularly hurtful. Having one's friendship broken up and unwanted sexual touching were seen as most hurtful behaviours by a large proportion of both boys and girls who had experienced them. It was apparent that relational forms of ill treatment tended to be the most distressing; for example, being deliberately excluded, having one's secrets told, and having rumours spread about one, which was common among girls.

Gender Differences

Gender differences in reporting being hurt by negative treatment were most evident. Some 21 of the 30 gender differences were statistically significant, and in each case it was girls who reported being more often hurt. However, contrary to what is sometimes thought, what tended to hurt or upset girls most also tended to hurt or upset boys most. Thus, both boys and girls reported that 'having one's friendships broken up' was the most hurtful thing to happen. The notion that only girls were upset by a deterioration in their social relationships—a myth promoted by the boys in the focus groups—was shown to be untrue when we examined data obtained from individual boys and girls under conditions of anonymity.

Absenteeism

Approximately one respondent in eight claimed to have avoided going to school because of conflict, at least once during the year. Many more 'thought of doing so'. More girls considered staying away and actually did stay away than boys (15% compared with 9%). This may suggest that girls are more seriously affected by conflict at schools than boys, but there may be other considerations such as peer pressure on boys not to admit to being affected.

Findings from the Survey of Conflict-Handling Styles

The aims of the conflict-handling styles section of the survey

In summary, the aims of this section of the study were to assess the conflict-handling styles of South Australian adolescent students by:

- comparing the degree to which the students report employing the different styles
- examining whether boys and girls differ in their use of the styles
- examining whether there are differences between schools in the extent to which the different styles are used by students
- examining the relationships between the use of conflict-handling styles and (a) how students report having acted in seeking to help others in conflict and (b) the kind of help students would like to receive when they are in conflict with someone.

It is well known that people react in different ways when they are in conflict situations, some in ways that help to resolve difficulties, some in ways that perpetuate or escalate the conflict. In Chap. 2 we described Johnson's five conflict-handling strategies that are commonly employed (See Fig. 2.2). He argued that although people may use different strategies on different occasions, they tend to have a dominant strategy, and he related each of these styles to a particular animal.

1. Problem-solving (*owl*) is a cooperative strategy and aims to arrive at an agreement that meets the needs, goals or interests of all parties to a conflict, at the same time maintaining the relationship at the highest level possible.
2. Compromising (*fox*) is a cooperative strategy and involves finding 'middle ground' in order to reach an agreement. It involves giving up part of one's needs, goals or interests and possibly sacrificing part of the relationship.
3. Forcing (*shark*) is a competitive strategy that places high importance on meeting one's own personal needs, goals and interests regardless of the potential for damage to the relationship.
4. Withdrawing (*turtle*) is a strategy that involves giving up on meeting one's own personal needs, goals and interests by avoiding the other person and/or the issue.
5. Smoothing (*teddy bear*) involves 'keeping the peace' by giving into the other party in a conflict in order to preserve a relationship (Johnson, 1997).

The extent to which adolescent school children made use of these strategies in conflict situations in schools had not been closely examined prior to our study. It was unclear, for instance, whether adolescents tend to use a so-called problem solving style more often or less often than a 'forcing' style. There was uncertainty regarding gender differences in conflict-handling styles. Given that males tend to act in a more forceful and aggressive way than females, one might have expected boys to make use of a 'forcing' conflict-handling style. Whether there were gender differences for the other kinds of conflict-handling styles remained to be seen.

Johnson suggested that people acquire a dominant conflict-handling style early in life. If that is so, one would expect that by the time children reach adolescence, the social environment would have little or no impact on how they seek to resolve conflict. Children in different secondary school environments might therefore not be expected to differ appreciably in their conflict-handling styles. On the other hand, if school children are influenced by the social ethos of their school, one might expect differences between schools in the extent to which students employ particular conflict-handling strategies.

Adolescent Conflict Style Scale

The measure used to assess conflict-handling styles in our research was the Adolescent Conflict Style Scale (ACSS), a 25-item scale Rigby and Bagshaw developed for the purpose of this research. It consisted of five sets of 10-items that were written to describe the kind of behaviour consistent with each of the conflict-handling styles proposed by Johnson. As far as possible, the items included were those suggested in the course of the preliminary discussions in focus groups with Year 9 students.

Twenty-five items in random order were included in a questionnaire. Students were asked: 'When you are at school and have a strong disagreement with a person of your own age on a matter which you care about, what do you do?' Students were asked to read through the items and indicate how they behaved by circling one of the following: 'I never or rarely do this'; 'I usually don't do this'; 'I do this about half the time'; 'I usually do this'; 'I always or nearly always do this'. Responses were scored from 1 to 5 in the direction of more frequently reporting the behaviour. The questionnaire contained two additional sets of items:

- *How students had helped others in conflict*
  Six items were included about how students had acted in situations in which they sought to help others in a conflict situation. The following ways of helping were listed: listening, taking sides, taking messages between people, breaking up or stopping the conflict, trying to resolve differences, and bringing in someone to help, such as a teacher or counsellor. Students could answer to each of these items 'never,' 'sometimes' or 'often'.
- *How students would like to be helped if they were in conflict*
  Thirteen items were about the kinds of help students would like to receive if they were in conflict with others. These comprised the following: mediation, taking messages, talking to the other person for you, simply listening, counselling, suggesting things, telling you what to do, deciding who is right and who is wrong, breaking up the conflict, punishing the guilty person, leaving you to sort the matter yourselves, telling your families, and taking your side in the conflict. Students could answer 'not at all', 'possibly' and 'probably'.

Differing Conflict-Handling Styles

We examined the extent to which students reported using different conflict-handling styles by computing the proportion of students who reported that they 'usually', 'nearly always' or 'always' responded in a particular style when they were in conflict

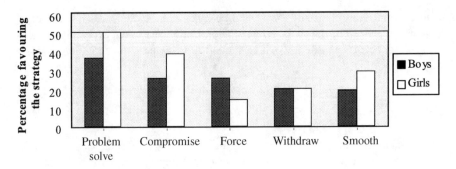

Fig. 7.1 Conflict resolution styles of Australian adolescents

with someone. This was done using the responses given to the five representative items given in Fig. 7.1.

At least 20% of the students surveyed commonly used each of the five styles. The most commonly used styles were compromising and problem-solving. About 30% of students reported using one or the other. A substantial proportion of students indicated that they often used less desirable ways of dealing with conflict, such as the use of force and withdrawal; approximately 20% indicated that the use of force was their dominant style and a similar percentage used withdrawal.

Discussion of the Findings

This aspect of the study demonstrated that the five conflict-handling styles suggested by Johnson can be measured with an acceptable degree of reliability among young adolescent students. However, some of the measures were not independent of others. This was evident in the moderately sized correlations between some of the measures and also in the finding that some measures have many of the same correlates with indications of past behaviours and how they would like to be helped. Notably, students uncomfortable with a dominant problem-solving style tended to engage in compromising and smoothing, but not in forcing.

We noted that the more positive styles of responding were evidently more commonly used than negative styles, although here we should recognise that some students may have wanted to appear more positive than they actually were. The school environment appears to have made a difference to the styles students reported using. There were significant differences between the schools on four of the five conflict-handling styles. This is an encouraging finding, as it suggests that improvements in the school environment or ethos may result in the employment of more positive ways of resolving conflict.

The gender differences were, in general, not surprising. The study confirmed that boys were more prone to use force as a strategy and girls to engage more in problem-solving, compromising and smoothing. However, contrary to the stereotypical view that girls tend to avoid conflict, there were no consistent differences between boys and girls as far as withdrawal was concerned.

The conflict-handling styles were related to how students said they had behaved in the past when they had sought to help somebody in a conflict situation. There was a particularly strong contrast between, on the one hand, those whose style tended to favour problem-solving, compromising and smoothing, and on the other hand, those who favoured forcing. The former tended to have a history of behaving in ways that are helpful in resolving conflicts, for instance by listening and trying to resolve differences, while the latter, the high forcers, had more often behaved in ways that are generally counterproductive, as in taking sides and not listening.

The kind of help adolescents wanted when they were in conflict also seemed to depend on their conflict-handling style. High problem solvers, high compromisers and high smoothers were more open to mediation, wanting to be listened to and counselled. By contrast, high forcers were keener to have people take their side, and were less interested than others in hearing suggestions about how the conflict could be resolved.

Finally, in view of the similarities between the correlates of some of the conflict-handling styles, it may be asked whether a set of five styles is too many. It is true that some are closely related and have similar correlates. However, there were indications that the different styles can be differentiated. Although high problem solvers were similar to high compromisers and high smoothers in a number of ways, they appeared to be different in their tendency not to want others to take their side and not to want to see the guilty punished. These qualities are important in avoiding an escalation of conflict. Similarly, although high forcers are in some ways like withdrawers—for instance, they are both more likely to favour wrongdoers being punished—the high forcers were unique in being more in favour of being left alone to sort things out and being more disinclined than others to have others listen to them. They appeared to maintain a uniquely tough façade that makes it difficult for them to be helped.

Conclusions from the Focus Group and Survey Research

The survey of aggressive behaviours experienced by students provided valuable information that enabled us to assess the extent to which adolescents are treated in negative ways by their peers at school. Clearly, a large proportion of adolescents were regularly implicated in painful altercations with their peers. These could take a wide variety of forms: physical, verbal and relational. It was evident that for many students, conflict was not being handled in a positive manner.

The survey of conflict-handling styles suggested that some students' predominant styles were positive: that is, they involved problem-solving and/or compromise approaches. However, a substantial number of students used negative or counterproductive methods, especially when using methods of forcing and/or withdrawing. There was also evidence that the styles identified in this study were, in fact, related to how students had behaved in conflict situations and how they would like to be assisted if they were in conflict with someone.

Finally, the fact that schools differed significantly in the extent to which their students practised positive or negative methods of handling conflict suggests that the school environment may be crucial.

This analysis helped us to recognise more clearly the distinctive features of alternative conflict-handling styles as practised by adolescents and the strengths and weaknesses associated with those styles in bringing about successful conflict-handling. We drew on this information for the next part of our study where we introduced the five styles of conflict handling to Year 9 adolescents through the medium of educational drama.

The Classroom Study

The second stage of the South Australian DRACON project analysed the effectiveness of teaching adolescents to handle conflicts in a cooperative manner through the medium of educational drama in one secondary school in Northern metropolitan Adelaide, South Australia. Our prior research had indicated that peer mediation strategies might not be appropriate for some adolescents, in particular for Year 9 students. The suggestion being tested in this part of the study was that conflict education and literacy can be provided through the medium of educational drama.

Introducing adolescents to Johnson's (1997) five styles or strategies of conflict handling through the medium of drama were central to the research. Johnson's typology of styles has two underlying dimensions. He assumed that we are concerned about two things in a conflict with others:

- getting what we need or want, and/or
- the relationship with the other person.

The five basic conflict-handling styles, which we have previously outlined, can be categorised as competitive or cooperative. Johnson explains that normally each person uses more than one style, depending on the situation they are in. However, the hypothesis is that we usually have one style we use most, particularly in a crisis, or in an argument with people we are close to.

Research Methodology

Research Aim

The aim of this stage of the South Australian DRACON subproject was to study drama-in-education approaches to teaching and learning cooperative conflict-handling strategies, involving Year 9 students in a secondary school in metropolitan

Adelaide. By choosing to work with a difficult class, which initially presented with subgroup conflicts, it was also possible to study the effects of the learning process on both the individual class members and the groups.

The School and Participants

A large school located in a low socio-economic area in the Northern suburb of Adelaide agreed to participate in the research. Half the students in this school came from disadvantaged backgrounds with one third of students from non-English speaking backgrounds. According to the findings of our prior research, and the findings of other researchers at the time, it was schools with these demographics that were predominantly reporting escalating problems with conflict.

During planning meetings with teaching staff from the school, the students in the assigned Year 9 drama class were described as 'difficult'—often uncooperative, seemingly uninterested in drama, boisterous and at times hostile. Initially, there were nineteen students in the class—eight boys and eleven girls. They had been in this drama class for the third term only and during this time the teacher had been unable to engage them in any meaningful way. The teacher indicated that some students in the class had chosen drama as an 'easy' option.

The Research Team

The Team involved two conflict researchers—the project coordinator Dale Bagshaw and co-researcher Ken Rigby—and two drama facilitators, Rosemary Nursey-Bray and Myk Mykita, who were directly involved with the students on a weekly basis. Two other members of the DRACON team acted as consultants. The drama facilitators took alternate classes while the conflict researchers designed and implemented the research strategies. The researchers also acted as observers and recorders, occasionally facilitating small group activities and giving conflict theory input to the drama teachers and students as needed. The school drama teacher chose to support the researchers by monitoring attendance and completing other administrative tasks. The researchers began work with the class at the start of the fourth term. The commitment was for two 100-min sessions a week, for a period of eight weeks.

Focus, Ethics, Methods and Techniques

We decided that verbal abuse was an appropriate focus for the educational drama sessions, as it had been identified by Year 9 students in the school in our earlier survey as the predominant source of conflict. Our prior research in a range of secondary schools (including this one) had identified that verbal abuse between adolescents at school was common, was often ignored by teachers, can be more hurtful than physical abuse, can continue for a long period and is difficult to handle. It is important to reflect that verbal abuse had also been identified by many victims of domestic violence in South Australia as being the most destructive form of abuse in the long term (Bagshaw, Chung, Couch, Lilburn, & Wadham, 2000).

As manifestations of human behaviour, conflict issues and drama pose potential ethical problems and therefore demand sensitivity, trust and confidence among the participants. Participation in the project was informed and voluntary with formal permission sought from the University of South Australia and the Catholic and State Education Departments and from the schools, students, parents and teachers involved.

Educational drama approaches to be tested included a range of drama exercises, improvisations, and role-plays involving conflict situations typically experienced by students at school, especially conflicts involving verbal insults or abuse. The emphasis was on enabling students to develop their own conflict scenarios and to practise different styles of handling conflict, drawing on their experiences and creativity.

We employed an action research framework, allowing the researchers to work collaboratively with the participants and to constantly evaluate the process and modify activities. It involved 'the application of fact finding to practical problem-solving in a social situation with a view to improving the action within it' (Sarantakos, 1998:7). The process was fluid with continuous evaluation and feedback between the researchers and participants, through the medium of diaries, informing each stage in the development of the project.

We tried various research techniques to ascertain their usefulness; they included the following:

- Focused observation using descriptive techniques. One observer/recorder described the exercises and techniques used and student responses to each exercise and the overall session.
- Participants recording their impressions in journals immediately following each session. The rationale was to identify changes in understanding that might be attributable to the educational drama work. The students were asked to write briefly about three things for each session: what they enjoyed, what they did not enjoy and what they learned.
- Pre- and post-intervention questionnaires designed to ascertain changes in the target group's attitudes to conflict.
- Videoed-recordings of the drama activities, which were introduced in session five and used as a tool for ongoing critical reflection and for evaluation in the final session.

Each session was designed to introduce drama activities that facilitated the exploration of key concepts linked to conflict resolution, management and transformation. Most of the concepts were introduced in the earlier stages and were centrally important to the development of the group. These included trust, cooperation, listening, empathy, non-verbal communication, feelings and status/power. In which order the concepts were introduced was contingent on the stage of the group's development. Simple handouts were supplied at the beginning and/or at the end of each session, along with a brief discussion of the concept explored and how it related to the students' experience in the session. Drama exercises were designed to reinforce these concepts.

Students were then introduced to the five strategies for handling conflict—withdrawing, smoothing, forcing, compromising and problem-solving. Drama activities were designed to facilitate student exploration of the effect of each strategy, and to identify the potential destructive and constructive elements of each.

After each session, the team would debrief and share perceptions of student involvement, review the journal entries, evaluate the relevance of each drama activity used on the day, discuss personal responses and effects, and then plan the next session. We assessed and analysed the data collected using a reflexive approach, which acknowledges and incorporates the effect of the researchers' participation in the process, without assuming expert status. Through this understanding, the data from student feedback and researcher observations were contrasted in order to formulate ongoing and final evaluations.

The Educational Drama Process

Weeks 1 and 2: Establishing Trust, Mutual Respect and Collaboration

The team's first priority was to build a collaborative relationship with the students based on trust and mutual respect. The team used their first names with the class in an attempt to establish a sense of democracy. We assumed that cooperation would be facilitated by less formal personal relations than are usual between students and staff in schools.

In *Session 1*, the project coordinator and co-researcher introduced the project and implemented a pretest. Warm-ups and group building exercises were used to engage the students with each other, with the researchers and with the project. Initially, members of the class were hostile, distrustful, undisciplined and disrespectful towards the team. They had studied drama for ten weeks before the team's arrival. We had assumed that they would be an integrated class, familiar with each other and their teacher and having some basic understanding and experience of drama techniques, particularly in improvisation and role-playing. This was not the case; in fact, a great deal of resentment and resistance seemed to have accrued during the prior term.

From the beginning, the students positioned themselves in three distinct sub-groups:

- Group A—all boys who were mostly boisterous and aggressive, except for a sub-group of twin boys who were quiet, serious, tidy and clearly experienced in drama techniques.
- Group B—a smaller group of less confident girls, who we describe in this report as 'Shy', who were overtly excluded from the larger group of girls.
- Group C—the 'in-group' of girls, consisting of a larger group of more confident girls we describe as 'Cool', reflecting the students' language.

Within these subgroups each student appeared confident, but when isolated from others in their group, confidence waned, in particular among the Shy girls.

It was very difficult to get individuals to interact with students from the other subgroups. For example, in the first few weeks, most of the Cool girls were unwilling to engage with other class members who were not in their subgroup, or to work in pairs or a small group with a Shy girl.

In order to ascertain their willingness and ability to engage in a drama activity, we invited the students to form three single-sex groups to discuss the differences between the way boys insult each other and the way girls insult each other. The groups they formed were closely aligned with the groups we had identified above. We then asked each group to devise a scenario taking the role of a person of the opposite sex and to act out a typical conflict involving that same-sex group. Each group worked with one of the researchers or drama facilitators in rehearsal and devised imaginative, amusing and insightful scenarios. However, when asked to perform for the larger group, the boys participated but both groups of girls froze.

The knowledge gained from this first encounter provided us with a basis on which to proceed. The team would have to start from scratch. However, we questioned whether a difficult class like this one (antagonistic and dysfunctional) was exactly the kind of class that might benefit from some help with conflict-handling techniques? The students made it clear that they resented the written work by refusing to listen to instructions, loudly protesting and disrupting each other. However, in spite of this, their journal entries reflected that most were self-conscious about speaking or performing in front of their peers and most enjoyed learning about 'the differences in the way boys and girls insult each other'.

Sessions 2–8 were formulated expressly to build cooperation and basic drama skills. The team described again to the students the idea behind the DRACON project. We felt it was important to restate that the team were looking to the students for guidance as to how to shape the program. The students engaged first in exercises that demanded individual action, such as walking in their own space. Then they worked in pairs, for example mirroring each other's behaviour and role-playing a master/servant scenario. This was followed by an observation game that required the cooperation of the whole group. Some of these exercises—like 'Touching Kneecaps'—were deliberately designed to be amusing. They were also designed to lead the class towards attitudes, disciplines and skills necessary for drama: cooperation, concentration, observation, reacting to a lead given by someone else and communicating without words.

Most of the students participated enthusiastically and their journal entries reflected that they were having fun.

It was much more fun than other lessons we have had

Week 2: Confronting Disruptive Behaviour and Resistance

Unfortunately, *Session 3* was held in the Dance Studio, an allocated room totally unsuited for drama, highlighting the importance of physical context. Sound echoed and reverberated; there was a hard, vinyl-covered floor, mirrors and walls with *barres* attached. Students reacted by being loud and boisterous, uncooperative and disrespectful to the researchers and to each other. Journal entries were negative, summed up by the statement: 'I thought today's lesson was boring'.

A problem presenting to the drama facilitators was the difficulty of timing sessions and therefore planning effectively. The students would thoughtlessly race through in five minutes exercises intended on average to take half an hour—or these would take an hour and a half, where instructions had to be repeated many times and students had to be constantly pressured into concentrating, cajoled and helped with ideas. Planning was problematic; the best approach seemed to be to come to class with a lot of ideas and proceed flexibly with whatever seemed to interest the class. It was crucial to emphasise to the class the reality of the team's desire to work in ways that were relevant to their needs and in areas they would find pleasurable, and that the team had no desire simply to impose structures from 'above'.

The priority for *Session 4* was to confront the students about their disruptive behaviour. One drama facilitator pointed out to them that the success of the project depended on the cooperation of all students. He established some basic group norms and made it clear that if the students did not wish to participate, the researchers would happily withdraw from the project. This proved to be a turning point—the students then realised that they had the power to terminate the project and the power to shape it. There was evidence of a shift when a student, well known for being late and disruptive, entered the classroom more than half an hour late. The facilitator asked him to apologise to the class for interrupting their activity and he refused to do so—choosing instead to storm out. Rather than support him (which they had previously done) the students ignored him and chose to continue with their activity.

At this stage in the process, the drama facilitators were beginning to explain the rationale behind the drama exercises and games. The student leader of Group C began to question both the project and the process, indicating a genuine interest. By answering her queries, the facilitator was able to address some of the questions that others had not been confident to ask. That leader's growing enthusiasm and acceptance of the project exerted a strong influence over the class in general and particularly over 'her' group, which was the larger and more confident 'Cool' girls' group. Student journals began to reflect dissatisfaction with class members who continued to cause disruption.

> I don't really like the fact that most of the class still haven't started to stop being all embarrassed and just do the activities
>
> I learned that if the whole class gets involved everything works better for everyone

Week 3: Building Interaction and Group Cooperation

During *Session 5* the Team introduced a video-recorder into the classroom; the students were comfortable about being filmed. We felt that a video of the role-plays would be a bonus, both as a record and as a tool for communication and feedback. The facilitator also put forward the suggestion that a video-recording could be used as an end product for the project, and invited the students to give this proposal some thought. This proved another turning point. The students were clearly excited at the possibility of 'making a film'. By this session, a pattern of activities began to be established. The drama facilitator would begin with warm up exercises, which were at times fast and involved the whole group—such as an Irish Jig—or at other times slow and meditative, allowing for individual reflection. Both approaches served to promote participation and large group cohesion.

The drama facilitators had noticed how physically active the boys liked to be; vigorous 'warm-ups' seemed popular. Some of the girls were enthusiastic dancers. Both sexes danced the Irish Jig with pleasure; however, we did not put the students in the potentially embarrassing position of having opposite gender partners—alternate dancers were 'apples' or 'oranges'. An added factor in the success of the Jig was perhaps the fact that the Irish show '*Riverdance*' had recently played in Adelaide, and had been televised to great acclaim. The students related to the glamour and the macho quality of this contemporary performance. The facilitators acknowledged the need to offer opportunities for energetic activity in future classes, and the attraction for students of engaging in exercises they felt to be 'with-it.' The final exercise in this session involved the groups making up a story where a bad event was followed by good, after being told the story of the Good Samaritan. The students enjoyed this and did it well. The boys devised a battle between England and Scotland—a piece of real Dance Drama. They fought in a stylised way, inventively using small plastic table tops as shields and the table legs as swords or clubs, sometimes in slow motion, with admirable discipline, until (one presumes) the 'good guys' won. Interestingly, this was the only piece not handled naturalistically.

The Team felt that some headway had been gained during this session. The dance had been a success in focusing and expending energy and building interaction. The class seemed nearer to grasping some of the techniques of drama; they had enjoyed improvising a play. The 'Shy' girls had begun to contribute more and the 'Cool' girls had begun to accept them.

To date, the focus had been on building relationships, establishing trust, developing confidence and encouraging cooperative behaviour.

In *Session 6*, the researchers began to explore concepts relevant to conflict, namely the differences between cooperation and competition and recognising and naming feelings. We used a page of cartoon faces expressing different emotions as an amusing stimulus. Handouts describing how one expresses feelings verbally and non-verbally through tone of voice, facial expression, eye contact and touching were discussed. Drama activities were introduced to enable students to explore these concepts—for example an arm-wrestle exercise, acting out feelings, and theatre sports. The students were still reluctant to contribute to large group discussion; however, their journals indicated that many were recognising the importance of teamwork and cooperation.

> I learnt that if everyone cooperates more and doesn't compete with each other then the group works better and is much more enjoyable

Week 4: Transforming Attitudes and Behaviours—Trust, Participation and Cohesion

Session 7 introduced a communication exercise and a 'trust walk' in the school grounds that tested the relationships between some students. Student journal entries identified the value of trust.

> I enjoyed doing the trust activity. It was a bit scary to do but it was still fun

The students were improving but still finding it difficult to listen to and follow instructions. They were unwilling to admit to gaining any knowledge. Any attempt to reflect on the meaning of exercises met with resistance. The team, however, noticed that the students were in fact beginning to learn how to interact with each other. What discussion did occur indicated that there was an increase in both their willingness to participate and their understanding of concepts. We also had a growing sense that the students were beginning to trust the team.

The class decided they would eventually like to devise short plays in groups, showing how a certain conflict was resolved. These would be videoed as an end product of the project.

By *Session 8*, the group dynamics were altered by the suspension from school of the two most disruptive boys in the class. Their absence saw a shift in the behaviour of the rest of the boys from indifferent participation to enthusiastic contribution. Although the small groups still operated autonomously, there was greater class cohesion. Students were beginning to take an overt and constructive interest in the activities of others outside their subgroups. In this session the drama facilitator explored dimensions of conflict through discussion of contemporary plays. This led into group discussion about the students' own experiences of conflict. A communication exercise later required the students to devise a scenario which demonstrated a conflict situation but in which the dialogue was fixed and restricted.

All the students devised scenarios that clearly demonstrated the power of non-verbal communication. They all acted out their particular scenarios confidently and watched the work of others respectfully. Some were also willing openly to discuss the knowledge they had gained, risking ridicule from others. Trust was beginning to manifest itself in changed attitudes and behaviour. All students, even those consistently fearful of being required to participate in a public performance, reported enjoying the exercise.

> I enjoyed getting up and acting out a scene involving conflict without going psycho killing each other

> I sort of enjoyed performing our play—I am getting more confident

Most clearly identified that they had learned about the importance of non-verbal communication.

> I learnt how to read how people are feeling

At the end of these preliminary sessions, the team felt that there had been an appreciable growth in cooperation and interest and a considerable improvement in drama skills and discipline. The students' listening skills and willingness to contribute were significantly enhanced but their behaviour was still problematic.

Week 5: Learning Conflict Transformation Concepts and Play-Making

Sessions 9–13 concentrated on concepts of conflict transformation and play-making.

In *Session 9* a student challenged an attempt to organise an exercise that required students to work in pairs. Her protest was supported by many in the class. This provided the facilitator with an opportunity to demonstrate further that the students could influence the direction of the project. That significantly altered the group dynamics. Increased communication and cooperation across subgroups began to emerge.

This session was designed by the team to explore the related concepts of status and power. The students were required to develop a scenario about the abuse of power—called *The Worm Turns*. Students were given prepared cards with some suggested power combinations—student/teacher, mother/father, child/parent—but took the initiative to create some imaginative scenarios beyond the choices offered. They demonstrated that they understood the concepts and were taking charge of their own learning.

Members of the team helped provide ideas and structures. The 'Shy' girls created a courtroom scene where there was a confrontation between Lawyer and Client. The girls giggled but were prepared to show their play to the others. The boys were unable to maintain a dialogue but got their point across in a player/referee altercation at a soccer match. A school counsellor/student interview was presented by the 'Cool' girls. The other 'Cool' girls were children playing Mum and Dad off against each other. The Twins presented a humorous scene where, through a misunderstanding, a police man harassed a 'suspect'—who turned out to be the pizza delivery boy.

Student journal entries for this session were much more informative than previously. There was overwhelming support for working on 'plays' and for being able to choose whether they worked in small groups or pairs. Some reflected that they 'enjoyed performing in front of everyone and working in pairs', while others commented that 'we should be able to go with as many people as we like'. From this point on the students made an effort to listen to instructions and took responsibility for their actions.

Weeks 6–8: Preparation and Presentation of Role-Plays

The final sessions were devoted to the preparation and presentation of role-plays that required each small group or pair to develop a scenario involving verbal insults or abuse and to demonstrate different conflict-handling styles or strategies. We introduced the students to the five conflict-handling strategies or styles and they were asked to identify their own dominant conflict style by completing an exercise from Johnson (1997: 229–249). The students related with amusement to Johnson's animal archetypes, which proved very effective in illuminating the approaches described.

Students were given simplified handouts and explanations in class to assist them to understand the concepts. By this time, the class had experienced or used most of the conflict strategies but had not previously been able to label them. However, they were initially unable to demonstrate an understanding of the strategy of problem solving, or an ability to apply it. The facilitators explained that each of the strategies could be appropriate for a particular situation. Everybody agreed that in most conflict situations between peers at school, the cooperative strategies of compromising and problem-solving have the potential to generate the most satisfactory outcomes for everyone involved, as they preserve the relationship(s) and attempt to satisfy everyone's needs and goals.

The students chose to work on developing their own role-plays in small groups, with the Twins opting to work together as they wanted to expand on their *The Worm Turns* scenario. Despite a suggestion that previous scenarios could form the basis of a final piece of drama, most of the students decided to create new conflict situations. Each group developed its own sets, organised props, devised scripts and successfully demonstrated the different styles of handling conflict in various scenarios.

In *Session 10*, the students began to develop their scenarios for the final presentation and some groups showed their scenarios as 'Work in Progress'. For example, a scenario involving two of the 'Cool' girls and two boys was as follows:

> Two boys and a girl—Wayne, Chuck and Amelia—are sitting on the school oval. Another girl, Rachel, approaches angrily. Rachel is angry with Wayne who had been going out with her but had also secretly taken out Amelia. Obliged to make a choice between the girls, Wayne prefers to go off with Chuck. (This was a witty and interesting approach, perhaps designed to test the tolerance level of the team, as the hint of homosexual preference was present.)

The team helped students to develop their ideas by giving feedback and contributing suggestions. The facilitators pointed out that most of the scenarios used Shark or Turtle techniques to solve the conflict, and challenged the students to explore other approaches. Most of their scenarios were very short and basic. Students clearly did not understand how to 'flesh out' the skeletons. From this point, individual members of the team (including the researchers) worked with each group as a drama facilitator, using improvisational techniques and discussion to help the students develop the plot and structure of the scenario and enriching the dialogue and characterisations. All groups (especially the 'Shy' girls, who needed the boost in confidence that this can bring) were keen to 'set' their plays and use costumes and props. The 'Shy' girls relied on a formally written script more than the others who were relaxed about improvising words within a carefully structured scenario.

Many changes occurred in this period, including the dissolution of the subgroups, initiated by two boys and two of the 'Cool' girls (Group C), who elected to work together on a scenario. All students opted to help students from other groups by volunteering to be 'extras' in each other's plays. They also acknowledged and included the research staff, asking for support and feedback on their ideas. They all demonstrated a marked increase in self-confidence and were not afraid to present their ideas for public scrutiny.

> I enjoyed being able to have the freedom to make up a short performance with our own ideas

All the students, even those who consistently reported hating 'doing plays' and 'performing in front of the class', wrote in their journals that they enjoyed developing their play and rehearsing for their final performance. After several rehearsals each subgroup performed, with confidence, for the rest of the class.

> I really enjoyed performing the play and I think we did it well

In addition, each scenario demonstrated that they had understood and responded to the requirements, which were to devise a typical scene to illustrate a conflict involving verbal abuse or insults, and to demonstrate various styles or strategies to handle the conflict. The journal entries continued to reflect the students' learning about conflict, cooperation, expressing feelings and 'how to work together and not stuff around'.

In the final scenarios devised by the students, where conflict was the subject of the drama, they were each able to experience different aspects of conflict and to experiment with different strategies of conflict handling. The end products had developed considerably from the initial scenarios. The plays were set imaginatively, using rostra and other resources of the Drama room. The students had gone to a lot of trouble to construct props and found appropriate costumes on their own initiative.

Each small group performance was videoed and the edited video was played back to the students on the last day. Following this, students were videoed as they interviewed each other in pairs (*vox populi* style), asking each other two questions:

- What style of conflict did you demonstrate in your play?
- If you were to demonstrate a problem-solving style, what would you have done differently?

Responses to these questions demonstrated an improved understanding of key conflict styles and concepts. The students were all able to identify the conflict strategies that they used in their role-play. Those who had used withdrawal, forcing or smoothing strategies were also able to describe more cooperative approaches they could have used, involving the use of compromise or problem-solving. This ability had not been evident in earlier sessions.

Participant Evaluation

A special session was arranged in the last week to review the edited video, to thank the students for their participation and to present them with a specially prepared certificate of attendance. All students made a special effort to attend and the mood of the group was positive, cheerful and cooperative, in marked contrast to the first two sessions. In this and the previous session, oral feedback given to the researchers by students (in front of their classmates) indicated that their confidence levels had increased and that they appreciated learning about conflict through drama, especially through devising their own scenarios. They spoke of growing confidence, having fun, learning different conflict solving methods, improved acting skills and improved communication skills. These examples from their final journal entries illustrate the potency of drama as a medium for learning about conflict.

> I learnt about different ways to loosen people up so that they aren't shy
>
> I learnt how to communicate better and how to resolve conflicts more civilized
>
> I learnt how to bow and curtsy and how to use different problem solving methods during conflict
>
> I learnt confidence I never had and how to be myself a little more

Members of the team felt that they had made great progress in transforming a dysfunctional class of students, with separate and conflicting subgroups, into a viable and cooperative drama class with increased conflict literacy. This had been achieved by using strategies to establish egalitarian staff/student relations, which built trust, and by persuading the students that they genuinely had a crucial role in the structuring and development of the project and that their needs and interests were the priority. We used various techniques to encourage cooperation between the subgroups, techniques that also empowered students to take charge of their own learning.

The drama facilitators were flexible in their approach and willing to adapt to the preferences of the class. Exercises were devised that allowed for the expression of physical energy, were concerned with contemporary issues, were 'with it', exciting and amusing. No pressure was exerted to form or break up existing groups; however, some melding occurred naturally as class cohesion improved. The making of a video of the final performances as a permanent record was an effective stimulus for students to present a worthwhile production of which they could be proud.

It seemed clear to the Team that at the conclusion of the project interpersonal understanding and friendship had begun to grow between members of what had initially been discrete groups in the class. The indications were that this improved understanding could lead to more pleasant social relations in the future between members of the class.

Discussion

This pilot project was ambitious given the limited time frame, the large, difficult student group involved and the conflict between the three distinct subgroups within the class. However, we observed a profound shift in levels of attentiveness and self-confidence in the individual students and the cooperation between the subgroups, given the high level of disruptive behaviour initially displayed. Action research strategies enabled the research team to respond flexibly to the needs and interests of individual students and to affirm their abilities, thereby gaining their respect and trust. They appreciated the confidence that we placed in their ability to be self-directed—'I enjoyed having a choice on what we wanted to do—not having the teachers choose what we have to do'. This finding is not surprising, given the push for autonomy typically displayed by adolescents at this stage of their development.

During the first few sessions, the students' behaviours challenged us. They tested boundaries and our tolerance levels by arriving late, refusing to be involved, and by being disruptive and disrespectful to other students and to the drama facilitators. This behaviour was challenged in turn by one drama facilitator and it was from that point that the journals became more informative and useful. One student who had previously written negative, monosyllabic responses now disclosed a difficulty—'sometimes I didn't understand what he [the drama facilitator] was talking about'.

The one-page journals were designed to elicit student feedback immediately after each session—what they liked and disliked about the activities engaged in and what they had learned. Despite their general reluctance to write about each session in their journals (e.g. 'the only thing I didn't like about this term was writing the feedback at the end of the lesson'), the information they provided over time gave us useful material for ongoing and final evaluations. This was the most important action research tool we used, as the students were often reluctant to verbalise their ideas and opinions in front of each other. Information we gained from observations and the journal entries we used to modify and shape each session. Oral feedback in the final session indicated that the students' considered their ability to influence the project was a very important aspect of their experience.

It was valuable to record our focused observations of each session, as our evaluation of the student feedback in the journals needed to take into account the context of the session. For example, the large group's behaviour and the feelings of dissatisfaction they reported in session three could not have been adequately explained without reference to the unsuitable surroundings of the dance studio.

The use of written pre- and post-tests as a research strategy was inappropriate for this group of students. They initially registered their protest at being required to complete written work by providing misinformation and very little comment in the pre-test questionnaire. The students were still not comfortable about completing the post-tests at the end, complaining that they hated writing. The post-test results were inconclusive, indicating little or no shift in their attitudes to conflict or verbal abuse. In both the pre- and post-test, when asked about their attitudes to another student being called hurtful names, half of them claimed it was of concern to them and the other half that it did not concern them. Similarly, there was no significant fall in the numbers of those who admitted to being perpetrators of abuse on other students, nor any evidence of a shift in their attitude to this practice. The pretest and post-test findings, moreover, did not tally with the feedback in the students' personal journals, with the observer's notes, or with the oral feedback they gave in the *vox populi* interviews with their peers and in the final session.

The use of the video as a tool for evaluation and feedback was invaluable with this age group. They encouraged its use and were very keen to view themselves performing. On reflection, the video would have been more effective than written tests as a tool for evaluation. Given the students' aversion to writing and to completing tests or questionnaires, we conjectured that individual student interviews, videotaped before and after the project, would have been more effective. Recording the *vox populi* interviews between the students was an effective way of ascertaining the students' understanding of the different conflict-handling styles, but without a benchmark, it was difficult to measure changes in attitudes to conflict over time.

This exploratory research project demonstrated the potential for educational drama to engage adolescents in problem solving and cooperative action. Although the project was limited to one class in one school (making inferences difficult) there were strong indications that drama is an effective medium for introducing possibilities for change, by widening the experiences of adolescents and allowing them to explore conflict, and its management, resolution and transformation, from a variety of perspectives.

Conclusions

Conflict played an important part in the lives of the South Australian schoolchildren in our study. This was evident from the comments of the students in focus groups and the subsequent survey conducted in a wide range of schools. Some schools were located in communities where there were high levels of aggression and violence, and where members of the community were involved in the conflicts at school. Such schools cannot be expected to implement conflict transformation strategies and programs in isolation—broader, structural issues need to be addressed for a lasting change in attitudes and behaviour to occur. Macro-level strategies for conflict transformation, involving families and the broader community, may be more appropriate in these areas. However, in the current political and economic climate in Australia, which is contributing to the increasing marginalisation of some schools and communities, this will be both challenging and difficult.

Conflict in South Australian schools continues to give rise to substantial numbers of students being subjected to hurtful forms of aggression—physical, verbal and relational. We need to pay attention to adolescents' comments about their experiences of conflict at school and the sort of helping strategies they need. Adolescence is a time when young people begin to form intimate relationships with their peers and are striving to create an independent, adult identity. It is typically a time of turmoil when adolescents test themselves, their relationships with other people and the boundaries of those relationships. It is important to provide early intervention and prevention strategies that will assist them to deal constructively with conflicts that arise in these relationships. A range of strategies will be needed.

It is clear that adolescent students use a variety of conflict-handling styles—some constructive, such as problem-solving and compromise, and others that are likely to produce negative outcomes for individuals, groups and the school community at large, such as forcing and withdrawing. It is a matter of concern that substantial numbers of students in our study were using negative styles.

Peer mediation may be helpful for less serious conflicts involving adolescents in schools, at the micro-level. Teachers, counsellors and students would benefit from learning the skills. However, some Year 9 students in our study indicated that peer mediation is not always a useful strategy nor acceptable for their age group, especially where the conflicts are serious, where there is an imbalance of power and where forcing styles are being employed by bullies. International research related to bullying in schools and colleges strongly supports this contention (Rigby, 2010, 2011).

Drawing upon the understandings derived from what Year 9 students in this study told us about their conflict experiences in a range of schools and how they seek to handle conflict, we believe that educational drama has an important role to play with this age group as a strategy for teaching conflict literacy and conflict-handling skills. In this study, we have demonstrated that with a difficult 'out of control' class in a disadvantaged school there were indications that drama can provide a creative medium for the teaching of constructive conflict handling skills to individuals and for the development of cooperation between groups.

References

Australian Government. (1994). *Sticks and stones: Report on violence in Australian schools*. Canberra: House of Representatives Standing Committee on Employment, Education and Training.

Bagshaw, D., Chung, D., Couch, M., Lilburn, S., & Wadham, B. (2000). *Reshaping responses to domestic violence*. Canberra.

Collins, C. (1999). The school gender game narrows choices and behaviour. *Refractory Girl* (53), 18–21.

Connell, R. W. (1995). *Masculinities*. Sydney: Allen & Unwin.

Gilbert, R., & Gilbert, P. (1998). *Masculinity goes to school*. St Leonards: Allen & Unwin.

Johnson, D. W. (1997). *Reaching out: Interpersonal effectiveness and self-actualisation* (6th ed.). Boston: Allyn and Bacon.

Kenway, J., Willis, S., Blackmore, J., & Rennie, L. (1997). *Answering back: Girls, boys and feminism in schools*. St Leonards: Allen & Unwin.

Rigby, K. (2011). *The method of shared concern: A positive approach to bullying in schools*. Camberwell: ACER.

Rigby, K. (2010). *Bullying interventions in schools: Six basic approaches*. Camberwell: ACER.

Rigby, K. (2002). *New perspectives on bullying*. London: Jessica Kingsley.

Rigby, K. (1996). *Bullying in schools—And what to do about it*. Camberwell: ACER.

Sarantakos, S. (1998). *Social research* (2nd ed.). South Yarra: MacMillan Education Australia.

Chapter 8
Brisbane—Cooling Conflicts and Acting Against Bullying

The Background

This chapter describes Brisbane's DRACON project of nine one-year-long cycles of ongoing action research in a whole-school setting, aimed at empowering students to take control of their own and their school's conflict management agenda. The core of the applied research was the combination of drama techniques and peer teaching to enable school students of all ages to understand and address conflict. This decade of research was carried out by the Griffith University Centre for Applied Theatre Research.

Drama is a strong and popular subject in senior schools in New South Wales (NSW) and particularly in Queensland, where it has the status of a full university entrance subject and tends to be as popular in private schools as in state schools. Both states have long-standing drama teacher education programs and strong drama teachers' associations. In both states, as in the 2013 National Curriculum, drama is categorised within the Arts Key Learning Area, along with Dance, Media Arts, Music and Visual Arts. Notionally, all those subjects have parity, though in NSW and in the primary schools in both states music and visual arts have been long and thoroughly established, while drama has been taught only in some schools. In the secondary schools, drama is sometimes seen as a civilising balance to the science and mathematics 'staples', as a useful option for the 'non-academic' students, or as a way of enhancing the school's cultural image. Some schools in low socio-economic areas see drama as a way of raising their students' self-esteem and confidence in public, of broadening their horizons, and of giving them a means of imaginative self-expression.

Genesis of the Project

In 1993, Shirley Coyle, the Director of the New South Wales Whole School Anti-Racism Program (WSARP), which was then being finalised (Coyle and French, 1996), approached the authors and Chief Investigators of our project. Coyle is an experienced drama teacher herself and had identified several possibilities for the extensive use of drama in anti-racism programs in schools that were outside the scope of WSARP—though a little drama had been trialled successfully. Between 1994 and 1996, we jointly planned a major research and development project, initially for the Northern Territory and then for NSW; however, in both cases the funding fell through.

In 1996, we were invited to join the DRACON project—which at that early point was intended to study 'Drama and Conflict Resolution in schools'. The preliminary preparation and reading for the two projects above had already focused our drama thinking on issues of conflict and harmony. Under the aegis of DRACON, we started to investigate what we believed were new approaches to conflict management in schools, using drama.

The Research

Research Premises

We approached the project design with a number of underlying hypotheses that we used to drive the research:

- Educational drama techniques have considerable potential to motivate and assist students to understand the causes of conflict, including its cultural aspects.

    – For this, we coined the phrase 'conflict literacy'.

- Conflict literacy would assist students to manage their own conflicts and perhaps mediate in those of their school community.

    – The extent of transferability of the learning into practical applications in their own lives became a major criterion for success of the project.

- Drama is more appropriate for learning new approaches to conflict management than for resolving conflict directly.

    – We based this hypothesis on our experience in drama education which indicated that drama's twin demands on participants for empathy and emotional distance make it unsuitable to use as a direct approach to mediation, conflict transformation, management or resolution, especially in school contexts.

- Students could be empowered to take some responsibility for the management of their individual and communal conflict agendas in schools.

Research Aim and Questions

These hypotheses informed the initial aims of our project, which were:

- to investigate whether drama can contribute significantly to conflict management in secondary schools on a whole-school basis;
- to investigate whether drama can assist in empowering students to take more responsibility for their own and the school's conflict management agendas.

From the start, we had a generic vision for the improvement of conflict management as a result of conceptual understanding of conflict and approaches to it, learned through drama. However, we waited to see where our early experiments would take us before formalising our aim. This is why we chose action research as our method, structured in annual cycles.

Our aims and the Research Questions had clarified by Year 2, with the introduction of the empowerment motif and the peer teaching that became a central component of the project in theory and practice (Table 8.1).

As is typical of action research, a number of Research Questions emerged at various times in the ten-year life of the Griffith program. The following three Questions have remained constant throughout:

1. *Can educational drama create conflict literacy, and reveal to students how conflicts are handled in schools and the wider community?*
2. *Can drama pedagogy within the curriculum empower students to take responsibility for their school's conflict management?*
3. *Can drama empower diverse whole school communities to sustain constructive conflict management agendas?*

Table 8.1 Brisbane project research questions

Cycles and dates	RQ	Question
Cycles 1–9: 1996–2005	1	*Can educational drama create conflict literacy, and reveal to students how conflicts are handled in schools and the wider community?*
Cycles 1–9: 1996–2005	2	*Can drama pedagogy within the curriculum empower students to take responsibility for their school's conflict management?*
Cycles 1–9: 1996–2005	3	*Can drama empower diverse whole school communities to sustain constructive conflict management agendas?*
Cycles 2–9: 1997–2005	4	*Can peer teaching enhance learning in conflict management through drama and democratise teaching?*
Cycles 4–9: 1999–2005	5	*Can students construct a multi-cultural perspective through drama to improve their management of cultural conflict?*
Cycles 7–9: 2002–2005	6	*Can peer teaching and drama also empower school students to deal with bullying?*
Cycles 7–9: 2002–2005	7	*What professional development do teachers need to teach conflict literacy and bullying management through drama?*

Prior to experimentation with peer teaching in Cycle 2 (1997), we added this Question:

4. *Can peer teaching enhance learning in conflict management through drama and democratise teaching?*

Then, for our work with the NSW WSARP Project (1999–2001), we added a fifth Question:

5. *Can students construct a multi-cultural perspective through drama to improve their management of cultural conflict?*

Following the first six years' work, we added two further Questions for the project's continuation in Queensland (2002–2005):

6. *Can peer teaching and drama also empower school students to deal with bullying?*
7. *What professional development do teachers need to teach conflict literacy and bullying management through drama?*

Evolution of the Research

The terms of reference of our 'mother' DRACON project were for each research team to investigate conflict with adolescents in schools, which meant that our research would be in secondary schools. The parameters of the research were and remained dependent on the extent of funding. In the first instance, the work was carried out on a small scale in one school in Brisbane, Queensland. There were a number of local schools, some with excellent drama programs and potentially interested teachers. However, the research needed both school and systemic approval to go ahead.

The project started with just John O'Toole and Bruce Burton as the investigators in one school classroom. However, two other key researchers were also involved—the classroom teacher involved in that first year's research, Morag Morrison, and one of our preservice teacher education students, Anna Plunkett, who was coincidentally doing professional practice in the classroom at the time. Both became involved in the project. Morrison became the first Key Teacher, and Plunkett our first research assistant. Both have subsequently completed PhD theses inspired by and connected with the Project (Plunkett, 2002; Morrison, 2009).

In 1996, a small university grant led to subsequent funding from the Australian Research Council that covered all the phases of the project, though its long-term continuance was precarious throughout and led to changes of direction to chase the funding. However, we were able to sustain the Research Questions and add to them as previously indicated.

Research Design and Methods

Participant, interventionist action research (Reason & Bradbury, 2008; Zuber-Skerritt, 2016) was the main research method used, because of both the Project's aims and the limitations and uncertainty of the funding: The research problem was deficiencies in conflict management in schools. Our vision was to empower students to manage and mediate in their own and their community's conflicts. As experienced drama teachers with considerable experience in exploring conflict through drama, the Chief Investigators were well placed to be participant–researchers. The fact that there were two of us—then later five, including a second research asssistant—also permitted some measure of ethnographic observation, though at various times each of us was involved directly as a participant in the program.

The Brisbane project created and applied a series of nine successive annual action research cycles that became larger and more complex with each iteration. We designed these cycles to answer the Research Questions in terms of the needs of the schools and their students.

In all, 2140 students participated, or—since the project worked on a whole-class basis—99 classes in 25 schools. All year-groups from Year 3 (eight-year-olds) to Year 12 (sixteen- and seventeen-year-olds) were represented at some point. The majority of the project work was carried out by Year 11 Drama classes, Year 8 or 9 English classes, and Year 5 and 6 primary classes.

We used a range of methods for data gathering and analysis, both qualitative and quantitative.

- Documents included the journals and diaries of participants, researchers, teachers and observers; school assignments; student tests, some with multiple-choice answers, some qualitative, along with other documentation relating to assessment and evaluation. These provided a range of evidence sources.
- Extensive interviews were conducted with informants from all participant groups (project classes, teachers, etc.), and other active stakeholders (such as administrators, parents, community members). We sometimes conducted the interviews ourselves, but when we needed objective feedback, the interviewers were unknown to the participants. The selection process and interview type varied according to the context, and each variant threw up different and useful kinds and patterns of response. In some cases, we interviewed all students in the class; in others, the class teacher and the research team selected five students; in others, we interviewed focus groups; in others, the research team selected specific students. A small number of the latter were followed up at intervals varying from one week to six months—and, in four case studies, 4 years later; in another case study, both 2 years later and 3.

In all, the interview participants comprised:

- 35 teachers
- 149 Key Class (senior drama) students
- 128 Focus Class (junior secondary) students

- 90 Relay Class (primary) students
- 20 focus groups—4 of teachers, 4 of community groups and 12 of students.

The researchers used a range of quantitative measures, especially formal questionnaires, which provided longitudinal data to investigate significant elements, such as: the kinds and amounts of conflict the students identified within their classes, the success of the program across whole schools within the cluster, and comparisons with other schools and other conflict management programs.

In the first 6 cycles, we administered pre-project questionnaires to 82 teachers and 1236 students. These provided data to guide the research team in structuring the project and to provide material for the peer teachers in devising their own work for their client groups. In addition, some of the Key Classes administered their own questionnaires to prospective Focus Class students, to provide materials and stories for their own prospective peer teaching episodes.

In the final 3 cycles, which focused specifically on bullying as the source of conflict for students, we administered pre- and post-project questionnaires at the beginning and end of the project in each school. The data from these questionnaires gave detailed information about the students' and teachers' perceptions of the project; the students' explicit understanding of bullying concepts; their ability to articulate them both in terms of the project; and in their own terms, the students' sense of the difference (if any) the project made in their experience of bullying, and how they dealt with it. As an instance of this, over 90% of the 216 secondary school students involved in *Acting Against Bullying* who were surveyed during the final two years of the project were able (a) to define bullying, (b) to identify the three types of people involved in bullying (bullies, bullied and bystanders) and (c) list the stages (latent, emerging and manifest).

Video records proved to be valuable but frustrating anecdotal records, owing to the limits and selectivity inevitable with one fixed camera. Nevertheless, close analysis of sections of videotaped class action revealed many aspects of behaviour, classroom relationships, language use and paralanguage that could not be identified live from observation or from their written reflection. In all, the team scrutinised over thirty-five encounters from 21 class groups.

The Action Research Cycles

The Project comprised nine action research cycles, which increased in size, scope and complexity over the ten years of the research. Cycles 1–3 were conducted in the same Brisbane school over two to three months each year, and involved considerable experimentation in the planning, implementation, and re-planning of the research. Cycle 4 took place over six months in a very different, rural NSW school where intercultural conflict was a major problem. Cycles 5 and 6 occurred over a two-year period in and around Sydney, primarily involving eight secondary schools and their feeder primary schools. The final three cycles (7–9) ran for three years in twenty-five schools in Brisbane and regional Queensland, with a specific focus on bullying as the cause of conflict (Table 8.2).

The Research

Table 8.2 Brisbane project action research cycles

Cycle	Year	Location	Schools
1	1996	Brisbane	1 urban high
2	1997	Brisbane	(same) 1 urban high
3	1998	Brisbane	(same) 1 urban high
4	1999	Regional NSW	1 rural high + feeder primary
5	2000	Sydney	4 urban high (2 co-ed, 2 girls') + at least 1 feeder primary for all (total 6)
6	2001	Sydney & surrounds	(same) 4 urban high + 2 urban high (boys) + 1 inner-city high + 1 rural high (total 8) + feeder primary for all (10)
7	2002	Brisbane & SE Queensland	4 urban high + 1 regional high + feeder primary (5)
8	2003	Brisbane & SE Queensland	(same) 4 urban high + 1 regional high + feeder primary (10)
9	2004–5	Brisbane & SE Queensland	(same) 4 urban high + 1 regional high + feeder primary (10) + 10 urban primary schools (not feeder)

In Cycle 1 (1996), we instituted a small-scale project within one class of Year 12 students, teaching drama and conflict concepts. We used the standard action research format of Contextual Identification, Planning, Observation, Reflection and Evaluation, then Re-planning. This was primarily to address Research Question 1: *Can educational drama create conflict literacy?*

In Cycle 2 (1997), we expanded the project to incorporate four other classes and peer teaching, which had emerged as a possible strategy in Cycle 1. This continued to address Question 1 and added Questions 2 and 4: *Can drama and/or peer teaching empower students in conflict management and (2) also democratise the classroom (4).*

In Cycle 3 (1998), we made a change to the focus and the drama techniques, extending the work in this school into an in-house community theatre setting, to start specifically addressing Question 3: *Can drama empower whole school communities in conflict management?* We conducted this cycle as an interactive theatre-in-education project performed by the students for their parents and families.

In Cycle 4 (1999), we returned to the classroom, but expanded the drama and the peer teaching. Now working through Shirley Coyle in the NSW Multicultural Programs Unit, we shifted the research site and the focus of conflict, locating the project in a different cultural and socio-economic milieu from School 1 in order to address Questions 1–4 together, and added a new Question (5): *Can drama affect the cultural aspects of conflict?*

The new school site was a country school with a recent and bitter history of inter-racial tension. The purpose of the research was therefore twofold. Firstly, we aimed to investigate whether the drama and peer teaching structures we had developed could address the serious and long-standing cross-cultural conflict in the school. Secondly, we wanted to create and refine an effective, stable practice and a useable set of teaching structures and materials that would have wider applications in conflict handling. At a functional level, we then expanded the project, to incorporate, for the first time, primary schools as third level 'Relay Classes'.

The Project gathered extraordinary momentum during this year, partly owing to increasing success in addressing the significant logistical problems we faced, and partly because of the sustained support of the school community. During this cycle, we instigated a detailed draft Handbook, a manual of practice for the teachers and students in the project, which became an official component of all following Cycles.

In Cycles 5 and 6 (2000–2001), we further expanded the Project, moving to Sydney and the surrounding area of central New South Wales, and incorporating eight new schools. This placed greater distance between ourselves, as researchers, and the participants in the schools. They were using the Handbook as their primary resource, rather than ourselves as teachers and mentors. All five Research Questions were invoked in this section.

In Cycle 6 (2001), the second year of the Sydney research, we extended the program into a number of new schools and included two major innovations: we structured the primary schools into the main program and consolidated the central drama techniques into one common drama-teaching structure. This cycle continued to investigate all five of the Research Questions.

In Cycles 7–9 (2002–2005), the project moved to Queensland with a quite different focus, aimed at specifically addressing bullying as a cause of conflict and answering Research Questions 6: *Can the combination of peer teaching and drama to investigate conflict also empower school students to deal with bullying?* and Question 7: *What is needed for the professional development of teachers in teaching conflict literacy and bullying management through drama?*

In Cycle 8 (2003), at the suggestion of their principals, four primary schools became lead schools for the first time. In Cycle 9 (2004–2005), we instigated a Master Teacher program for a select group of the teachers, to investigate Question 7 more closely.

Selection of Schools, Teachers and Students

We explain the reasons for our selections of particular schools, teachers and students in the detailed description of the cycles. The project structure crystallised into this basic sequence:

- A 'Key Class' at a senior level (15–17-year-olds) started the process.

- Peer teaching by the Key Class brought in Years 7, 8 or 9 'Focus Classes' (12–14-year-olds).
- In Cycles 4 and 5, Years 5 and 6 'Relay Classes' (9–11-year-old primary students) were added to the peer teaching.
- From Cycle 6, a second tier of Years 3 and 4 Relay Classes (8–9-year-olds) completed the peer teaching.

The effectiveness of the teachers was a major factor in the smooth running of the program, but turned out to be less significant to the students' learning than we had expected. In several cases, the teachers' **in**effectiveness even appeared to have a beneficial effect on the learning, and certainly on the autonomy of the students. The teachers took part with varying degrees of willingness—most were willing participants, and many were eager or engaged, but just a few proved consistently resistant, doubtful or antagonistic, even after volunteering. Some, particularly the primary teachers, were self-selected, because they were 'attached' to the desired Relay Class. We strongly discouraged any coercion to participate.

Until 2003, the schools were all chosen individually, and primary school participants were from the high schools' feeder primary schools. The prime selection criterion was the school's willingness to participate. This proved problematic; in some cases, the enthusiastic Principal urged the program on to teachers who were less enthused, at least initially. All secondary schools also had to have a senior drama program and a drama teacher willing to be the Key Teacher. Other criteria included:

- The geography (in Cycles 5–9 a range of inner-urban, suburban, outer-suburban and rural schools were selected);
- sociocultural and racial mix;
- socio-economic profile;
- gender profile (in Cycle 5 two all-girls' schools were included, and so Cycle 6 included two all-boys' schools).

The Pedagogy

Teaching Conflict Literacy

From the start of the project, our aim was to develop conflict literacy. In the action research, a variety of conceptual approaches to conflict and mediation were trialled, especially in the first three cycles. We developed these in association with a conflict management specialist academic, Dr. Merrelyn Bates. As the research evolved, a number of key concepts regarding conflict emerged as particularly valuable; we abandoned a few of our original ideas and integrated some new ones into the Project. By Cycle 4, the following concepts formed the basis of the theoretical content to be understood by the students and transmitted through the peer teaching to younger students. In addition, we designed the drama work to give them a thorough (experiential and three-dimensional) knowledge of the dynamics of conflict. The key concepts included the following:

- Conflict derives from clashes of interests, rights and power.
- Not all conflicts are destructive—conflict can be healthy.
- In clashes of interests, rights and power, the central participants are named the protagonists. To each protagonist, the person or persons with whom they are in conflict are named their antagonists.
- Conflicts are often fuelled by participants' assumptions and stereotypes of each other. For example, cultural conflicts can be fuelled by stereotypes based on recognising difference but not commonalities, combined with fear or ignorance of the perceived difference.
- Conflicts have three identifiable escalating stages: 'latent', 'emerging' and 'manifest':
  - latent, where there are potentially conflicting interests, rights, values or misunderstandings, but these have not yet led to conscious clashes;
  - emerging (or brewing), where some, but not all, of those affected by the conflict are aware of it;
  - manifest, where there are clashes of interests, rights, values or power imbalances for all those affected, and outsiders, to see.
- Conflict tends to escalate because of the emotions involved, and de-escalation has to take account of the emotional conditions as well as the clashes and misunderstandings.
- Some conflicts need third-party intervention, such as mediation.
- Mediation can involve separating the parties, removing them from the site of the confrontation and the heat of the moment, and exploring what can be conceded or negotiated.

Acting Against Bullying

In Cycles 7–9, with the additional focus on bullying, a number of new concepts derived from the current literature on the issue were included in the formal teaching.

- Bullying is always harmful.
- It involves the imposition of power by individuals or groups on those who are less powerful, with the intention of causing harm.
- It can be physical, verbal, psychological, social or sexual.
- There are normally three parties to bullying: the bully, the bullied and the bystander (The 3 Bs). Besides the alliterative value of the neutral noun participle 'bullied', we consciously avoided the more commonly used word 'victim' for the bullied party, as we perceived that it carried strong emotional and attitudinal associations and preconceptions that could affect both action and discussion.

- All parties have some power to change the situation, but the bystander has the most potential.

However, the idea of an escalating conflict through the three stages—latent, emerging and manifest—and the need to de-escalate the conflict proved equally relevant to bullying management. This formed the basis of the teaching and provided the framework for the enhanced forum theatre in the project.

Teaching Drama Techniques

In Cycle 1, we experimented with a range of drama techniques and genres, mainly improvisation, rehearsal and role-play structures. This was done within a school unit in Greek tragedy.

From then onwards, the range of techniques was consolidated into two classroom drama approaches—process drama and forum theatre—then further consolidated into one, where drama process techniques were incorporated into enhanced forum theatre (EFT). These genres are described in detail in Chap. 3.

In Cycle 3, to investigate the question of community impact, the Project stepped sideways, and the Key Class developed and performed a piece of community theatre-in-education (TIE), also using some techniques from both process drama and forum theatre.

In Cycles 2, 4 and 5, students learned one or both genres of process drama and forum theatre. We taught both to all the Key Classes; each group then made the choice to use one of them with their Focus Class. In Cycle 5, we also used this approach with the Relay Classes. The advantages and disadvantages of the two structures became clearer in the evaluations of each cycle. At the end of Cycle 5, a large focus group of participating teachers and students confirmed our observations that process drama was the more difficult strategy to grasp and to manage effectively, but it provided a deeper exploration of conflict. They perceived forum theatre as much simpler and clearer to manage, but felt it was superficial in terms of the students' understanding of conflict, compared with what the students learned from process drama.

We had ourselves become concerned about the number of students who were unable to fully comprehend or effectively manage process drama. We had also observed that forum theatre as practised in the project classes tended to remain superficial because, as part of the convention, the audience was encouraged to intervene with insufficient background and in the heat of the confrontation, which could actively encourage and teach bad conflict mediation practice. Consequently, we redesigned the drama component of the program for Cycle 6, consolidating the two techniques into the hybrid form that we named 'enhanced forum theatre' (EFT).

Peer Teaching

In the second year of the research, peer teaching emerged as a major technique in the implementation of DRACON. It was initially raised in a discussion with Morag, the class teacher, about reshaping the first year's experimentations in Greek theatre into what we felt was a more appropriately contemporary unit in terms of exploring conflict handling—'Social and Political Theatre'. Our desire to explore the socially engaged genre of process drama and the politically engaged work of Boal quickly led us to think of participatory performance with younger students, and we hit on peer teaching. This idea resonated perfectly with our overarching democratic teaching aim to use drama to give students the knowledge and cognitive tools to deal with their own real conflicts; these were already beginning to show up in our research evidence. We put together the sequence described in our Selection of Schools section above (Sect. "Selection of Schools, Teachers and Students"), and then sustained and extended this structure through all the remaining cycles.

The efficacy of peer teaching as a powerful pedagogy is outlined in Chap. 4. In our project, we found that peer teaching combined seamlessly with drama: the students were able to learn the drama techniques and through them learn the conflict concepts. These were clear, simple and congruent enough for them to master well enough to teach younger students, who could then do the same with minimal adult assistance. The peer teachers reinforced their own learning in the process. In almost every case, the younger students responded positively and productively to being taught by other students who had very recently undergone their own experiences, rather than by teachers who they felt were impersonal and far removed from experiencing conflicts as an adolescent. This was a constant theme in interview and survey responses. Our own research reinforced the weight of global research evidence that indicates that peer teaching can change habits of behaviour and increase self-esteem and a sense of mastery in participants.

In the Brisbane DRACON project, peer teaching proved crucial to the positive outcomes of the research, and the combination of drama and peer teaching became the core of the project. There was clear and continuing evidence throughout that the students involved in peer teaching were able to more effectively identify and manage conflict and bullying in their own lives than those with just drama, or with no tuition. The Swedish DRACON team also introduced peer teaching into their research, following its success in Brisbane.

Implementing the Programs

The Brisbane DRACON project was continuously implemented from 1996 until the end of 2005, as described. Because of the substantial number of schools involved, we are not giving each school an identifying pseudonym (as in the Swedish and

Adelaide chapters), to further complicate the reader's task. Instead, where relevant, we describe the schools in terms of their profile.

Cycle 1, 1996 Queensland—An Urban Brisbane High School

Cycle 1 took place in a Brisbane high school with a multicultural population. Together with the class teacher, Morag, we experimented with drama techniques and structures for teaching about the causes of conflict and ways of mediating and managing conflicts in the lives of the students.

In order to give the project every chance of success, we initially selected a performing arts high school, strongly supportive of drama, with a coherent and effective school conflict management strategy, an exceptionally competent drama teacher and a senior drama class (Years 11/12 combined; 29 students) as our Key Class of high achievers. We expected these drama students to be comfortable and competent in empathising with protagonists in conflict—'stepping into the others' shoes'—and in using drama techniques to explore conflict.

The Key Class was already involved in exploring conflict as part of their senior syllabus work on Greek tragedy for one school term (ten weeks of approximately three 45-min classes). Our experiments were constricted less by the time available than the unit content. These students found it difficult to relate classic tragic conflicts to their own domestic conflicts; moreover, our attempts to teach mediation concepts and skills were undermined by Greek tragedy itself, where the conflict is not resolved by human agency!

However, the results of this pilot clearly suggested that drama was an effective way of teaching students to understand the causes, nature and structures of conflict. Even in this first year, evidence of them applying this understanding to their own lives started to emerge. The following was typical of almost half the students who mentioned without prompting their real conflicts in the light of what they were learning:

> If I know there's going to be an argument with my mum, I'll just walk off, and I'll just think of a few things to say, and then I'll come back with a few different points. And I've talked to my sister about it and stuff like that. She's in Year 9. I've used some of our techniques on her—thinking of things she could say to a student instead of going in fighting. (Year 11 student)

Cycle 2, 1997 Queensland—The Same Brisbane High School

The results of Cycle 1 encouraged us to expand the work to investigate the Project's influence on conflict management throughout the same school and Key Drama teacher. During Cycle 1, we had noticed that some of the students had effectively peer-taught their classmates the techniques that they had previously learned. Accordingly, for Cycle 2, the team experimented with adding to the pedagogy large-scale peer teaching (class-based rather than the more common individual peer tutoring), with the intention of empowering the students to take over their own conflict management agendas.

Although the syllabus constraints of Cycle 1 had hindered the full implementation of the project, we still felt it was important to work within the normal curriculum, broadening out from the Drama class to include other younger groups, our first cohort of Focus Classes. In the interests of working towards a 'whole-school approach' and infusing the whole curriculum, we decided that it would be preferable not to confine the Focus Classes to Drama classes and Drama teachers. We split the Key Class students into four groups and trained each group to implement the same drama techniques and teach the same conflict concepts to one of four classes of Year 9 English classes. Fortunately, this time we located a Key Class with a flexible drama unit: 'Political theatre and drama', which was more appropriate to the project than Greek Tragedy, and where improvised drama techniques could be explored again. Fortuitously, the chosen Focus Classes were to study a theme-based unit in English called 'Conflict Resolution' at just the right time of year!

The Project team and our drama colleague provided a one-day in-service workshop for the four Focus Class teachers. Initially, two of these expressed strong resistance to the use of both drama and peer teaching. However, all the teachers ended up voluntarily extending the drama work with their classes.

In Cycle 2, we implemented and evaluated drama techniques explicitly designed to (a) develop understanding of the causes of conflict and its cultural components and (b) train the students in the basic demands of mediation. The Key Class—including a few of the 1996 students—spent a term learning about conflict and experimenting with transforming conflicts within the safe, fictional but realistic models that drama provides (see Chap. 4, Sect. "Towards an Integrated Model").

During this period, four major categories of conflict emerged through the drama work itself and through questionnaires administered to the Key and Focus Classes:

(a) peer conflicts;
(b) family conflicts;
(c) conflicts with teachers and administration;
(d) cultural conflicts.

We incorporated these categories into our program structure and used them in all later cycles.

Process drama, forum theatre and play-building were used in developing students' understanding of conflict. Two groups chose process drama and two chose forum theatre to work with the younger students. Each group met their class in advance to identify the topics and contexts of conflicts that the younger students were most concerned about.

After the peer teaching, we held follow-up interviews with all the Key Class students and with selected students from all the Focus Classes. In addition, one Focus Class teacher administered a questionnaire to all students in one her class. The data collected provided strong and unmistakable evidence that:

- Key Class students had reinforced their own learning by having to teach it to other students.
- Key Class students were again applying their learning to their own real-life conflicts.
- Focus Class students had enjoyed the experience and felt they had learned from it.
- Focus Class students had learned quite accurately the basic concepts about conflict from the Key Class students.
- Focus Class students strongly felt that, in the school context, peer teachers were preferable to adult teachers, because they were much closer to themselves, and better understood their problems, attitudes and conflicts.

In our evaluation of this cycle, we considered a possible extension of the project, with Focus Classes peer teaching primary students.

Cycle 3, 1998 Queensland—The Same Brisbane High School

In 1998, without an external grant, limited financial resources and timetable restrictions prevented the planned expansion of the project. Instead, for Cycle 3, the research team investigated Question 3: *whether the drama learning might be able to be applied in the broader school community*—beyond the school gates. A Key Class (incorporating some of the 1997 students who were now in Year 12) identified and researched through interviews a community group with specific conflict problems, then devised and presented to them a piece of participatory theatre-in-education, scripted and directed by a visiting British TIE director, Dr Steve Ball. The community group they chose was close to home—senior students in three other local schools, and their conflicts with parents related to leaving school. This subproject had little direct scrutiny from the research team, though it featured significantly in the class teacher's own research and subsequent PhD study (Morrison, 2009). However, it did establish that this was at least a practicable structure, with strongly positive feedback from performers and audience alike.

The preliminary findings of all three cycles demonstrated that the use of drama to teach conflict transformation concepts and approaches was both motivating and illuminating for students, with an overwhelming majority of Key and Focus Classes indicating they wished to extend their responsibilities for managing the school's conflict agenda. Over 50% of the 1997 Key Drama Class, unsolicitedly and explicitly, identified ways that they were applying their new understandings about conflict from the project to their school and home lives. There were very few negatives and, in the end, virtually no mitigating results. However, we had specially chosen the school for its strongly affirmative multicultural and conflict resolution agendas and the high status given to Drama in the school. The project team felt it necessary to give the drama and the peer teaching a tougher road-test in the next Cycle.

Cycle 4, 1999 New South Wales—A Rural High School and Feeder Primary Schools

In Cycle 4, our DRACON project came together with its other progenitor, the NSW *Whole-School Anti-Racism Project (WSARP)*. The continuation and extension of the peer teaching that we had originally planned for 1998 we instituted in 1999 as part of WSARP. Our action research method was essential here, since WSARP required the production of usable materials and resources. Through the action research, we were able to synchronise our continuing research into the interaction of peer teaching and drama in the teaching of conflict with the production of resource materials. We also added a new Research Question (5) as we were funded by the Multicultural Programs Unit: *to what extent can drama help students deconstruct cultural stereotypes and reconstruct a multi-cultural perspective, and what effect does this have on their management of cultural conflict.*

We made the following changes from 1997:

- We added the step of Focus Classes teaching primary children. This meant incorporating the high school's feeder primary schools into the project.
- We intended to withdraw from the day-to-day teaching of the project to give the Key and Focus Class teachers the opportunity of using the new resource materials for themselves.

We extended the one-day in-service course that we had held for the Focus Class teachers in Brisbane to a two-day residential in-service and invited all teaching staff. Almost 50% came, which was to prove significant in the informal school-wide on-the-ground support for the Project, where staff who were not directly involved in the program provided encouragement, especially for the Focus Class students.

There were other major differences from Cycle 2. We chose a school with a quite different cultural profile—a rural school rather than urban, and a much lower socio-economic catchment. Instead of a broadly multicultural student body, it had a bicultural profile comprising a white Anglo-Celtic majority and a significant Aboriginal minority. The school had a bad reputation for racial conflict, which students and teachers alike were trying hard to live down.

The Key Class was a very timid group of 12 (later 10) students, all girls (though the school was co-educational), with serious absenteeism. The Key Class teacher, though competent and experienced, had no experience of the process drama and forum theatre techniques we were using. The two Focus Classes consisted of:

- one Aboriginal Studies class of fifteen Year 9 students, about half of whom were themselves Aboriginal;
- one English class of twenty-eight Year 8 students, specially chosen by the school (against our advice) from among those students in the year-group with the most serious conflict problems.

The overall results were similar to Brisbane, and in the main, the expanded peer primary teaching worked successfully. However, as anticipated, there were more problems than in the Brisbane school. Through the expanded in-service, both the school administration and the other teachers were better informed than those in Brisbane, and were very supportive. However, chronic absenteeism by both staff and students was a severe problem, leading to a periodic loss of understanding and motivation. Sometimes there were fewer than four out of the ten Key Class students present. Their Key Teacher's family illness problems resulted in him abandoning the project, leaving the students to their own devices or to relief teachers, who were not briefed.

On at least three occasions, our observation was that our own ad hoc interventions (including a three-week full-time residency in the school by our research assistant, Anna) effectively 'rescued' the Project at the Key Class level, and our presence tended to keep it on task and schedule. These issues, however, gave us a rich research site as all the research team had to make constant visits, sometimes to run the classes in the absence of their teacher, which gave us the opportunity to witness, closely analyse and record some astonishing transformations, and to observe the overall success of the project, in varying degrees, despite the obstacles.

The results of the Focus Class peer teaching episodes were very positive. For once there was no absenteeism among the Key Class, a feature that we were to see repeated several times in later cycles. In the unavoidable absence of the two most highly motivated and informed Key Class students, other quieter and less active students took over calmly and efficiently, and surprised us all (another feature of later cycles). Their reflective responses indicated that the experience had significantly reinforced their own learning about conflict, as we had found in Cycle 2.

The Focus Classes participated with the same wholehearted enthusiasm as in Brisbane. Post-project interviews with the students evidenced the same pattern of approval and sense of having learned useful knowledge that would assist in their personal lives. We observed changes of behaviour, especially in the Aboriginal Studies class, with several normally withdrawn and passive students taking part assertively. We had anticipated problems with the 'special' Year 8 class, which did not eventuate as most of the students regarded it as an honour to have been chosen for the project.

The second-tier peer teaching caused logistical difficulties that threatened to derail the project, but also gave us the biggest surprises. The problem was again absenteeism, only teachers' this time. The enthusiastic Aboriginal Studies teacher was frequently absent, leaving the students to their own devices for most of the peer teaching preparation lessons. There did not appear to be a properly briefed teacher assigned at all to the Year 8 class at this point, and sometimes there was not even a teacher in the classroom, so we needed to intervene frequently, and sometimes run the whole session.

The peer teaching cohort comprised five groups of Year 6 and 7 students from two different schools, with each group, to our alarm, consisting of from forty to sixty students. They were assigned to the two Focus Classes, who taught in turns, each for an hour. Throughout the entire day, neither Focus Class had their teacher present. We and the accompanying primary teachers were the only adults present. We had asked them not to intervene, and we were intent on doing so only in emergency. To our astonishment, the students coped with these enormous classes and managed to complete the peer teaching. No formal results are available, but informally the student responses were positive. The most significant effects were on the peer teachers themselves. All the Aboriginal Studies students took an active and willing part in the peer teaching and managed their sessions without intervention. We observed culturally interesting patterns of Aboriginal communication, and several participants said that the sessions had changed their way of thinking about conflict, and about each other.

The Year 8 Class peer teaching was more inconsistent. Most of the boys showed little motivation. Two of the most seriously disturbed girls in the school who were on the brink of expulsion effectively ran the classes. Both managed the whole event and the large primary group with confidence, intelligence, resourcefulness, co-operation and teaching skill. We were forced to make only one rescue intervention.

For these two girls at least, the program was a life-changing experience. Follow-up interviews (immediately after the event and annually for the next three years) confirmed that the students' behaviour changed in school and beyond. Their orientation to the school and their teachers changed, they became positive and popular members of the school community and they became much less violent and instinctual in their response to conflict. The participants and their parents ascribed these changes to the Project.

> I've learned to be myself, to deal with my anger in different ways. DRACON taught me to stay calm, you know—take a few breaths and think about things. I've improved out of sight. More confidence, my attitude—just my attitude towards schoolwork, towards my family, towards the teachers, everything's just changed. It's great. It's made me feel like I have got to listen to others and there are other ways to deal with conflict. (Year 8 student—recorded in Year 10)

At the end of the project, we had come to the strong conclusion that the combination of peer teaching and drama was indeed a powerful and empowering pedagogy. On the other hand, logistical difficulties in schools and inconsistent approaches by teachers now loomed as major potential problems. However, we had not been able to establish the full picture of the teachers' capabilities and the effects of their absences. The knowledge we gained was channelled into the production of drama-based resource materials to be implemented state-wide in WSARP and used for further projected reflective practitioner research within the DRACON project. These materials, entitled the *DRACON Handbook*, provided the resources for the next stage of the project.

Cycle 5, 2000 NSW—4 Sydney High Schools and Feeder Primary Schools

We were disappointed that the rural school chose not to repeat the project the next year, due to those logistical barriers. In 2000 and 2001, with a new Australian Research Council (ARC) grant we expanded the Project into four urban Sydney high schools and their feeder primary schools. Chosen for their diversity in socio-economic and cultural profiles, two of these were girls' schools in middle-class inner suburbs and two were working-class outer-suburban co-educational schools. This entailed a new configuration of the project to meet diverse needs and school curricula. However, we retained many of the major features and consolidated them into a formal three-phase program lasting for about one and a half terms.

- In Phase I, with our assistance, a drama teacher introduced a Year 10 or 11 Key Class in each school to conflict theory and conflict management through drama.
- In Phase II, the Key Class worked with junior secondary Focus Classes, helping them to develop effective drama-based responses to conflict situations.
- In Phase III, the Focus Classes then taught the concepts and the drama techniques they had learned to classes of Years 5 and 6 primary students, which were now named Relay Classes.

The drama techniques used were again process drama and forum theatre, with Key Classes being given the option of choosing either for their own peer teaching. The program was preceded by a two-day practical in-service workshop with the participant teachers, school guidance officers and regional consultants, modelled on the previous year's workshop.

There were a number of key differences too, mainly designed to cope with the research team's greater distance (1100 km), and therefore the impossibility of our on-the-spot availability. We appointed DRACON Coordinators in each school, at the level of deputy head, who were responsible for the project's logistics and support. Several regional WSARP and Performing Arts consultants, who were mostly experienced seconded teachers, were also involved and became important liaison personnel between the Department, the research team and the schools. We appointed Christine Hatton, an experienced local (Sydney) teacher as our research assistant, who was able to intervene when necessary, as well as gather data. This was a direct outcome of our concern about the vulnerability of the program when not directly operated by ourselves.

In general terms, this cycle corroborated and added to the observations of previous years in nearly all respects. The Key, Focus and Relay Classes all took place with some measure of success. All levels of students in all four schools were uniformly positive about the program, with the exception of only one Focus Class—see below. All the others enjoyed the drama and the peer teaching, and they felt that it had helped them to understand conflict. Some students once more disclosed that they attempted to use what they had learned in their real conflicts. Again, the research assistant, the advisers and the teachers observed and reported notable individual transformations, particularly among Key Class students. The school principals and administrations all approved of the program's achievements—though some had kept a closer eye on its achievements than others.

As well as collecting evidence of success, the research team examined the project data for problems and potential barriers to what was now evidentially a powerful and successful pedagogy for conflict transformation. Student and occasionally teacher absenteeism was once again a problem that seemed to cancel itself out: in all cases, the students turned up in full for the peer teaching sessions and contributed, even if they had barely attended the preparation sessions. Most of the teachers needed support and assistance, from the WSARP advisors, occasionally from the Brisbane team on visits to Sydney, and particularly from the research assistant Christine Hatton, who intervened effectively when necessary, and produced valuable supplementary resource materials based on local curricular demands.

New logistical problems did emerge, such as the inflexibility of school timetables, which made it hard to organise the Focus Class peer teaching within the school and particularly the visits by or to the primary Relay Classes; these were sometimes at the high school and sometimes in their own schools. Perhaps the biggest continuing problem was the research team's communication with the schools. We established a protocol that we would communicate primarily through the school's DRACON co-ordinator, but the busy deputy principals who usually filled this role were often unable to make the project a high priority. This was compounded by erratic official communication, as none of the teachers had personal e-mail addresses or a personal school telephone number, and sometimes by unreliable responses from the Key Teachers. Those problems were greatly alleviated by the multicultural consultants, who became an important support group to the whole program.

Another ongoing problem that took us by surprise was the difficulty of getting the teachers to consult the DRACON Handbook, which was clearly laid out, but rather bulky and not user-friendly in layout. We stressed the importance and comprehensiveness of this document at the in-service training and constantly during our visits. However, anxious teachers still frequently consulted the team about matters that were explained within the document—particularly the drama techniques. We were also surprised by the Key Teachers' lack of experience with these techniques, and in some cases with drama itself and its place in the curriculum. Once more, research assistant Hatton often came to the rescue.

With the larger numbers and types of schools, personnel problems became more noticeable, if not more frequent. Surprisingly, there was some resistance and/or obstruction from our Key Teachers. One had volunteered for the program, then obviously regretted it and did not implement most of his Key teaching, nor encourage his students. Another, effusive in person, was notable for her frequent absences, which the students mirrored. The same teacher had a predilection for favourites, which deflected the students' attention from DRACON and created divisions in her class. A few other teachers lacked enthusiasm or belief in their students' peer teaching capabilities. In all bar the one case already mentioned, these peer teaching episodes ended up observably successful, sometimes with a little help from the consultants or ourselves. In that solitary case, the class had poor group dynamics, little group trust and low self-esteem as a group, which were all exacerbated by their complete lack of respect for the teacher. To their own relief, they were pulled out of the project by the school DRACON co-ordinator. Some later expressed regrets.

An innovation in this cycle was a feedback day involving nearly all the participating teachers and selected Key and Focus Class students. This valuable and mutually appreciated event resulted in several changes being implemented in the following cycle.

Cycle 6, 2001 NSW—8 Sydney and Regional High Schools and Feeder Schools

In Cycle 6, we retitled the program *Cooling Conflicts*. However, informally, many of the participants continue to call it DRACON.

Double the number of schools was involved. All four of the Cycle 5 high schools volunteered to continue with the project, three with new Key Teachers and Focus Classes from different curriculum areas. In one school, the two Focus Classes became the new Key Classes (setting a precedent, because they were only Years 9 and 10, not senior classes). At the request of WSARP, four new high schools joined the project, each with at least one feeder primary school. This enabled us to fill some of the gaps in the school selection criteria: two boys' high schools with different socio-economic profiles, a tiny inner-city high school with severe sociocultural problems, and a school in a regional country town.

On the advice of the teachers and Educational Department personnel, there were several changes, three of them major, for this year's cycle. Two of these were structural. We fully incorporated the primary school Relay Classes and included their teacher in the preliminary in-service to give them full information and ownership of the Project. We also extended the peer teaching downward to second-tier Relay Classes of Years 3 and 4 students. Our observations showed that when properly peer-taught, the Relay Class children were quite capable of understanding the conflict concepts and implementing the drama, and decided that the first level Relay Classes should be given the same opportunities for reinforcing their own learning through peer teaching.

The third major change was pedagogical; we consolidated the drama techniques into enhanced forum theatre, following the strong advice from teachers and students on the Cycle 5 Feedback day.

In addition, we made further changes to attempt to improve the communication channels and to try to give the teachers more support with less direct intervention from us. We updated, clarified and simplified the Handbook. We fine-tuned the in-service training to enable teachers to give more effective assistance and to enable them to contribute more to the project. We got direct telephone access to the participant teachers. The multicultural consultants' role was clarified, and their direct involvement encouraged.

A notable outcome of this cycle was our production of a professional-quality DVD: *Cooling Conflicts*. This was used as a teaching tool in future cycles and as an instrument for advocacy.

This cycle concluded our official engagement with NSW and WSARP and provided unmistakable evidence that drama and peer teaching worked to give students both understanding of the nature of conflict and competence in handling it.

> Before, I didn't know the three stages of conflict, but now I know how to stop a fight if it's started.
>
> I have learned to manage my conflicts better because my fighting has gone down.
>
> I have learned by me trying to stop the fight instead of making it worse.

(Year 5 questionnaires)

The NSW MPU continued to run the Project for at least the next decade. Follow-up research that we were able to carry out after six years indicated that some form of the *Cooling Conflict* program was running in over 135 schools; in many of these it was incorporated into their school behaviour management policy and programs.

Cycles 7–9 Queensland 2002–5—Twenty-Five Brisbane and Regional Queensland Schools

In 2002–2005 (Cycles 7–9), a new ARC grant permitted what was effectively a new DRACON project, entitled *Acting Against Bullying (AAB)*. This was based in five high schools, four in Brisbane and one in a regional centre, with their neighbourhood primary schools. Initially planned for three years, the three cycles effectively ran as one continuous cycle over four years, which is why we have consolidated their descriptions under one heading. This Project was instigated by the Queensland Department of Education and enthusiastically endorsed; *Acting Against Bullying* was launched by the State Premier at one of the Project Schools. However, after this welcome publicity, all that enthusiasm quickly dissipated, when the relevant official moved and nobody else in the Department knew how to categorise us, nor wanted to take responsibility for the Project. After 2002, no division of the Department aided or acknowledged the Project, so it remained centred in the participating schools and entirely dependent on them.

Another major structural shift that happened in 2004 involved beginning the Project in several additional primary schools (Years 1–7 in Queensland). This was at the behest of some primary school principals because either their 'home' secondary school was not involved in the Project, or they were frustrated that their own school's involvement had to wait until the second half of the year, when the downwards spiral of Focus Class teaching reached their students.

In general, this experiment did not work well, partly because of the lack of support from the Department but more significantly because the teachers in those schools, apart from the keen Project initiator, who was usually the principal, rarely had sufficient confidence in either drama or peer teaching to give the Project the time, energy and prioritisation it needed. By the end of 2005, this version of the Project had petered out and had been discontinued in almost all the schools.

Just like the NSW school in Cycle 4, it can be said that AAB produced notable positive findings despite the odds: its apathetic and at times hostile official settings, lack of sponsorship, and the limited success of the primary-first experiment. For the whole of this Project, we added and addressed two significant Research Questions to the five already explored; the first a natural successor to the earlier cycles, the second quite new:

6. *What is needed for the professional development of teachers in teaching conflict literacy and bullying management through drama?*

7. Can the combination of peer teaching and drama also empower school students to deal with bullying?

Professional Development of Teachers—A New Model

For Research Question 6, unmistakable evidence had emerged from the large-scale, two-year Sydney cycles that a small but significant proportion of teachers lacked the basic skills, knowledge and confidence to use either drama or peer teaching effectively, where they only had the assistance of a teaching manual and/or brief in-service training. Many were also unable to find ways of incorporating either form within their normal curriculum. The research team observed that while for the students the Project had been democratic and empowering, ironically for the teachers it was often the opposite, especially when imposed 'top-down' by the school administrators.

To investigate this question, we fashioned an in-service professional development model that incorporated the teachers from the outset, in their own classroom, as joint decision-makers with the School DRACON co-ordinators and the research team. The model we used had been identified as a highly effective professional development structure (Ball, 1982) and entailed a series of professional development workshops for a range of teachers in five pilot schools (one trial school in 2002 and an additional four in 2003). Following their professional development, the teachers introduced an anti-bullying program to their classes. The students were trained in drama techniques and peer teaching that focused specifically on countering bullying rather than on conflict management.

When interviewed after the Project, most teachers indicated that they had been empowered by their participation in the Project, and were able to recognise bullying much more clearly, including the distinct types of bullying behaviour and the differences between genders. Over 80% of teachers believed that the Project should be a part of a whole school anti-bullying program in their schools.

Encouraged by this, in 2004, we instigated a Master Teacher training program with four Key Teachers, enthusiastically endorsed by them. Its purpose was to build their capacity not only to lead the Project in their own school, but also to set up networks in their local areas. Unfortunately, the Department's enthusiasm had long-since dissipated and the Master Teachers initiative received no encouragement or assistance—financial, in-kind or logistical; it quickly became impractical and officially petered out. However, three of those teachers were able to build on their own understanding and confidence over the next few years to sustain and expand their own programs, at least locally—in effect, they did become master teachers.

Acting Against Bullying—A New Approach

For Research Question 7 (*drama and peer teaching to counteract bullying*), the three action research cycles each took a year, as for the earlier cycles. The aim was to develop a whole-school anti-bullying program that could be applied and disseminated within the standard school curriculum.

The same structure was employed, beginning with a senior secondary Key Class teacher introducing through drama activities and then EFT a simple set of concepts and definitions about the nature and consequences of bullying, and a range of bullying management techniques. They then began the peer teaching through EFT spiral exactly as in Cycles 5 and 6, through the Focus Classes and down to the Years 3 and 4 Relay Classes, each peer teaching episode with students usually two years younger, which we had established was the most effective age gap. A range of curriculum areas was invoked, so that the Project was cross-curricular (sometimes primarily for timetable logistics) and included English, Social Studies, Health and Physical Education, occasionally Indigenous Studies, Science and Mathematics.

Where available, the school's own records of the incidence and nature of bullying provided our baseline data. We administered and analysed over three hundred pre- and post-questionnaires to participant students and teachers. In each cycle, we conducted focus group interviews with students from all year levels, and summative one-on-one interviews with selected students and their class teachers. Some students, especially in the high schools, wrote reflective journals. We collected these data sets during each of the three years of the action research in the five high schools and their neighbourhood primary schools, along with ancillary data.

Findings and Outcomes

Rather than providing definitive findings and quantifiable evidence, during the first six cycles most of our accrued action research data was informing and developing better research and pedagogical procedures from a range of volatile contexts, with many uncontrollable variables. Accordingly, for Cycles 1–6, we have described discursively for the reader these developing understandings and their indicators, rather than metrics or evidentiary outcomes. However, from Cycles 7–9, we were able to collect both qualitative and quantitative data, as well as conducting longitudinal case studies in the participating secondary schools.

Outcomes from Cycles 7–9

The research findings from each action research cycle, and from the summative data collected, clearly and consistently revealed significant impacts on major manifestations of bullying in the subject schools. These impacts involved an increase in awareness about bullying itself, and positive changes in the attitudes and behaviours of bullies, those being bullied, and bystanders.

All our research data sets over the three years consistently showed that students feel that when they can experiment within the drama they are able to empathise with students being bullied and understand the behaviour of bullies, and to intervene in role appropriately for both parties. Furthermore, many students involved in the *Acting Against Bullying* Project identified that the third party, the bystander, usually has the greatest opportunities for de-escalating the situation, which is crucial in a bullying situation. In EFT performances, students intervened more often as bystanders than as both bullies and bullied combined.

Over 90% of the 216 secondary school students who were surveyed during the final two years of the Project were able to define bullying, identify the three types of people involved in bullying (bullies, bullied and bystanders) and list the stages of conflict escalation (latent, emerging and manifest).

In the final surveys and questionnaires, 87.2% of all the students surveyed in the project stated that they were better able to recognise when bullying was taking place, and 87.1% believed that bullying could be de-escalated or stopped. Asked if they were more likely to do something in response to a bullying situation to de-escalate or end it, 64% of all students involved in the Project replied 'yes' and 33% said they were 'not sure'; only 3% responded negatively. Questioned whether they had learned how to manage bullying situations better, 70.3% students replied 'yes', 19.3% stated they were 'unsure' and only 10.4% responded 'no'.

> Bullying can cause major physical and psychological damage. The victims in a bullying situation can suffer more than people realise. These people have the power to stop the bullying. If they don't let themselves be bullied or give the bully power it may stop. (Year 11 Student)

In primary schools where the project was implemented successfully from the neighbourhood high school, teachers noticed greater awareness in their students of the nature of bullying and increased confidence in their ability to deal with it. Teachers generally agreed that they saw positive changes after the Project in their more problematic students' attitudes towards bullying. Interestingly, students who had previously displayed bullying tendencies often became leading advocates of the Project during the peer teaching sessions, confirming our findings from Cycles 3 onwards. Teachers and students noted that students who were being bullied were empowered to take more responsibility for their situations, through their new understanding of the nature of bullying and their experience through drama of managing bullying situations. Inevitably, our classes frequently contained youngsters who in real life were currently being bullied, and were or had been bullies and bystanders. Many students were able to recognise and acknowledge that they had been a bullied, a bystander and even a bully—and sometimes all three in different contexts.

The conceptual framework of the *Acting Against Bullying* research particularly emphasised the role of the bystander. When exploring bullying situations through drama, the students portraying bystanders were encouraged to experiment with strategies to de-escalate the bullying. In a survey of the 124 secondary school students involved in the Project in 3 schools in 2005, 59% identified the bystander as the person most likely to change a bullying situation, while only 20% named teachers, and 14% the bully or the bullied. The outcomes of the research consistently indicated that students, especially secondary school students, were far more likely to become competent at dealing with bullying in their own lives if they were empowered to do so by confronting it through drama and then teaching what they had learned to their peers.

Conclusions and Projections

The summative evidence from all our action research project clearly indicates that the combination of peer teaching and enhanced forum theatre can assist individual students to deal more effectively with both conflict and bullying in their own lives. Other noteworthy evidence of the positive impact of our action research project on the schools themselves continues to emerge. One school initially became involved in the research in 2003 because of an ongoing series of serious bullying incidents in the school that attracted the attention of the State Education Department and the media. From 2004 to 2008, *Acting Against Bullying* was established in this school as the centre of its behaviour management program. In this period, the school began to keep accurate records of the incidence and seriousness of bullying behaviour throughout the school. The school records indicated a significant decline in reported bullying, and the teachers and school management staff reported the disappearance of major bullying incidents as a behaviour problem. At the time of writing, this school continues to run its behaviour management program with *Acting Against Bullying* as its core.

The data from Cycles 4–9, from the inception of primary peer teaching in 1999, consistently indicated that students as young as eight years old found no difficulty in remembering the parties to conflict and bullying, and the terminology of 'latent, emerging and manifest conflict'.

> Latent is when you are like just talking or like arguing; emerging is when it gets a bit more serious; and then manifest is like when you start punching or you hurt them emotionally really badly or something. (Year 5 student)

Early primary students involved in the research were also able to describe the nature of each party to bullying and the key features of each of the three conflict escalation stages and could identify and discuss their representations in specific scenes in improvised plays they created or watched.

Over 300 questionnaires were administered during the three years of *Acting Against Bullying* and these recorded a consistent rate of 99% in students' ability to remember and define the three stages of conflict escalation and bullying, and identify these stages in their own drama work within the project and beyond. As a result, a clear outcome of the research has been that almost all students recognised the need to intervene in bullying before it becomes manifest, and students were able to articulate a valid understanding of the nature and implications of bullying. Most students surveyed also identified the bystander as being the party best able to intervene to change a bullying situation.

Finally, the longitudinal data collected in Sydney in 2007 as part of an ongoing evaluation provided evidence of the outcomes of the earlier *Cooling Conflict* project carried out by the research team and managed by the Industry partner—the NSW Department's Multicultural Programs Unit. This data indicated significant positive changes in the whole culture of some of the schools who implemented the Project for five years or more, with improved student relationships and a decline in the incidence of conflict in schools. There have been several tangible and practical local outcomes to the project in NSW. Firstly, in the participating schools, in the years following the project, the students and administrators had access to many trained reflective practitioners, both teachers and students. In addition, the schools had the opportunity to develop a coherent and sensitive approach to conflict and cultural harmony, both in the schools themselves and in the local communities. The NSW project was supported by the Department of Education and Training and then continued to expand, with four new schools introduced per annum. A 2003 follow-up to one of the Cycle 6 schools revealed that the Project had survived the withdrawal of external support, in-service and funding, but had mutated and was embedded in the Year 6–7 primary-to-secondary school induction program and subsequent Year 10 mentoring. The teacher and DRACON co-ordinator from this school also reported that some of the new secondary Year 7 students had experienced the initial Relay teaching as primary students in Year 5, and were still familiar two years on with the terminology and using it in their normal interaction:

> Miss! Miss! There's a conflict happening over by the pool! [As the teacher started to scramble to her feet:] *Don't hurry Miss, it hasn't got to manifest yet*
>
> [Year 7 student]

In addition, the Project had repercussions in other areas. In 2002, the Department organised a major multicultural education conference, with a demonstration of EFT from four of the *Cooling Conflicts* schools as a centrepiece.

Over the years since the Project, the Brisbane research team has received enquiries from youth drug awareness leaders and adult education organisations, specialist schools, Indigenous Youth schemes, as well as conflict management, peace education and corporate management organisations in USA, UK, Hong Kong and Kazakhstan among other overseas places. Those follow-ups that led to sustained new programs have been described in Chap. 9.

The long-term outcomes and significance of this project could have considerable implications in several other fields. For example, drama methods are currently being used in industry training in fields ranging from medicine to business management. In particular, the findings from our project will add to the growing body of research literature on the effects and effectiveness of drama methods in learning in a range of professions and fields, and, we hope, in the pedagogy of schools.

Postscript

I used to get angry and use violence all the time but now I just go for walks or take deep breaths, talk it through with my mum or who I'm angry with, and just stop and think of the consequences...and then you think, 'Yeah, latent, emergent, it's only got to emergent'—you know because you then step in—the actual words don't go through my head but the stages do, like. It's great. It has made me feel like I have got to listen to others and there are other ways to deal with conflict. Ever since I've been doing DRACON I haven't been getting into trouble at school lately. My results have been really good and so I think it must have done something. My pleasure and thank you for helping.

(Year 8 student interview)

All Photographs: Robert Weismantel

Brisbane 1: Acting Against Bullying... Will the bystanders intervene?

Conclusions and Projections 211

Brisbane 2: Acting Against Bullying... Enhanced forum theatre—emerging conflict

Brisbane 3: Cooling Conflict... Manifest conflict—who can de-escalate it?

Brisbane 4: Cooling Conflict... Enhanced forum theatre—hot-seating a protagonist

Conclusions and Projections 213

Brisbane 5: Cooling Conflict... Spotting a latent conflict

Brisbane 6: Cooling Conflict... Year 8 peer teachers demonstrate manifest conflict

Brisbane 7: Acting Against Bullying... The mediator investigates

Brisbane 8: Acting Against Bullying... The mediator intervenes

References

Ball, S. (1982). *Brisbane South region drama project: An evaluation*. Brisbane: Queensland Department of Education.

Coyle, S., & French, D. (1996). *The NSW whole-school anti-racism project*. Sydney, NSW: Department of Education and Training.

Morrison, M. (2009). Shouts and whispers: Re-engaging disaffected girls through peer-teaching drama. PhD thesis: Griffith University.

Plunkett, A. (2002). *The art of cooling conflict: Using educational drama and peer teaching to empower students to understand conflict* (PhD thesis). Griffith University.

Reason, P., & Bradbury, H. (2008). *The Sage handbook of action research: Participative inquiry and practice*. London: Sage.

Zuber-Skerritt, O. (2016). The action research planner: Doing critical participatory action research. *Educational Action Research, 24*(1), 150–154.

Part III
Past, Present and Future Impacts

Chapter 9
After DRACON: Persistence, Sequels and Echoes

The DRACON project was formally wound up in 2005, with the comprehensive final report appearing in 2007. However, this project has demonstrated a marked sustainability factor—it won't go away… which is part of the reason for this book. There have been some examples of continuity and many extensions. Some of the work has been continued for years in its original locations, and a little still exists in modified forms as batons picked up and passed on by others after the official research teams left. There have been immediate follow-ups, longer-term sequels and indirect offshoots of DRACON carried out by most of the participant researchers. All the authors of this book have incorporated the DRACON insights into their own practice and research, and consciously modelled aspects of later projects on DRACON. So too, many of our research associates, PhD students and colleagues, who have been influenced and inspired to start their own research or practical teaching projects, forming a 'second generation' of DRACON. Moreover, numerous other entirely independent new initiatives and spin-off projects using drama for conflict transformation have emerged around the world in a diversity of contexts ranging from Kazakhstan to Sierra Leone, and from remote indigenous communities to university management training courses. All of these have been inspired and influenced by what their leaders have seen and read of this work, either from direct contact with DRACON participants or from our earlier publications. This chapter tracks some of them.

Most of these have been practical projects and initiatives, some with an explicit research component. Many of them have been documented and written up individually in books, theses and research journals, or appear on websites. For readers wishing to find out more about any of these projects in this chapter, a complete list of all of them, including all the in-text references, can be found in **Appendix B**, under the project titles in the relevant subheading.

© Springer Nature Singapore Pte Ltd. 2019
J. O'Toole et al., *Researching Conflict, Drama and Learning*,
https://doi.org/10.1007/978-981-13-5916-3_9

Persistence: What Happened in the DRACON Schools?

From its initial conception, we have viewed and organised DRACON as a finite research project. Each of the four research teams identified and scoped their project, carried it out according to their plans, and formally wound it up. The whole DRACON collaboration was itself formally concluded at the Penang meeting of 2005. Nevertheless, some elements of the DRACON project did continue and prosper in their original locations after the formal project finished. All of these have been a bonus for the research teams, and this record is one of occasional rather than expected continuity. By definition, a university-based experimental research project like this, even if it has been welcomed and encouraged, is imposed on schools and disrupts their normal functioning. The very nature of schools, with frequent moves by committed teachers, changes of scheduling and timetabling, and shifts and replacements of management staff, makes vulnerable any initiative introduced and supported from outside—particularly ventures like the peer teaching in the Brisbane and Swedish projects that imposed constraints on the school's 'normal' logistics. These internal volatilities are often compounded by larger shifts in the educational environment that have their impact on schools' organisational structures, such as a new government's post-election 'restructuring' of education.

Some of the researchers designed their DRACON project as a one-off intervention in the first place, like the Malaysian theatre-in-education performances; to fly in and fly out is the essence of TIE. Some were limited experiments of differing durations, like the eight weeks of teaching in Adelaide, or the year-long Cycle 4 of the Brisbane Project in rural New South Wales. These were both set up specifically to allow the researchers to investigate and examine through drama how students deal with conflict in contexts that tied in with the researchers' earlier investigations. In Adelaide, these had been through field surveys and theoretical conclusions; in Brisbane, through action research. The criteria for school and class selection in both projects fitted this—both those research projects chose as their research site a cohort of socially disadvantaged students in locations dubbed 'conflict-rich' by a teacher in one of them with a strong sense of irony. Both were set up with a finite timeline, so continuity was never the intention.

In Adelaide especially, the timeline was extremely short and pressing as the team structured the drama work to finish in one term, with a final coming together of the work in a formal presentation at the end. The team produced a video to show the students and for the researchers' future use, but there was no discussion on continuing the drama after the research team had left. This would have been difficult as the research team facilitators planned and taught the lessons and the class drama teacher had chosen not to take an active part in the lessons as either teacher or observer.

In Brisbane's Cycle 4, the much longer timeline and the unexpected involvement of almost half of the teaching staff in the preliminary in-service training, together with their continuing informal support, did raise the research team's hopes that the project might continue in that school. However, those unavoidable constraints of schools—in this case the drama teacher's long absence during the project, new and pressing priorities for the principal, and no obvious successors for the Key Classes—meant that the project died when the DRACON team left.

Elsewhere there is evidence of considerable and admirable (though patchy) continuity, either of ongoing research into the project, or of the practical drama-and-conflict-transformation work in the DRACON schools. In Sweden, for instance, some school students with experience from the 2004 DRACON program had the opportunity to participate in a film added to the Swedish DRACON text book (see below), which was another direct outcome of the project. Nine years later, a drama teacher, Hanna Sjöstedt, met with a focus group of five of the students from this group. Her 2014 analysis showed that the students remembered all the important parts of the program, such as the ABC model, the animals representing conflict styles, mediation, third-party role-plays, video-recording and peer teaching. They also described glowingly the positive impact of their DRACON experiences on their whole class. Exclusive subgroups of boys and girls had disappeared, communication had increased, and they solved conflicts with each other's help. The atmosphere in the classroom had changed 'from restlessness to peacefulness'.

In the years after the Brisbane project too, although the rural NSW high school was not able to sustain the *Cooling Conflict* momentum in spite of its good intentions, a couple of the other cycles of the Brisbane project have shown evidence of greater longevity. Notwithstanding the almost complete lack of systemic support or encouragement in Queensland, one of the high schools participating in the later *Acting Against Bullying* subproject (Cycles 7–9) found so much evidence of the success of the drama and peer teaching from their own statistics on incidents and behaviour management, that they expanded their program to include the whole school. They have continued the program to this day (sixteen years from its inception to the time of writing), as we reported in Chap. 8. It is no coincidence that the original Key Teacher is still at the school, in a senior management position.

In NSW, the Department of Education Unit that had supported *Cooling Conflict* from 2000 to 2003 continued to support it officially for a number of years after the research concluded, first hiring the research team members to run the annual preliminary in-service workshop for their participating schools, then using one of their own original Key Teachers to lead the workshop. By the time the DRACON researchers followed up once more on this component in 2011, the explicit systemic funding had stopped, but the former NSW coordinator estimated that between 100 and 150 schools were still using some aspects of DRACON or its principles—the drama or the peer teaching, or both. By this time, the programs were usually embedded in the school's behaviour management programs and protocols. We have not been able to gather data since then, though the later NSW project has produced at least one spin-off program with troubled Aboriginal teenagers, described below.

Sequels: The Continuing Impact

It is hardly surprising that in one way or another, the majority of the researchers who were involved in the DRACON project in the three countries across the world have continued the work ever since, either to further investigate the research implications or to promote the practice, or both, including all of the authors of this volume. We have documented most of DRACON's research outcomes, mainly in the form of academic journal articles and chapters. **Appendix A** comprises a comprehensive list of the publications directly or indirectly emanating from DRACON and the theory behind it. This chapter therefore concentrates on the later effects of DRACON and its principles surviving in practice: how DRACON has continued to make an impact on schools and communities to this day.

In reviewing all the examples of where and how the spirit and principles of DRACON have been perpetuated, five overarching themes of primary intention emerge:

- Behaviour change in schools and with children
- Training the next generation of DRACON teachers
- Training in broader educational contexts
- Adult training and professional development
- Building resilience in individuals.

These themes are not watertight, and as believers in integrated programs we would be sad if there were not considerable overlap: for example, behaviour change with children may also build resilience in the individuals; teachers' professional development can often assist in both of those. When originally structuring this chapter, we settled on a sixth category that seemed clear at the time: 'community and cultural change'. However, in the writing, we realised that just about all of the examples and projects described, which neatly fit into the other categories, also had this theme, at a micro- or macro-level, as part of its underlying purpose, so it more properly forms the conclusion of this chapter.

Behaviour Change in Schools—DRACON: The Next Generation

Schools were at the centre of the DRACON research, and they have been the settings for much of the ongoing work. The theoretical research has continued for some years, particularly in Adelaide, where the DRACON team used the insights derived from DRACON in substantial further research and publication, mainly into bullying in schools and cultural conflict. In all four locations, the practical outcomes and follow-up projects that are the focus of this chapter have been embedded in, or accompanied by, action research.

New Uses for DRACON in Swedish Schools

The need for conflict and bullying management in Swedish schools has increased in the years following DRACON. Those years showed a national decline in the formerly highly rated education system as measured in the OECD *Programme for International Student Assessment (PISA)* tests, and though the 2015 PISA report indicated that the decline had begun to reverse, other findings were more worrying. Predictable governmental responses to the PISA decline—promoting a 'back-to-the-basics and increased testing' regime—had further exacerbated the problem, increasing the levels of student alienation. The sense of belonging in school had decreased more than in most of the other 72 countries participating in the PISA tests. The difference between advantaged and disadvantaged students was increasing. In addition, Sweden's exceptionally high level of acceptance of refugees and migrants during the period inevitably caused intercultural stresses, misunderstandings and conflicts.

In the years following our initial project, the DRACON program has been tried out with different age groups, with positive results. DRACON follow-up work with children as young as Year 5 primary classes has been documented over months. A typical comment was:

> 'This was the funniest day of DRACON but still the worst, for it was the last […] I recommend this for restless classes!' (Lundberg, 2014, p. 2)

At the other end of the age spectrum, the program has also been documented in the textbook *DRACON i skolan* (2005, see below) by one of the theatre teachers involved, Kristina Karls (dubbed 'Ingrid' in the book), as being entertaining and of good practical use among students in upper secondary theatre classes. Reports to the DRACON team from other schools and in other regions of Sweden, at different school levels, indicate that the first part of the program (see Chap. 6) is frequently used, though the second, more demanding part of the program that included video-recordings and an introduction to mediation and peer teaching, is more seldom reported. In 2015, a website enticingly titled *Learn for Peace*[1] was launched. It includes an introduction to the Swedish DRACON program.

Theatre-in-Education for Transforming Conflict in Malaysia

In Malaysia too, work did not cease after the research. After the DRACON research phase was completed, team member Janet Pillai worked with a theatre group: *Young Theatre Penang*, and a women's organisation: *Women's Centre for Change* (WCC), to develop applied theatre projects that incorporated findings from DRACON. This resulted in two large-scale TIE projects, which played to school audiences in Penang.

These projects involved young actors between the ages of twenty and twenty-three who researched conflict situations experienced by young people, then used the information to devise highly interactive and participatory performances. The

---

[1] [laraforfred.se].

performances incorporated educational drama techniques, particularly forum theatre and image theatre, and involved audiences as 'spect-actors' (see Chap. 3). These performances were accompanied by a resource kit for teachers to discuss the issue in more depth with their students.

The first project, 1998–1999, entitled *OK! Tak OK! (Okay! Not Okay!)*, dealt with the subject of child grooming and child abuse. The performance aimed at building children's awareness of 'good touch' and 'bad touch' and how to handle such situations. The second project, entitled *RESPEK (Respect)*, 1999–2000, dealt with the subject of teenage gender relations. Both projects were highly successful. They were ultimately transformed into interactive educational videos for primary and secondary schools in Penang as the WCC organisation realised that the use of drama in conflict handling was more effective than poster campaigns or talks, which were informative but did not provide opportunities for practice and critical thinking.

Acting Against Relational Aggression and Cyber-bullying

The need for new approaches to bullying, if anything, is increasing. Ten years after DRACON concluded, the 2015 OECD PISA report expressed deep concern about the worldwide 'significant prevalence of all forms of bullying'. Moreover, those statistics did not explicitly take account of the spectacular rise in cyber-bullying during the decade. According to an IPSOS/Reuters survey in 2012, over one in ten parents (12%) worldwide stated that their own child had experienced cyber-bullying, and a quarter (24%) said they knew a child who had. According to online workplace analysts TAL Global, by 2017 the numbers had risen: 'Over half of adolescents and teens have been bullied online, and about the same number have engaged in cyber-bullying'.[2]

From 2009 to 2010, Brisbane team member Bruce Burton led an action research project of three cycles exploring cyber-bullying in Brisbane schools. At this time—two years before the celebrated IPSOS/Reuters 2012 report—cyber-bullying was just beginning to receive considerable local media coverage and official concern. He conducted his project in a large all-girls school, and his initial investigations revealed that bullying was endemic among the older adolescent girls in the school. The action research clearly demonstrated that the conceptual framework and techniques of the *Cooling Conflicts* and *Acting Against Bullying* programs were equally effective in uncovering and managing covert cyber-bullying among adolescent females. However, just as in all previous implementations of both programs, it was necessary to adapt the structures and techniques to the specific context.

Acting Against Bullying at the Islamic School of Brisbane

Australia has also been experiencing many of the same geosocial changes in schools as Sweden: a similar slide in PISA ratings; governmental responses of 'back-to-

---

[2] http://talglobal.com/cyber-bullying-the-facts/, accessed 17 April 2018.

basics' and a new testing regime; and a sharp rise in refugee migration. The stresses of the last factor were deeply exacerbated and magnified by conflicted government policy decisions and openly hostile political rhetoric that have increased intercultural stresses within Australian communities, particularly for some migrant groups—most notably Muslims.

In 2010–2011, Burton led a mixed group of university students in implementing the *Acting Against Bullying (AAB)* program in a Brisbane Islamic high school, over two years, with students from Year 11 down to Year 8, at the school's request. The program produced strongly positive data right across the four-year levels on reductions in bullying and increased students' awareness of it. However, the most remarkable outcome was the way the Year 11 Muslim girls used the project to assert their equality with their Year 11 male counterparts, insisting on scenarios and explorations of bullying that addressed the male-dominant culture in the school and in their community. By the end of the project, the girls were running the implementation of *AAB*, and organising and controlling the behaviour of the boys.

Bullying and Cultural Conflict Mediation in Adelaide

Adelaide team members Ken Rigby and Dale Bagshaw both used the insights derived from DRACON in substantial further research and publication, mainly into bullying in schools, and the impact of verbal abuse and bullying on adolescent identity and gender. In the same multicultural spirit as the Brisbane Islamic project above, Bagshaw has conducted workshops making extensive use of DRACON-type role-plays for Year 10 students from the Adelaide Islamic College, and various groups of New Australian youths from Afghanistan and Africa, funded by Multicultural South Australia.

The Indra Congress Peace Project

Of all the young people's projects directly employing the principles and practice of DRACON, probably the most inspiring is the Indra Congress. This is described as a 'growing, global network of young people, artists, educators and others who share a commitment to the development of the arts as a crucial resource for peace-building and the non-violent transformation of conflict' (Indra Congress, 2018). Indra Congress was launched in 2010, the brainchild of English drama educator David Oddie and international collaborators, and aimed to link and bring together youth theatre groups from round the world in this cause. Oddie was himself inspired to use the DRACON techniques by reading the Brisbane team's textbook *Cooling Conflict* (See below). From the start, the *Cooling Conflict* model has been the Congress's central modus operandi, particularly the use of enhanced forum theatre (EFT) and the accompanying conflict analysis model. One of Indra's offshoot foundations in Derry, Northern Ireland, is even entitled *The Art of Cooling Conflict*. Indra's network includes young people's theatre groups from Brazil, Cyprus, Greece, India, Ireland,

Kosovo, Nigeria, Palestine, Portugal, Sierra Leone, South Africa and the UK dedicated to using drama and theatre in the cause of world peace. Their congresses so far have brought these young people together through drama and theatre in England, Northern Ireland, Palestine and South Africa.

Chinese Puzzles

Cross-cultural germination of the seeds of DRACON is no bed of roses. We have underlined the importance of adapting the specific pedagogy and drama techniques devised for the DRACON projects to their particular contexts. This is illustrated by examining in slightly more necessary detail one of DRACON's less immediately successful manifestations, in one of DRACON's sequels in China.

Chinese applied theatre practitioner Au Yi-Man has had some success working through Oxfam with Chinese village adult groups, using some of the DRACON techniques she originally embraced at a demonstration in a drama conference in the UK. Making DRACON work for Chinese secondary school children is the problem that is currently perplexing her. At the time of writing, she is attempting to establish the Brisbane model of EFT and peer teaching with 14-year-old secondary school students in Yunnan province. The school appears willing, yet not entirely committed, because drama and open discussion of conflict are both a long way from the school's conventional Chinese curriculum and pedagogy, which is strongly one-way transmissive and content-driven. Au reports that the students are enjoying the experience but display embarrassment; they are not taking it seriously nor fully engaging in the drama and conflict transformation structures. Peer teaching has not yet been possible. She has described her bewilderment in ongoing correspondence with Brisbane team member John O'Toole, who also mentored her much more successful earlier work with adult NGO trainers (see below). Together, they are endeavouring to diagnose whether her own and the students' difficulties are due one or both of the following:

– the students' 'Chinese-ness', including commonly identified national characteristics that are reinforced by their systemic education: fear of loss of face; reluctance to speak or assert themselves in class; obedience to authority; and comfort with given answers rather than open-ended questions;
– Au's own lack of familiarity with teenagers, and the relevant pedagogical skills, because she is trained and experienced as a teacher of adults, not children.

This example in particular raises a significant new question, still to be answered:

– to what extent is the success of DRACON affected by cultural factors?

Adopting the principles and theory of DRACON has sometimes been easier than adapting the DRACON teaching techniques to particular contexts. Cross-cultural situations demand answers to the two vital and complementary questions:

– To what extent is the success of DRACON dependent on the teacher's competence in adapting the pedagogy to the cultural context?

Sequels: The Continuing Impact

– Which culture are we talking about: the macro-culture of the participants' national identity, or the micro-cultures of the students' classroom and their expectations, or both?

These questions recur in more than one of the post-DRACON projects recorded here and may be a factor in some of the well-meaning attempts of teachers to implement projects inspired by DRACON that have disappeared without leaving evidence of why... which also makes our next category of the purposes of post-DRACON initiatives a vital one.

Training the Next Generation of DRACON Teachers

DRACON Textbooks and Their Effects

Among the earliest manifestations of the ongoing momentum of DRACON was the publication of school textbooks written by two of the research teams, both appearing in 2005. The first of these, by Grünbaum and Lepp (2005), was in Sweden: *DRACON I SKOLAN. Drama, konflikthantering och medling (DRACON in School. Drama, Conflict Management and Mediation)*. The book is accompanied by a demonstration video and introduced the Swedish DRACON project to teachers and drama educators in Sweden. Some schools purchased the book for all interested teachers. In addition, the authors ran DRACON courses for teachers to add to their knowledge about how to practise drama for learning about conflict management and mediation. The ideas spread to some extent, but this did not lead to a 'whole-school' approach that had been the team's ambitious aim from the start of DRACON Sweden.

In Australia, the comprehensive teachers' handbooks that had formed part of the *Cooling Conflicts* project in NSW and *Acting Against Bullying* in Queensland were also transformed by John O'Toole and Bruce Burton into a book, *Cooling Conflict* (O'Toole et al. 2005), which tells the story of the projects and provides models and guidance for teachers. Perhaps because the book was trying to do those two disparate things, or perhaps because of the delay, when teachers' interest in the projects had also cooled, it did not have nearly as much local success in sustaining the project as the Swedish textbook. However, it did have some longer-term and more far-reaching effects, most notably on the *Indra Congress*. Like the Swedish researcher-practitioners, the Brisbane team has continued to hold demonstrations and in-service workshops for some years, in Australia and overseas. As in Sweden, however, the whole-school approach that was also the Australian researchers' dream has only eventuated in a tiny handful of cases.

Training Teachers in Sweden Today

Systematic teacher training of the DRACON program can be found especially at the Västerberg Folk High School, Storvik, where Grünbaum worked; since 2000 all the students have received five to six days intensive training. Whether through this or their textbook—or probably both—the flame of interest in DRACON is still alive and well today in Sweden. At the time of writing this chapter, 24 drama teachers, representing preschools, primary schools, cultural schools and Swedish folk high schools, had just participated in a three-day DRACON workshop for 14–15-year-olds, run by Grünbaum and Lepp, organised by the major Swedish association of drama pedagogues, RAD .[3] The leaders implemented all the steps of the Swedish DRACON program (see Chap. 6, Section "Third-Party and Mediator Roles") except the video-recording and peer teaching. Analysis of the participants' dramatic interventions proved they were ready to try their hand at being impartial mediators.

Mediation for Teachers and Administrators in South Australia

A similar approach has been used in Adelaide since the end of the DRACON project. The South Australian Education Union has mounted yearly five-day workshops for teachers and administrators on mediation as an approach to conflicts and bullying in schools These have been run by Bagshaw, using DRACON theory and practice. The workshops have used a range of school-based scenarios in role-plays, to give participants the opportunity to develop their skills as mediators, conflict parties and observers.

Developing Mentoring Skills for Conflict in Kazakhstan

Australian team member Morag Morrison, currently working at Cambridge University UK, was invited to become involved in Kazakhstan's national teacher development project on a recurrent annual basis from 2013 to 2016. Working with 20 experienced teachers undertaking school leadership training, Morrison utilised EFT to help these teachers develop and manage classroom scenarios of conflict. These scenarios were then incorporated into an exploration of drama and conflict for all 90 teachers undertaking this level of training over one week of their program. Kazakh teachers were not familiar with working through the medium of drama, but they embraced its potential and were thoroughly engaged in the activities. Although this was only one small component of a series of training activities, it is interesting to note that many of the international trainers, after seeing the levels of engagement among the teachers, began to introduce some drama and role-play into their own sessions.

---

[3]RAD: Riksorganisationen Auktoriserade Dramapedagoger. www.dramapedagogen.se.

Enhancing Teachers' Interpersonal Skills

Closer to home in Cambridge, Morrison recognised that while teachers in all secondary disciplines may receive some guidance on classroom management, little in their training prepares them for developing an understanding of the often complex interpersonal contexts in which they will work. She conducted a 'mini' action research project with a mixed group of 64 postgraduate secondary preservice students, who were preparing to teach across a wide range of subjects, including Maths, Science, the Humanities and the Arts. Her two three-hour sessions of action research utilised strategies and techniques drawn from the DRACON work, in particular EFT, to support trainee teachers in their understanding of professional situations and sources of conflict. The workshops bridged the gap between theory and practice as students explored alternative perspectives on a problem towards developing deeper professional understanding. Her findings indicated that the workshops offered a dynamic form of engagement and reflection that proved to be a powerful learning medium for professional development of those students.

Broader Educational Contexts

Not surprisingly, since most of the drama researchers in the original DRACON teams came from teacher education, these are the adult training contexts that have been most strongly—though not exclusively—focused upon. However, DRACON has also been used by those researchers, and others, for a widening range of educational purposes. The pedagogical value of DRACON goes well beyond the training of teachers.

Training Disability Workers in Japan

In the most recent of these professional outreach initiatives, a drama and conflict management project was introduced in Japan in 2018, in a collaboration between Kochi University (Kanako Korenaga) and Gothenburg University (Margret Lepp). The overall aim was to understand the methodology underlying drama pedagogy as it applied to the support of children with developmental disabilities. This was to improve the participants' practical knowledge of how to intervene and how to advise local childcare centres, kindergartens and schools about online support for developmental and other disabilities. The target groups were staff from children's support groups, graduate students and other senior education consultants. A more specific aim for the two-day workshop was to design and implement future drama workshops for care staff and teachers that would assist the development of their own communication, interaction and conflict management skills when working with children, students and patients with special needs.

Child Care Workshops in Japan

Well after we started on the writing of this final chapter, Lepp found herself leading a drama education workshop as part of the above Kochi/Gothenburg collaborative agreement. Held at a child welfare facility in Takaoka City, Japan, the workshop's aim was to help mutual understanding and conflict management in everyday life, by giving participants the opportunity to 'play the other'. Approximately 20 people, including teachers and child care staff, learned the importance of drawing out the feelings of the other person through playing the roles of children and adults. As one of the teachers summed it up:

> Classroom management is important to build relationships between children and parents, so that we could learn the importance of having a broad perspective to deal with various ideas though drama education.

Mediator Accreditation in Australia

Supervised role-plays demonstrating mediator competence are a requirement for the training of all Australian mediators who apply for accreditation with the Australian National Mediator Standards Board. Dale Bagshaw has trained for this accreditation hundreds of mediators from a wide range of disciplines and cultural backgrounds, incorporating DRACON principles and practice in her training. She and other trainers in Australia have used DRACON-style role-play to provide opportunities for student mediators to apply their knowledge and skills under supervision, as mediators, participants and observers.

Training Academic Supervisors in Sweden

DRACON principles are also applied at a high level of university educational training at Mälardalens University, Sweden, by Margret Lepp. A course entitled 'Supervisors—Third Cycle Programs' is offered within the Competence Centre for Students, the Labour Market and Personnel. The participants are already PhD supervisors, or at least on their way to becoming associate supervisors. In addition, they represent different fields such as engineering, education and health care education. For several years, *Drama as a tool towards a deeper understanding* has been an appreciated component of the course. The drama content includes group process activities, cultural understanding and forum theatre. All the drama activities are designed to enhance understanding of the significance and implications of being a supervisor for PhD students with problems, dilemmas and conflicts.

Training the Trainers in Chinese NGOs

In China, from 2013 to 2015, Au Yi-Man found that—unlike her experiences with school students—using the DRACON theory and some of its techniques with adults was doubly successful. She was working on a three-year PhD research project, designed to increase capacity-building among approximately 20 trainers employed in a range of non-government organisations (NGOs). Her action research fieldwork involved training them to utilise applied theatre techniques, including some of those pioneered in DRACON—notably EFT. Her first win was to come up with conclusive evidence that the participants' dramatic understanding of, and pedagogical skills to teach, applied theatre had been raised—though to different levels that directly correlated with their previous familiarity with drama and applied theatre techniques. Importantly, they themselves were also aware of this improvement. The other part of the double win was a quite unexpected result—and as it sits squarely within our final category of Building Resilience, it will be described there.

Adult Training and Professional Development

Not surprisingly, DRACON has caught on in nursing and nurse education contexts just as successfully as in schools and among teachers. Just like schools, hospitals and other medical settings are social contexts full of incipient conflicts, competing interests and high-stakes dilemmas. Like schools, medical organisations often prefer to underplay or conceal the existence of conflicts, for the sake of their clients or their own reputations. They may even pretend conflicts are not happening, rather than take active and explicit steps to deal with them. It has helped in DRACON's dissemination into this field that Margret Lepp is both a nurse educator and drama teacher, and she has been influential in disseminating DRACON in many countries besides Sweden. As a result, quite a number of the post-DRACON projects, both practical and theoretical, have been set and continue to take place in the field of nursing, sometimes involving her DRACON colleagues.

Nursing Education in Sweden

Four recent practical research projects have been carried out to establish drama in nursing education through research under Lepp's leadership, the first three by Susanna Arveklev Höglund at the University of Gothenburg, that also involved Morrison and Burton.

In one study, the aim was to provide undergraduate nursing students with illuminating experiences related to learning about conflict and conflict management through drama. The study concluded that through participating in drama, nursing students develop a personal understanding of theoretical concepts of conflict and conflict management, as well as their readiness to approach and manage future conflicts.

In another study, the aim was to use drama to help undergraduate students describe their experiences of learning about nursing. Among other things, this study showed that drama provides a safe environment for students to try out their future professional role as a nurse and also offers opportunities to explore different caring strategies and communication styles.

In a third study with students in the specialist postgraduate nursing program in paediatric care, the conclusion was similar: that drama can support postgraduate nursing students in achieving several of their formal and specific learning goals, such as involving the child and family in their own care, and handling complex situations in nursing care.

A fourth study by Maud Lunden relates to the different field of radiography. The aim this time was to explore the use of applied drama as a learning medium, focusing on the use of forum theatre, to foster team work and collaboration in the field of radiography and learning. Once more, the study demonstrated that drama is a useful learning medium to promote teamwork and collaboration in the radiological intervention field.

Nursing Education in Norway

Over the border in Norway, similar action research using drama in nursing education in the first and second cycles is ongoing at the Høgskolen i Østfold (Østfold University College). In one study, the aim was to describe how forum theatre was applied as a reflective pedagogy, focusing on nursing students' practical experiences in mental health care. This study also concluded that forum theatre can be used to enhance nursing students' learning of alternative ways to manage interpersonal conflicts. The aim of a second study focused more on the nursing students' experiences of participating in a drama workshop with forum theatre. Similar to the second Gothenburg study above, the major finding from the students' statements was that 'feeling safe' is a prerequisite for fully participating in drama. The study also showed that drama makes experienced-based knowledge visible by performing then reflecting on authentic caring and nursing situations.

International Explorations in Australia and Indonesia

The DRACON researchers have used their long-standing relationships with each other to set up international collaborations. *Drama in Acute Care* (DIAC), taking place between Griffith University in Australia (Burton) and Gothenburg University (Lepp), has as its aim to develop and enhance essential capabilities of communication, empathy and conflict management in nursing students and professional nurses in the field of Intensive Care, in both Sweden and Australia. The project comprises drama workshops, filming of scenarios for teaching material, questionnaires and interviews.

In 2017, drama and research into its effects were also introduced into nursing education at Jogjakarta's Universitas Gadjah Mada in three master's courses—(a) Paediatric, (b) Medical and Surgical and (c) Maternity. The aim of each of the three different discipline studies is to explore and describe students' experiences of drama as a medium for developing cultural understanding in difficult caring situations. Another current study is looking at drama, conflict management and leadership for teachers, nurses and doctoral students. The aim of that study is to explore the use of applied drama as a learning medium to promote leadership and conflict management in nursing education and learning.

Clinical Practice Training in Jordan

Perhaps the most ambitious and far-ranging of the nursing initiatives to be mentioned here was a program for clinical teachers, preceptors and nurses directly modelled on the Swedish DRACON project, as part of a larger collaborative training project between Jordan and Sweden. In this project, some of the DRACON theory, including the ABC conflict model (see Chap. 2) was explored in practical activities including 'third-party sculptures' and paired role-plays, which prepared the ground for EFT based on real situations from the participants' lives. These situations were then used for further exploration and discussion. The students' experiences and the research findings were positive and affirmative of the core values of this international intercultural collaboration, which required the careful establishment of relationships built on trust, teamwork and acknowledgement of the cultural commonalities and differences.

Beyond teacher education and nursing, DRACON approaches have been applied in a number of other adult education settings, with varying success.

Business Training in Hong Kong

DRACON knowledge and techniques have been applied in Hong Kong's commercial world, for human relations training in business management courses. This particular initiative was in sharp contrast to the invariably successful cross-cultural collaborations in nursing education we have already recorded.

The leaders of a local community education provider,[4] Tracey Lau and Matchy Choi, attended an intensive DRACON workshop in 2012 and were inspired to develop a course for business managers to help them deal with conflict in their workplaces. Their first commercial attempts to implement a model based on the Brisbane Project foundered on the same cultural issues with which Au is struggling in her school-based workshops. The participants were reluctant to engage physically or psychologically, fearful of losing face. They had enrolled expecting the passive transmission of trust-

---

[4]The Merit Minds Workshop: http://meritminds.com.hk.

worthy knowledge (facts and tips) rather than dialogue and autonomy. In collaboration with the Brisbane team, Lau and Choi diagnosed some problems resulting from their own inadequate mastery of the techniques and the theory, and withdrew the courses for the time being, while they rebuilt them (and their own confidence) by using their drama techniques in schools. Unlike Au, as experienced schoolteachers in their former lives, they were much more at home with school students.

This raw and optimistic experiment with hard-nosed adult business executives in China raised exactly the same questions about the cross-cultural applicability of Western-derived drama techniques and models of conflict as Au Yi-Man experienced with the secondary school students in Yunnan. Perhaps these two examples show no more than that it is 'horses for courses' when it comes to running DRACON—Au and Lau ought to have swapped their participant groups!

University Senior Management Training

A high-status and therefore high-stakes professional implementation of DRACON principles and practice was carried out between 2007 and 2009 at the University of Melbourne. Working with two colleagues and a small team of professional actors, John O'Toole devised and carried out more than a dozen half-day training programs focusing on higher education leadership dilemmas and conflict transformation as part of a five-day leadership course for senior university management. The participants numbered between 10 and 25 and came from universities across the nation, from all faculties and disciplines. Their ranks ranged from pro-vice-chancellors, deans and faculty managers, to heads of school and program directors. The drama facilitators devised a special performance depicting a fictional situation involving stress, professional dilemmas or academic problems, which was accompanied by a range of the 'relevant' fictional documents. They then used drama techniques including enhanced forum theatre to assist the participants to explore and resolve the problems. Aspects of the DRACON conflict theory frequently emerged. These workshops were consistently rated by the participants as the most valuable and productive session of their week-long training program. In the third year, the team made a specimen video that could be recycled interstate, to lessen the considerable expense of employing and transporting the whole acting team. The video-based sessions did not have quite the same magic—though they were still positively rated. However, the program's labour-intensive demands in preparation proved its undoing. After the third year, the Leadership Centre decided that the experiment was beyond its budget and scrapped it, in spite of the positive feedback.

Professional Drama and Theatre Training in Malaysia

Back to more sustainable successes. Creating conflict can actually be good for you… if you are a dramatic artist, that is! With conflict as the object rather than the subject of her participants' attention, DRACON team member Janet Pillai has been using its theory and practice in Malaysia since 2000 for learning purposes quite specific to drama and theatre. Her focus has been in strong contrast to all the other projects' aims, such as improving pedagogy, clinical understanding or personal and interpersonal competencies. Instead, she has worked with a range of adult students of drama and theatre, including budding independent writers and film-makers, as well as Performing Arts students in universities, Speech and Drama instructors and Literature teachers in secondary schools. These ad hoc lectures or training sessions have aimed to help students and practitioners in performing arts to understand and apply the theory of conflict when devising or analysing scripts and directing actors—in other words, to help them make more and better conflicts! Feedback from participants who have applied this approach continues to be encouraging, and many have said that the conscious application of conflict theory has strengthened their understanding and approach to literary criticism, play building and directing.

Building Individual and Community Resilience

Reading this chapter thus far, it can be readily seen that, like 'community and cultural change', 'resilience' has been one of the recurrent themes of DRACON's aims and purposes for many of the diverse groups of participants in the post-DRACON initiatives. Building resilience has also found a number of more specialised and less obvious manifestations.

Toughening up the NGO Trainers in China

As we have foreshadowed, the second triumph of Au Yi-Man's applied theatre research in China was to build a crucial type of resilience in her NGO trainers, namely the ability to think reflectively, in particular in coolly analysing failure and redesigning for success.

China has over half a million NGOs, most of which employ teachers and trainers, for instance in village education for HIV-AIDs, sanitation, etc. A feature of this profession is a startling and unacceptable rate of drop-out and burn-out. Au and others have recognised that those dedicated, usually idealistic and mainly young workers are products of China's passive, positivist and didactic education system. They are used to being given sets of facts, procedures and 'truths' to deliver to their clients. As successful and compliant graduates of the Chinese education system, when they encounter unexpected resistance they have no resources to fall back on. This resistance might come, for instance, from village elders who are outraged that their time-honoured customs are to be trashed in the name of something called sanitation or from other villagers who 'know' that AIDS is a curse sent by the magic woman in the next village; or from children with physical, mental or social disabilities that render them non-compliant. In such cases, many NGO trainers have no skills to enter into real dialogue, to listen to the villagers or the children and engage in two-way communication with them; nor do they have the strategies to reflect on their failed encounter and to find an alternative or oblique way of getting round the problem. Au discovered that her participants, in learning to utilise the dialogical and reflective tools that are part of drama pedagogy in applied theatre, also developed these skills in themselves. They vividly recorded that they had learned to reflect, to analyse, to treat failure as an opportunity rather than a disaster, and to learn to listen as well as to talk to their clients. To Au, this was a more important form of capacity-building than her original objective which was to teach them how to use applied theatre.

Building African Male Leaders in Preventing Domestic Violence

A current project of Adelaide's Catalyst Foundation, focusing on African males, is developing a 'Partnering with Men Toolbox' to build men as leaders in the prevention of domestic violence. In this project, Dale Bagshaw is researching prevention programs and conducting workshops with African male leaders, to find with them ways of working with the males in their communities to challenge and change cultural and patriarchal attitudes, which are contributing to high rates of domestic violence. The knowledge and skills gained from DRACON will inform the development of the toolbox and assist in training the community leaders.

Re-engaging 'Negative Leaders'

Truancy, disruptive behaviour and general disaffection from school are an ongoing challenge in Western schools across the world—not least in the UK and Australia. A common feature of this is the growth of 'negative peer leaders', disaffected children of high energy and potential leadership capacity, but who put those qualities into effect by leading the disruption. Morag Morrison's 2010 study into this phenomenon was partly inspired by her own experience as a Brisbane DRACON Key Teacher and researcher, and partly by the emerging stories from other project schools, reflected in this statement from a Year 8 negative leader, turned positive by her experience of peer teaching drama in a NSW school:

> DRACON taught me to stay calm… I've improved out of sight. More confidence, my attitude—just my attitude towards schoolwork, towards my family, towards the teachers, everything's just changed…

In Morrison's study, drama and peer teaching were used as effective strategies to support the re-engagement of negative leaders with school learning. Peer teaching had been identified as one of the most powerful elements of the DRACON project in Brisbane. In both of her case study contexts (Australia and the UK), disaffected adolescent girls became peer teachers, using drama with younger students. Outcomes of the study suggested there was a strong link between democratic teaching and learning processes, risk and emotional engagement. Her research clearly demonstrated that peer teaching was a potentially powerful strategy for positive change, and suggested that it might be a way to address the challenge of adolescent disengagement and disaffection in schools.

Moving on from the Trauma of Childhood Abuse

From 2004 to 2006, while the Brisbane *Acting Against Bullying* component of DRACON was still happening, Bruce Burton and some Griffith University colleagues were simultaneously engaged in a three-year action research project, *Moving On*, using drama and theatre performances with adult survivors of childhood abuse. Naturally, the two projects complemented each other, and insights from each filtered into the other. Despite their long-term struggle with serious trauma, the *Moving On* participants developed a range of skills and new and effective behaviours, and succeeded in developing and performing a play about the abuse they had suffered as children in institutions. There was clear evidence that they had been enabled to deal more effectively with the psychological disorientation and disorganisation of their lives.

Enhancing Resilience in Adolescent Refugees

From 2011 to 2013, Burton and his university colleagues also carried out an action research project, *Refugee Resilience*, using drama strategies with thirty-two teenage refugees, newly arrived in Brisbane from diverse war-torn countries, to address conflict and bullying and encourage resilience. This project was situated in an English language unit in a large Brisbane secondary school and the research team used the DRACON conflict model and many of the techniques. Three of the four key research outcomes were closely akin to those of the earlier Brisbane DRACON projects, particularly the *Cooling Conflicts* programs in the disadvantaged Western Sydney schools. The newly arrived adolescent refugees learned to identify conflict and bullying situations and how to manage them. They demonstrated an increased interest in and commitment to their schooling and were able to realise and articulate that they could change their behaviour not just in drama, but in the school and in their lives. The fourth outcome, specific to these young people, was an impressive development in their mastery of spoken English through the drama work.

Developing Resilience to Bullying in Schools

A recent and direct spin-off from the *Refugee Resilience* program was carried out by Cindy Sykes, aimed at increasing resilience in a Queensland Christian school in which she teaches. She ran the *Acting Against Bullying* program in her school, and subsequently developed an after-school program for students from Years 8–12 to build resilience through process drama, EFT and verbatim theatre. This project provides the basis for her own Masters research.

Echoes: The Quest for Community and Cultural Change

The DRACON Quest Goes on

To conclude these accounts, rather than reiterate the research results or hypothesise about possible futures for DRACON, we will give a couple of contemporary snapshots. The first is a cameo case study. This time, we will provide more detailed human interest than we did in the other accounts in this chapter, as a reminder that DRACON is human research, and not just research-based and focused on collecting data, though this has been a key component. Post-DRACON projects, like the original, have been grounded in action research in order to focus on understanding a human problem, and on creating real change. That has meant welcoming and incorporating the affective components of the action, the human impact and social effects on the people involved, researchers and participants alike. This has inevitably led to change in communities and cultures, at a macro-level, micro-level, or occasionally both.

Costa's Story

Our first cameo describes a series of initiatives by a teacher who joined the DRACON project towards the end. His experiences with the 'ups and downs' of implementing DRACON between 2004 and 2015 typify the idealism, intelligence and perseverance necessary for conflict transformation in schools and educational systems and for the corresponding changes in the communities and cultures of the participants.

Costa is a high school drama teacher in Sydney. He first heard about the DRACON project from his university lecturer, who had himself been the local Arts Advisory teacher when the Brisbane DRACON project came knocking on Sydney's door. Intrigued, Costa read the *Cooling Conflict* Project Handbook, watched the video and persuaded his school to take part. Though the local DRACON research had finished, the state education authority was still strongly supporting the work, and the Brisbane team first met Costa at the 2004 in-service workshop. That same year, he led the project in his school as Key Teacher. In the process, a Year 9 Focus Class teacher, Louise, from Health and Physical Education (HPE) became enthused. Though the project was a great success, it was not sustained, because of timetable disruptions, grumbles from competitors in the crowded curriculum, and logistical difficulties with the primary school. Those difficulties exactly mirror the sustainment challenges of all the original DRACON projects.

Louise moved to a school with a 30 per cent urban Aboriginal population, many of them disadvantaged and conflicted, and some of them officially 'at-risk'. With the school's Aboriginal Education Officer, she made a tentative effort to implement *Cooling Conflict*. However, with the extreme levels of trauma experienced by some of the children, compounded by their own very limited experience of the program, the two educators found they did not even get to the drama component. They called in Costa, and together they worked out an ambitious plan to bus the students to a community program called *The Young Mob* in Redfern, the Aboriginal epicentre of Sydney. For this, they decided to revise radically the drama technique, turning their previous whole-day slow-burn EFT structure into a two-hour competitive game. This was a resounding success—in Louise's words, 'It really, really, really, really worked! If you want to give those kids a genuine voice, that's how to do it and we saw the results!'

The revised *Young Mob* program ran successfully for at least four years, attracting the attention of World Vision, for whom the team ran a successful demonstration program. At the outset, the charity was keen to adopt and expand the program to bring in other Aboriginal communities from across Australia. Then something happened. Suddenly, the proposal was cancelled with no explanation, just reluctant and evasive feedback from the charity. Both Costa and Louise hypothesise that management changes in World Vision were partly responsible, or perhaps even that giving too much voice and empowerment to those communities might have threatened the power of the charity itself... though they have no hard evidence.

Undeterred, our heroes focused their attention back on *The Young Mob* in Sydney and gained the attention of a national employment agency specialising in 'support and guidance to some of the most disadvantaged communities in Australia'.[5] Under their aegis, Costa and the team travelled to Mornington Island, a remote Aboriginal community in far Northern Australia. The community welcomed them warmly as they began carefully and sensitively to share knowledge and ideas with the elders. The DRACON concepts of conflict and how to handle it were entirely compatible with the elders' intentions, and the drama was intriguing to the community. The team threw themselves into designing a program for the community, still based on the revised 'game' version of the drama. Then something else happened. A new Federal Government in 2013, with a hard-right agenda towards dealing with social disadvantage and Aboriginal aid programs, resulted in the prospective agency funding being cancelled. Once more, they were back to Square One.

The team tried to refashion their plans into more of a commercial business model, offering their services, rebranded as TrueQuest Pty Ltd. This too sparkled briefly, flickered a while, but then had a short life—partly because the team, as they admitted, were teachers rather than business people or sales representatives. The team went back into full-time education, with Costa taking a brief detour into university teaching, where he managed to inspire some of his students to try out aspects of the DRACON program. He reports that remnants of this work, particularly the drama techniques, are still extant among those followers. He is currently teaching drama in a school where the conditions are not suitable to introduce DRACON, either his version or the original, but he still says: 'I would **love** to do it again—you never know, when there's a chance...'

In spite of all the setbacks over the years, when interviewed both Costa and Louise strongly affirmed their DRACON experiences, particularly for vulnerable children such as the troubled Aboriginal teenagers in extreme 'at-risk' family situations in the tougher social wastelands of Sydney. As Costa and Louise both pointed out, though

---

[5] Angus Knight Group: http://angusknight.com.au.

the program might not have attained its ultimate grail of sustainability, all those students who did experience it gained precious knowledge and tools for handling conflict. They acknowledged the richness of the experience for all those lucky enough to experience it, including themselves.

Costa's experiences are a kind of microcosm of the whole DRACON experience—opportunities seized and opportunities missed, success, triumphs and a few disappointments, deep permanent learning and ephemeral interest, official support and arbitrary withdrawal. Many of the seeds sown, sometimes metamorphosed and almost unrecognisable, are still growing and flourishing.

Stop Press: Today's News

As we are copyediting this final chapter, one of the authors has just informed the team that tomorrow she will be leading a drama and conflict transformation workshop in Yogykarta, Indonesia. Another is starting *Cooling Conflicts* training with a theatre company in Singapore. A third is bidding for an ARC grant on building resilience in Australian Aboriginal communities using DRACON techniques.

All seven of the authors of this book are still actively responding to enquiries about the research or requests for workshops. Five of the seven are now retired, but the spirit and the ideas of DRACON persist. More than twenty years since we became involved, we are all still committed to its ideals and have seen it working in principle and practice in many different contexts.

These final snapshots—of respectively one of DRACON's most recent recruits, and several of its originals soldiering on—show the persistence and longevity of DRACON, and its continuing potential for effective conflict transformation through drama in schools and beyond. We hope that this comprehensive and detailed account of the full story of DRACON—the research, the practice and its aftermath—will inspire readers to promote this work in their own contexts. For those who have the means, we hope the book will provide the impetus to establish DRACON-inspired projects in schools, hospitals, universities and beyond. DRACON has demonstrated that the careful and confident use of drama can provide individuals, groups and communities with the knowledge, skills, techniques and tools for the effective understanding and transformation of human conflict.

References

Grünbaum, A., & Lepp, M. (2005). *DRACON I SKOLAN. Drama, konflikthantering och medling (DRACON in School. Drama, conflict management and mediation)*. Lund: Studentlitteratur. Tr. Danish (2008).
Indra Congress. (2018). www.theindracongress.com/about-us/. Accessed 1 June 2018.
Lundberg, N. (2014). *Evaluation of DRACON lessons in Year 5 during the school year*. Unpublished.
O'Toole, J., Burton, B., & Plunkett, A. (2005). *Cooling conflict: A new approach to managing conflict and bullying in schools*. Sydney: Pearson Educational.

Appendix A

Documentation of the original (1996–2005) DRACON Project

Bagshaw, D. (2006). 'Language, power and gendered identities: The reflexive social worker'. *Women in Welfare Education, 8*, 1–11.

Bagshaw, D. (2004). *Verbal abuse and gendered adolescent identities*. [PhD] thesis, The University of Melbourne Library, Melbourne.

Bagshaw, D. (2003). 'Creative approaches to teaching conflict resolution skills'. *Association for Conflict Resolution Newsletter*. Feature Article, Spring, 35.

Bagshaw, D. (2003). 'Language, power and mediation'. *Australasian Dispute Resolution Journal, 14*(2), 130–141.

Bagshaw, D., & Halliday, D. (1999). 'Teaching adolescents to handle conflict through drama'. *NJ (Drama Australia Journal), 24*(2), 87–104.

Bagshaw, D. (1998). 'What adolescents say about conflict in schools.' *Children Australia, 23*(3), 17–22.

Bagshaw, D., Lepp, M., & Zorn, C. (2007). 'International collaboration: Building teams and managing conflicts'. *Conflict Resolution Quarterly* (Jossey-Bass), *24*(4), 433–446.

Bagshaw, D., & Lepp, M. (2005). 'Ethical considerations in drama and conflict resolution research in Swedish and Australian schools'. *Conflict Resolution Quarterly* (Jossey-Bass), *22*(3), 381–396.

Burton, B., & O'Toole, J. (2009). 'Power in their hands'. *Applied Theatre Researcher* No 10. https://www.intellectbooks.co.uk/MediaManager/File/ATR%20back%20issues/ATR%2010_2.pdf.

Burton, B., & O'Toole, J. (2005). 'Enhanced forum theatre: Where Boal's theatre of the oppressed meets process drama'. *NJ (Drama Australia Journal), 29*(2), 49–58.

Burton, B., & O'Toole, J. (2002). *Cooling conflicts*. Video. Sydney: Roc Productions.

Burton, B., Lepp, M., Morrison, M., & O'Toole, J. (2015). *Acting to manage conflict—Evidence-based drama strategies*. Dordrecht, Neth.: Springer.

Lepp, M. (2010). 'Drama for conflict management – DRACON International'. In: S Schönman (Ed.) *Key concepts in theatre/drama education* (pp. 99–104). Sense Publishers: Rotterdam.

Lepp, M., & Bagshaw, D. (2003). 'Journals as a tool for learning and evaluation in drama and conflict research projects involving adolescents'. *NJ (Drama Australia Journal)*, 55–68.

Löfgren, H., & Lepp, M. (2001). 'Students' basic strategies for handling conflicts: A study of Grade 8 students in Sweden'. In C. Day & D. van Wee (Eds.), *Education research in Europé. Yearbook 2001* (pp. 383–396). Leuven Apeldoorn: Garant Publisher.

Löfgren, H., & Malm, B. (Eds.). (2007). *DRACON INTERNATIONAL: BRIDGING THE FIELDS OF DRAMA AND CONFLICT MANAGEMENT. Empowering students to handle conflicts through school-based programmes*. Malmö: University of Malmö.

O'Toole, J. (2015). 'Rigid morals lead to quarrels'. In Shifra Schonmann (Ed.) *International yearbook for research in arts education: The wisdom of the many*. New York: Waxmann. (pp. 471–475).

O'Toole, J. (2015). 'En équilibre sur le manteau de la cheminée'. *L'Annuaire Théatrale*, Vol 55. Quebec: Érudit. (pp. 117–132). https://www.erudit.org/fr/revues/annuaire/2014-n55-annuaire02143/1033706ar/

O'Toole, J. (1997). 'Rough treatment: Teaching conflict management through drama.' *Teaching Education Journal, 9*(1), 83–88.

O'Toole, J., & Burton, B. (2005). 'Acting against conflict and bullying'. *Research in Drama Education, 10*(3), 269–283.

O'Toole, J., & Burton, B. (2002). 'Cycles of harmony: Action research into the effects of drama on conflict management in schools. *Applied Theatre Researcher* No 3. https://www.intellectbooks.co.uk/MediaManager/File/ATR%20back%20issues/ATR%203_1.pdf.

O'Toole, J., Burton, B., & Plunkett, A. (2005). *Cooling conflict*. Frenchs Forest NSW: Pearson.

Rigby, K., & Bagshaw, D. (2005). 'Helping students to counteract bullying by the use of educational drama and bystander training'. In Helen McGrath, & Toni Noble (Eds.) *Bullying solutions: Evidence-based approaches to bullying in Australian schools*. Pearson Education: Sydney, (pp. 133–146).

Rigby, K., & Bagshaw, D. (2001). 'What hurts? The reported consequences of negative interactions with peers among Australian school children'. *Children Australia, 26*(4), 36–41.

Appendix B

Documentation of Chapter 9: Post-DRACON
Persistence: What Happened In The DRACON Schools?
Sjöstedt, H. (2014). *Undervisning i DRACON. Fem elevers upplevelser av undervisning i konflikthantering med dramapedagogik som metod. (Teaching DRACON. Five students' experiences of learning conflict management with drama as a method.* Bachelor thesis*).* Högskolan i Gävle.

New Uses for DRACON in Swedish Schools
Karls, Kristina. (2005). 'DRACON at upper secondary. The experiences of a theatre teacher'. In Grünbaum A., & Lepp. M. (2005) *DRACON I SKOLAN. Drama, konflikthantering och medling (DRACON in school. Drama, conflict management and mediation).* (pp.145–150). Lund: Studentlitteratur.
Learn for Peace. (2018). *Lära för Fred: Learn for Peace* (http://www.laraforfred.se). Accessed 2 April 2018.
Lundberg, Nicklas. (2014). *Evaluation of DRACON lessons in Year 5 during the schoolyear 2013-14.* Unpublished.
Organisation for Economic Cooperation and Development (OECD). *Programme for International Student Assessment (PISA)* – Sweden. https://www.oecd.org/pisa/PISA-2015-Sweden.pdf Accessed 6 June 2018.

Acting Against Relational Aggression and Cyberbullying
Burton, B., Lepp, M., Morrison, M., & O'Toole, J. (2015). *Acting to manage conflict and bullying through evidence-based strategies.* New York: Springer. (pp. 155–172).

Bullying and Cultural Conflict Mediation in Adelaide
Rigby, K. (2011). *The method of shared concern: A positive approach to bullying in schools.* Camberwell: ACER.
Rigby, K. (2010). *Bullying interventions in Schools: Six basic approaches.* Camberwell: ACER.
Bagshaw, D., & Porter, E. (Eds.). (2009). *Mediation in the Asia-Pacific Region. Transforming conflict and building peace.* New York & London: Routledge.

The INDRA Congress Peace Project
Oddie, D. (2015). *A journey of art and conflict: Weaving Indra's net.* London: Intellect.
The Indra Congress. http://www.theindracongress.com Accessed 6 June 2018.

DRACON Textbooks and their Effects
Grünbaum, Anita & Lepp, Margret. (2005). *DRACON I SKOLAN. Drama, konflikthantering och medling (*DRACON in school. Drama, conflict management and mediation*).* Lund: Studentlitteratur. Tr. Danish (2008). *DRACON i Skolen. Drama, konflikthåntering och maedling.* Fredrikshavn: Dafolo.

O'Toole, John, Burton, Bruce, & Plunkett, Anna. (2005). *Cooling conflict: A new approach to managing bullying and conflict in schools.* Sydney: Pearson Educational.

Training Teachers in Sweden Today
Arveklev, S. H. (2017). Drama and learning in nursing education. *A study in first and second cycle.* Dissertation. University of Gothenburg: Sahlgrenska Academy Institute of Health and Care Sciences. http://hdl.handle.net/2077/53616. Accessed 18 April 2018.

Developing Mentoring skills for Conflict in Kazakhstan
Burton, B., Lepp, M., Morrison, M., & O'Toole, J. (2015). *Acting to manage conflict and bullying through evidence-based strategies.* New York: Springer. (pp. 129–134).

Enhancing Teachers' Interpersonal Skills
Morrison, M., Nilsson, E., & Lepp, M. (2013). 'Bringing the personal to the professional: Pre-service teaching students explore conflict through an applied drama approach'. *Applied Theatre Research, 1,* 63–76.

Training the Trainers in Chinese NGOs
Au, Yi-Man. (2017). *Changing practice?—exploring the potential contribution of applied theatre training to capacity-building for NGO workers in China.* Unpublished PhD Thesis, University of Melbourne.

O'Toole, J., Au, Y-M., Baldwin, A., Cahill, H., & Chinyowa, K. (2015). Capacity-Building Theatre (and Vice Versa). In Tim Prentki (Ed.) *Applied theatre: Development.* London: Methuen. (pp. 122–134).

Nursing Education in Sweden
Arveklev, S. H. (2017). *Drama and learning in nursing education. A study in first and second cycle.* Dissertation. University of Gothenburg: Sahlgrenska Academy Institute of Health and Care Sciences. http://hdl.handle.net/2077/53616. Accessed 18 April 2018.

Arveklev, S. H., Berg, L., Wigert, H., Morrison-Helme, M., & Lepp, M. (2018a). 'Learning about conflict and conflict management through drama in nursing education'. *Journal of Nursing Education, 57*(4), 209–216.

Arveklev, S. H., Berg, L., Wigert, H., Morrison-Helme, M., & Lepp, M. (2018b). 'Nursing students' experiences of learning about nursing through drama'. *Nurse Education in Practice, 28,* 60–65.

Arveklev, S. H., Wigert, H., Berg, L., Burton, B., & Lepp, M. (2015). 'The use and application of drama in nursing education – an integrative review of the literature'. *Nurse Education Today, 35*(7), 12–17.

Berg, L., Burton, B., & Lepp, M. (2015). 'The use and application of drama in nursing education – An integrative review of the literature'. *Nurse Education Today, 35*(7), 12–17.

Ekebergh, M., Lepp, M., & Dahlberg, K. (2004). Reflective learning with drama in nursing education – A Swedish attempt to overcome the theory praxis gap. *Nurse Education Today, 24*(8), 622–628.

Lundén, M., Lundgren S. M., Morrison-Helme, M., & Lepp, M. (2017). 'Professional development for radiographers and post graduate nurses in radiological interventions: Building teamwork and collaboration through drama'. *Radiography, 23*(4), 330–336.

Nursing Education in Norway

Antonsson, E. B., Femdal, I., & Lepp, M. (2017). 'Dramapedagogikk med fokus på forumspill i psykisk helsearbeid. Sykepleierstudenters refleksjoner over praksiserfaringer'. (Dramapedagogy with focus on Forum Theatre in mental health care. Nursing students' reflections on practical experiences) *Tidsskrift for psykisk helsearbeid, 14*(2), 121–133.

Femdal, I., Antonsson E. B., & Lepp, M. (2017). 'Studenters praksisrefleksjon med dramapedagogikk. "det är noe annet å reflektere gjennom å gjöre enn å snakke om det" '. Students' reflections on clinical studies using drama. "it is something different to reflect through action than to talk about it". *Nordisk sygeplejeforskning, 7*(2), 152–165.

Clinical Practice Training in Jordan

Burton, B., Lepp, M., Morrison, M., & O'Toole, J. (2015). *Acting to manage conflict and bullying through evidence-based strategies.* New York: Springer. (pp. 143–154).

Lepp, M. (2015). 'Conflict competency in nursing education: An international collaborative project'. In Bruce Burton, Margret Lepp, Morag Morrison & John O'Toole. *Acting to manage conflict and bullying through evidence-based strategies* (pp. 143–154). New York: Springer.

Lepp, M., Abdalrahim, M. S., Halabi, J.O., Olausson, S., & Suserud, B-O. (2011). 'Learning through drama in the field of global nursing'. *Applied Theatre Researcher* 12, article 5.

University Senior Management Training

O'Toole, J., & The Complete Works Theatre Company. (2007). *God moves in a mysterious way* (2007). Performed playscript (Writer, Director). Melbourne: L.H. Martin Institute.

O'Toole, J., & The Complete Works Theatre Company. (2009). *Divided by a common language.* Performance and video (Writer, Director). Melbourne: L.H. Martin Institute.

Toughening up the NGO Trainers in China

See under *Training the Trainers in NGOs in China*

Re-engaging 'Negative Leaders'

Finney, J., Hickman, R., Nicholl, B., Morrison, M., & Rudduck, J. (2005). *Rebuilding engagement through the arts.* Cambridge: Pearson Publications.

Morrison, M. (2015). 'Negative leaders in school: Extending ideas'. In Bruce Burton, Margret Lepp, Morag Morrison & John O'Toole. *Acting to manage conflict and bullying through evidence-based strategies* (pp. 59–78). New York: Springer.

Morrison, M. (2009). *Shouts and whispers: Re-engaging negative leaders through peer teaching and drama.* Unpublished Doctoral Thesis, Griffith University, Brisbane, Australia.

Morrison, M. (2004). 'Risk and responsibility: The potential of peer teaching to address negative leadership'. *Improving Schools, 7*(3), 211–220.

Morrison, M. Burton, B., & O'Toole, J. (2006). 'Re-engagement through peer teaching drama.' In Pamela Burnard & Sarah Hennessy (Eds.) *Reflective practices in arts education* (pp. 139–148). Dordrecht: Springer.

'Moving On' from the Trauma of Childhood Abuse

Burton, B. (2015). 'Moving on from the trauma of childhood abuse'. In Bruce Burton, Margret Lepp, Morag Morrison & John O'Toole. *Acting to manage conflict and bullying through evidence-based strategies* (pp. 99–118). New York: Springer.

Enhancing Resilience in Adolescent Refugees

Burton, B. (2015). 'Conflict and bullying management in adolescent refugees'. In Bruce Burton, Margret Lepp, Morag Morrison & John O'Toole. *Acting to manage conflict and bullying through evidence-based strategies* (pp. 173–190). New York: Springer.

Index

A
Aboriginal, 158, 198, 200, 221, 238–240
Aboriginal Education, 238
Aboriginal Studies, 198–200
Absenteeism, 163, 198, 199, 201
Abuse, 22, 31, 36, 40, 160–162, 170, 176–181, 225, 237
    covert, 160, 161
    indirect, 161
    physical, 170
    relational, 161
    verbal, 160–162, 170, 177, 178, 180, 225
Academic problems, 106, 234
Acceptance, 39, 41, 76, 78, 92, 173, 223
Acute Care, 232
Adelaide, 5, 6, 9, 46, 59, 159, 161, 168, 169, 174, 195, 220, 222, 225, 228, 236
Adelaide Festival, 158
Adelaide Festival Centre, 158
Adjudication, 15, 19, 33, 75
Adolescent Conflict Style Scale (ACSS), 165
Aesthetic doubling, 51
Affective, 50, 52, 56–58, 68, 74, 79, 98, 111–116, 238
Affective rhetoric, 114
Afghanistan, 225
Africa, 63, 225
Agency, 61, 82, 84, 85, 195, 239
Alcoholism, 106
Aldinga, 5
Allwood, Jens, 4
Alternative dispute resolution, 16, 20
Alternative reality, 75, 76
American Alliance for Theater and Education, xix

Andersson, Jöns, 4
Anglican, 157
Anglo-Celtic, 158, 198
Antagonist, 22, 43, 58, 62, 68, 70–73, 100–103, 192
Anxiety, 97, 147
Applied theatre, 48, 60, 63, 183, 223, 226, 231, 235, 236
Arbitration, 15, 33
Aristotle, 44, 49, 71, 72
Artistically oriented perspective, 126
Arts-ED Penang, xx
Arveklev, Susanna Höglund, 231
Assault, 160
Australian National Mediator Standards Board, 230
Australian Research Council (ARC), 186, 200, 204, 240
Au, Yi-Man, 226, 231, 234, 235
Avoidance, 90, 114, 124, 129, 130, 133

B
Ball, Steve, 197
Bates, Merrelyn, 6
Birch School, 135, 142–147
Boal, Augusto, 47, 51
Body portraits, 100, 102
Bolton, Gavin, 45
Boman, Esther, 45
Boredom, boring, 139, 161, 173
Brazil, 225
Britain, British, 89, 91, 92, 197
Buddhism, Buddhist, 21
Bystander, 23, 28, 58, 68, 110, 188, 192, 206–208

C

Cambridge, 228, 229
Camel, 24, 137, 140, 142
Catalyst Foundation, 236
Catholic, 157, 158, 160, 170
Child care, 230
Childhood abuse, 237
Children's theatre, 126
Chinese, 19, 89, 91, 94, 158, 226, 231, 235
Chinese puzzles, 226
Choi, Matchy, 233
Christian, 91, 157, 237
Climax, 71
Clinical psychologist, 94, 99, 104, 108
Collectivism, 30, 114
Come Out! Festival, 158
Commonwealth, 158
Communication theories, 21, 26, 70
Compromise, compromising, 19, 23–25, 71, 72, 90, 112, 114, 124, 129–131, 133, 140, 164, 166, 167, 171, 177, 178, 182
Conciliation, 15, 17
Conflict
　A-component, 20
　ABC theory, 18
　asymmetric, 29–31, 77, 137, 140
　B-component, 21, 32
　bipolar, 18
　C-component, 19, 32
　constructive, 9, 17, 134, 140, 141, 149, 159, 182, 185
　contingency model, 33
　data-based, 14
　handling styles, 23, 114, 137, 140, 149, 164–168, 177, 181, 182
　interest-based, 14, 19
　intergroup, 18, 19
　intrapersonal, 18, 19
　language, 4, 14, 136, 139, 141
　literacy, 4, 7, 9, 85, 93–95, 108–110, 113, 134–137, 168, 179, 182, 184–186, 189–191, 204
　multi-party, 18
　multipolar, 18
　necessary, 5, 14, 138, 238
　positive-sum or 'win-win', 20
　reconciliation, 27, 32
　security approach, 22
　socio-cultural context, 23
　structural elements, 23
　symmetric, 28, 30, 32, 77, 137, 142
　termination, 27, 32
　transformative, 74, 81, 85
　triangle, triangular, 18
　unnecessary, 14
　value based, 13
　zero-sum or distributive, 20
Confronting, 129–131, 133, 208
Congruence
　cognitive, 83
　emotional, 83
　social, 83
Constructivism, constructivist, 17, 20, 21, 30, 40, 54, 74
Cooperation, 5, 7, 15, 20, 24, 44, 53, 67, 75, 171–174, 176, 178–180, 182
Costa (Loucopoulos), 238–240
Coyle, Shirley, 184, 189
Creative arts, 5, 89, 93–96, 99–101, 104, 106–108, 113, 116
Creative dramatics, 44, 92, 126
Creativity, 49, 57, 93, 97, 126, 159, 170
Crisis, 16, 25, 69–72, 80, 91, 168
Critically liberating perspective, 126
Critical reflection, 78, 79, 170
Cross-cultural, 4, 7, 23, 190, 226, 233, 234
Cultural change, 222, 235, 238
Curriculum, 44, 45, 48, 63, 91, 92, 125–127, 157, 159, 185, 186, 196, 202, 203, 205, 206, 226, 238
Cyberbullying, 224

D

Dance, 53, 85, 93, 94, 96, 97, 99, 100, 103, 127, 173, 174, 180, 183
De-escalation (of conflict), 27, 43
Democratic learning, 82
Democratic values, 125
Denmark, 124
Denouement, 71–73
Department of Education (Queensland), 204, 209, 221
Department of Peace and Development Research, 4
Depth-psychological theories, 20
Derolment, 52
Derry, 225
Deus ex machina, 72
Deutsch, Morton, 13
Develop, Analyse, Support, Intervene and Evaluate (DASIE), 112
Dewey, John, 45, 92, 126
Dialectics, dialectical, 98
Dialogue, 10, 11, 15, 22, 32, 38, 43, 46, 55, 56, 76, 78, 79, 144, 175–177, 234, 235
Diaries, 137–139, 147–149, 170, 187
Disclosure, 96, 101–104, 114
Divorce, 19, 31, 106

Index

Doctor of Philosophy (PhD), 5, 6, 186, 197, 219, 230, 231
Dracon Co-ordinator, 201
Drama-In-Education (DIE), 45–47, 52, 54, 59, 60, 63, 69, 70, 73, 74, 77, 149, 169
Drama literacy, 134
Drama pedagogues, 4, 126, 127, 136, 141, 228
Dramatherapy, 45
Dramatic contract, 53, 54
Dramatic curve, 43
Dual affect, 51, 68
Dunstan, Don, 158
DVD, 203

E

Educational drama, 4, 6, 7, 9, 28, 34, 41, 43, 51, 57, 58, 63, 89, 92, 93, 113, 123, 126, 148, 149, 159, 168, 170, 171, 181, 182, 184, 185, 189, 224
Education kit, 108, 109, 111, 112
Education Queensland, 204
Egalitarian, 30, 59, 70, 158, 179
Emergent conflict, 210
Emotional closeness, 51, 68, 75
Emotional distance, 46, 68, 73–76, 184
Emotional intelligence, 110
Empathy, 37, 49, 51, 52, 54, 57, 59, 68, 73–77, 82, 85, 101, 113, 124, 125, 171, 184, 232
Enhanced forum theatre (EFT), 9, 51, 53, 61–64, 193, 206–209, 225, 226, 228, 229, 231, 233, 234, 237, 239
Erlander, Tage, 4
Escalation (of conflict), 26, 28, 32, 33, 43, 44, 58, 68, 70, 71, 102, 110, 167, 207, 208
Ethics, 58, 170
Ethnographic observation, 187
European Union, 124
Everyday reality, 75, 76
Experiential, 59, 73, 102, 113, 116, 192
Experiential learning, 59, 98

F

Factor analysis, 128, 129
Feminine, feminine values, 22, 124
Feminist theories, 22
Fight, Freeze and Flee (FFF), 23, 137, 142
Finland, 124
Five Arts Centre, 5, 93
Focus Class, 187, 188, 191, 193, 196–199, 201–204, 206, 238
Focused observation, 170, 180
Folk high schools, 127, 227

Forum theatre, 9, 47, 60–62, 64, 93, 100, 102, 109, 126, 137, 193, 196, 198, 201, 224, 230, 232
Fox, 24, 25, 137, 140, 164
Friberg, Mats, 4, 25, 133
Fronting, 129–133

G

Games, 20, 49, 50, 54, 75, 77, 93, 96, 108, 109, 111, 139, 144, 172, 173, 239
Gandhi, 30
Gender, 21–23, 30, 31, 91, 95, 99, 125, 126, 132, 148, 158, 163, 164, 167, 174, 191, 205, 224, 225
Georgetown, 94
Germans, 158
Good Samaritan, 174
Gothenburg University, 229, 232
Greece, 225
Greek theatre, tragedy, 194
Griffith University, 6, 183, 232, 237
Ground rules, 32, 35, 36, 38

H

Handbook (DRACON), 147, 200, 202, 238
Harassment, 22, 28, 30, 159, 160
Harmony, 27, 43, 92, 98, 124, 184, 209
Hatton, Christine, 6, 201, 202
Heathcote, Dorothy, 45, 46
Hegemonic, 162
Heuristic, 96
HIV-AIDS, 235
Høgskolen i Østfold, 232
Holistic learning perspective, 126
Homophobia, homophobic, 161
Hong Kong, 209, 233
Hospitals, 231, 240
Host, 62
Hot chair, hot-seat, 62, 111
Hot-seating, 62, 63

I

Ice-breakers, 96
Iceland, 124
Identification, 32, 50, 51, 68, 77, 98, 99, 104, 107, 113, 189
Image theatre, 47, 63, 100, 101, 110, 224
Imagination, 44, 48, 49, 52, 56–58, 77, 84, 126
Imaging, 96
Immigrant, 144, 145
Impartial mediators, 31, 123, 228
Improvisation, 47, 49, 50, 58, 64, 75, 96, 101, 109, 110, 137, 170, 171, 193

Independent (education system), 157, 158, 160
Indian, 43, 72, 89, 91, 94
Indigenous, 89, 158, 206, 209, 219
Indonesia, 232, 240
Indra Congress, 225, 227
In-service, 91, 196, 198, 199, 201–203, 205, 209, 220, 221, 227, 238
Integrated conflict exploration, 115, 116
Intensive Care, 233
Interactive performance, 109, 111
Intercultural, 7
International Drama/Theatre and Education Association (IDEA), 5
Intuitive, 52, 56, 57, 95
IPSOS/Reuters, 224
Ireland, 63, 158, 225, 226
Islam, Islamic, 91, 225

J
Jambunathan, Paul, xi
Japan, 229
Jogjakarta, 233
Johnson, David W., 13, 25, 164, 168, 177
Joker, 62
Jordan, 26, 233
Journal, 170–173, 175, 176, 178–181, 187, 206, 219, 222

K
Kamaluddin, Latif, 5, 94, 95
Karls, Kristina, 223
Key Class, 63, 187, 188, 191, 193, 195–199, 201, 203, 206, 221
Key Drama teacher, 195
Kindergarten, 229
Kochi University, 229
Korenaga, Kanako, 229
Kosovo, 225
Kuala Lumpur, 93
Kuo, Pau Kun, 44

L
Latent conflict, 17, 18, 71, 114
Lau, Tracey, 233
Learn for Peace, 223
Leow, Puay Tin, xi
Liew, Kung Yu, xi
Likert survey, 128
Linden School, 135, 136, 142–147
Lion, 24, 137, 140, 142
LISREL-analyse, 129
Literature, 14, 32, 67, 92, 126, 192, 209, 235
Löfgren, Horst, 5
Longitudinal case studies, 206

Long-term effects, 134, 141
Louise (Gerondis), 238, 239
Low anxiety country, 124
Lunden, Maud, 232
Lutheran, 123
Lyric writing, 103

M
Macro-culture, 227
Magic, 62, 63, 234, 235
Maguire, Greg, xii
Mälardalens University, 230
Malay, 27, 89, 91, 94
Malaysian education system, 91
Malm, Birgitte, 6
Malmö University, 5, 6
Manifest conflict, 17, 18, 21, 71–73, 103, 110, 208
Mantle of the expert, 45
Masculine, 124, 160, 162
Master Teacher, 190, 205
Maternity, 233
MAYA, 92
Media arts, 183
Mediation, 13–17, 28–31, 33–36, 38–41, 58, 62, 68, 70, 71, 73–75, 77, 80, 84, 92, 134–136, 138, 141, 142, 144–146, 149, 162, 165, 167, 168, 182, 184, 191–193, 195, 196, 221, 223, 225, 227, 228
Memory recall, 96, 98, 101, 102
Merit Minds, 233
Meta-conflict, 27, 75–77
Metaxis, 51, 57, 58, 76
Method of Shared Concern, 31
Metropolitan, 159, 161, 168, 169
Micro-culture, 227
Moore, Christopher, 13
Moreno, Jacob, 44
Mornington Island, 239
Motivation, 58, 62, 68–70, 82, 83, 139, 199, 200
Moving On, 237
Multi-arts, 7, 94, 96, 97, 99, 107, 114
Multicultural, 159, 198, 202, 203, 209, 225
Multicultural Programs Unit, 189, 204, 209
Music, 85, 92–94, 96, 97, 99–101, 103, 114, 116, 127, 183
Muslim, 91, 225
Mykyta, Mick, 6

N
Narrative, 21, 34, 35, 39–41, 54, 55, 68, 70, 73, 74, 76, 85, 96, 99, 102
Narrative mediation, 34, 40, 70, 74, 75

Narrative theory, 14
National curriculum, 91, 183
National identity, 157, 227
Natya Shastra, 43, 55, 67, 69, 72
Negative leaders, 236
Negative treatment, 162, 163
New South Wales (NSW), 6, 183, 184, 186, 188–190, 198, 200, 203, 204, 209, 220, 221, 227, 236
Newspaper sculpting, 98, 102
New Zealand, ix, x
Nigeria, 225
Non-confrontational, 94, 114
Non-violent action, 30
Non-Government Organisations (NGOs), 226, 231, 235
Nordic, 124
Northampton, x
Northern Territory, 184
Norway, 124, 232
NSW Department of Education and Training, 209
Nursey-Bray, Rosemary, 6, 169

O

Oddie, David, 225
OK! Tak OK!, 224
Olenius, Elsa, 126
Oporto, 5
Organisation for Economic Cooperation and Development (OECD), 31, 125, 223, 224
Our Theatre, 126
Over-distancing, 107, 111, 112
Owen, Maureen, xi
Owl, 24, 25, 137, 140, 164
Oxford Committee for Famine Relief (Oxfam), 226

P

Paediatric, 232, 233
Palestine, 226
Parents, 40, 92, 96, 110, 125, 128, 140, 144, 148, 149, 160, 170, 176, 187, 189, 197, 200, 224, 230
Participant, 6, 11, 12, 17, 19, 20, 31, 33, 36–39, 41, 45, 46, 49–59, 61–64, 68–71, 73–77, 81, 84, 85, 94–104, 106, 110, 113, 114, 116, 136, 137, 139, 143, 145, 149, 160, 161, 169, 170, 179, 184, 187, 190–192, 194, 200, 201, 203, 206, 219, 227–231, 233–238

Partnering with Men Toolbox, 236
Paternalism, 90, 114
Peace education, 127, 209
Peace studies, 4
Peer-mediators, 39, 40, 123, 134, 141, 148
Penang, 5, 10, 89, 93, 94, 220, 224
Peripateia, 71, 72
Personal development perspective, 126
Phases of mediation, 36
Philippine Educational Theatre Association (PETA), 92
PISA tests, 223
Plato, 44
Play-building, 96, 196, 235
Plunkett, Anna, 6, 186
Polarization, 21, 26, 32
Politeness, 114
Portugal, 5, 226
Postmodernism, postmodernist, 14, 22, 158
Postupak, 53
Power distance, 90, 114
Pre- and post-tests, 142, 147, 180
Pre-text, x
Problem-posing, 96, 112, 113
Problem-solving, 15, 17, 20, 25, 27, 31, 34–37, 39, 47, 59, 70, 73, 74, 84, 92, 96–98, 108, 113, 114, 126, 138, 164, 166, 167, 170, 171, 177–179, 181, 182
Process drama, 9, 46, 51, 53, 59–64, 71, 94, 96, 98, 193, 194, 196, 198, 201, 237
Professional development, 185, 186, 190, 204, 205, 222, 229, 231
Protagonist, 43, 58, 61, 62, 68, 70, 71, 77, 100–102, 192, 195
Pro-vice-chancellors, 234
Psychodrama, psychodramatic, 44, 45, 51, 127
Public performance, 175
Pupil Voice, 83
Puppet theatre, 127

Q

Queensland Department of Education, 204
Questionnaire, 55, 99, 104–107, 109–111, 113, 128, 129, 133, 142, 148, 149, 160, 162, 165, 170, 180, 181, 188, 196, 204, 206–208, 233

R

Racism, 125
Radiography, 232
Realist theory, 19
Real life conflicts, 72, 123, 134, 140, 141, 148

Redfern, 239
Redza, Aida, xi
Reflection, 52
Reflection-in-action, 52, 53, 63
Reflection-on-action, 52, 53, 63
Reform pedagogy, 126
Refugees, 223, 225, 237
Relational aggression, 163, 224
Relay Class, 188, 190, 191, 193, 201–203, 206
Resilience, resilient, 8, 48, 222, 231, 235, 237, 240
Resolution, 4–8, 13–15, 17–21, 26–29, 31–33, 39, 43, 51, 52, 55, 58, 61, 62, 67, 68, 70–73, 84, 93, 101, 102, 115, 127, 166, 171, 181, 184, 196, 197
Respek, 224
Restorative justice, 15
Rigby, Ken, 6, 31, 160, 169, 182, 225
Riksorganisationen Auktoriserade Dramapedagoger (RAD), 228
Riverdance, 174
Role circle, 62
Role-play, 44, 46, 47, 50–52, 59, 64, 74, 75, 93, 96, 109, 110, 135–137, 140–142, 170, 174, 177, 178, 193, 221, 225, 228, 230, 233
Rosenberg, Marshall, 22, 34

S
Safe space, 32, 35, 36, 51, 53, 54, 68, 75–77, 140, 144
Sanitation, 235
School adjustment, 129
School attitudes, 128, 132, 133, 148
Schools of culture, 85, 209, 225
Science, 4, 12, 13, 15, 52, 183, 206, 229
Scotland, 158, 174
Self-esteem, 83, 84, 128, 132, 133, 148, 183, 194, 202
Self-reflection, 59, 79
Serendipity, ix
Sex, sexual, sexuality, 22, 23, 28, 30, 106, 157, 159, 160, 162, 163, 172, 174, 192
Shark, 25, 164, 177
Sierra Leone, 219, 226
Simulation, 44, 96
Singapore, 43, 240
Sjöstedt, Hanna, 221
Slade, Peter, 45
Smoothing, 25, 164, 166, 167, 171, 178
Socialisation theory, 19
Sociodrama, 44

South Africa, 226
South Australian Education Union, 228
South Australian Youth Arts Board, 159
Spect-actors, 61, 224
Speech and Drama, 235
Speech bubbles, 100
Spolin, Viola, 49
Stefaniuk, Hanya, xii
St John's College Cambridge, xx
Stockholm International Peace Research Institute (SIPRI), 4
Stockholm School of the Arts, 126
Stockholm University, 127
Stop!Look!Go!, 111, 112
Storvik, 5, 227
Storyboarding, 96
Subtext, 114
Swedish Council of Scientific Research, 6
Swedish Labour Party, 124
Swedish Parliament, 125
Swedish School Act, 125
Sydney, 6, 83, 188–190, 200–203, 205, 209, 237–239
Symbolic transformation, 80

T
Takaoka, Japan, 230
Tamil, 91
Tan, Sooi Beng, xi
Teacher competence, 128, 129, 132, 133, 148
Teacher training, 127, 227
Teater Muda, 93–95, 98
Teddy bear, 25, 164
Tension, 7, 14, 16, 17, 20, 27, 28, 43, 49, 51, 54, 55, 68, 70–73, 76, 97, 98, 107, 113, 124, 190
Text, 35, 52, 60, 101, 114, 221, 227, 228
Theatre for Development (TfD), 47, 77, 92
Theatre-in-education (TIE), 9, 46, 51, 53, 60, 69, 77, 84, 93, 95, 108–112, 193, 197, 220, 223
Theatre of the Oppressed (TO), 47, 49, 77, 93
Theatresports, 49, 53
The Worm Turns, 176, 177
Third-party interventions, 28, 35, 137, 138, 145, 148, 192
Third party roles, 28–30, 32, 123, 134, 145, 149, 221
Thought tracking, 62
Torres Strait Islanders, 158
Touching kneecaps (game), 172
Transformative learning, 52, 78, 79, 81, 85

Transformative mediation, 34, 70, 73, 74, 80, 81
Transpersonal theory, 19, 26
Trauma, 97, 237, 238
TrueQuest Pty Ltd., 239
Trust, 10, 24, 26, 36, 39, 49, 53, 54, 76, 83, 96, 99–101, 103, 170, 171, 174, 175, 179, 180, 202, 233
Trust walk, 175
Turtle, 24, 25, 140, 142, 164, 177

U

UK, 81, 209, 226, 228, 236
Under-distancing, 107, 111
UNESCO, xx, xxi
United States, 15, 39, 44
Uniting (Church), 157
Universitas Gadjah Mada, 233
Universiti Sains Malaysia, 94
University of Auckland, x
University of Borås, xii
University of Melbourne, 234

V

Västerberg Folk High School, 227

Video, video-recordings, 93, 109, 127, 136–140, 142, 147–149, 170, 174, 178, 179, 181, 188, 220, 221, 223, 224, 227, 228, 234, 238
Visual arts, 85, 92–94, 96, 99–102, 108, 116, 183
Vox populi interviews, 181

W

Ward, Winifred, 44
Warm-ups, 96, 171, 174
Way, Brian, 45
Welfare state, 124
Whole School Anti-Racism Program (WSARP), 184, 186, 198, 200–203
Wiechel, Lennart, 127
Win-win solution, 24, 138, 140, 145
Women's Centre for Change (WCC), 223, 224
World Vision, 239

Y

Young Mob, 239
Young Theatre Penang, 93, 223
Yunnan, 226, 234